Black Diamonds

Black Diamonds

Life in the Negro Leagues
from the Men Who Lived It

John B. Holway

Library of Congress Cataloging-in-Publication Data

Holway, John.
    Black diamonds : life in the Negro leagues from the men who lived
it / John B. Holway.
        p.   cm.
    Includes index.
    ISBN 0-9625132-3-7 : $
    1. Afro-American baseball players—Biography.   2. Baseball—United
States—History.   I. Title.
GV865.A1H613   1991
796.357′092′2—dc20   90-22284
                                                                              CIP

cop . 1

Stadium Books, distributed by the Talman Company, Inc.,
    150 Fifth Avenue, New York, NY 10011

Printed on acid free paper.
Printed and bound in the United States of America.

To Eileen
with love and thanks
for helping organize most of my mess
and cheerfully tolerating the rest.

Contents

A note on research methodology:

The Negro leagues rarely published statistics, and in some years when they did, independent research indicates the published stats are probably in error. Thus most stats used in this book are compiled from original research into newspaper box scores. These are certainly incomplete for two reasons: One, the research is continuing, and two, some box scores were never published in the press.

Post-season data and performance against white major leaguers are the result of original research.

Minor league and Mexican league stats were provided through the courtesy of Bob Hoie of SABR's minor league committee.

Cuban stats are furnished through the courtesy of Jorge Figueredo, the leading historian of Cuban professional baseball.

Puerto Rican stats are courtesy of Luis Alvelo of Caguas, Puerto Rico.

The Country of the Past

The past is another country, they do things differently there.
The film, *The Go-Between*

Imagine, if you can, a world in which Dave Winfield, Dwight Gooden, Kirby Puckett, Rickey Henderson, Dave Stewart, Darryl Strawberry, Andre Dawson, and Ozzie Smith did not play for the Yankees, Mets, Twins, A's, Cubs, and Cards. Imagine that most of us never saw them, never read about them, never even knew their names, because they were playing instead on the Black Yankees, the Eagles, the Monarchs, the American Giants, and the Black Barons, and our newspapers rarely, if at all, mentioned their exploits.

Then suppose that, 50 years from now, in the year 2039, some elderly black fans tried to tell you about them—how hard they could hit, how fast they could throw, how swiftly they could run, how nimbly they could field. You might be either incredulous or, perhaps at the most, skeptical: "How do you know? They never played against major leaguers."

Today this is a fantasy. But in my grandfather's day, and in my own childhood, baseball apartheid was the real world. This was baseball as it existed for 60 years, 1887–1947. The white half of that world is well documented and has been almost memorized by every fan who wants to relive the thrills of Mathewson, Cobb, Alexander, Ruth.

This book is about the other half, the hidden half, the black half.

As a 13-year-old boy in 1943 I caught a quick glimpse of the end of that blackball era when, out of curiosity, I joined a stadium full of Washington fans to see Satchel Paige face Josh Gibson in old Griffith Stadium. I wasn't "making a statement" by attending, for I went to a segregated Virginia high school, sat in the front of the Virginia buses, and indeed had only passing contact with the blacks with whom I coexisted. That was the world I lived in, the only world I knew.

Everyone my age or older comes from that other country named the Past. Al Campanis is a native of that land. He is not a bad man. He is a loving grandfather, a caring husband, a pillar of his church. His "crime," if you care to describe his recent verbal indiscretion as such, is due to the circumstances of his birth over which he had no control—being born into a country which the citizens of the Present would barely recognize.

I also learned about baseball in that country. I'll never forget the involuntary gasp when, in 1941, I walked out of the passageway in Yankee Stadium and into the lower first base stands and suddenly saw Jimmie Foxx, muscles bulging, teeth clenched, waiting for the pitch not 100 feet away from me! That was the year Ted Williams hit .406 and Joe DiMaggio hit in 56 games. I saw them both. There wasn't a black anywhere on the field, and it didn't seem strange at all.

My father came from that country; when he was my age, he said, he had seen Larry Lajoie. My great-grandfather was also a native of the Past. Born before the Civil War, he used to tell me of his memories of George and Harry Wright and Al Spalding of the old Boston Red Stockings.

Black kids my age probably got the same thrill I got at Yankee Stadium from their first sight of Willard Brown or Josh Gibson at bat. Their fathers may have seen John Henry Lloyd or Smokey Joe Williams in their primes. And their great-grandfathers may have seen the legendary Bud Fowler or Sol White.

> *I can't believe in* impossible *things.*
> *Alice in Wonderland*

After my own first trip to see Paige and Gibson, I began inquiring about stories and records of the Negro leagues. I found there were none to be read. In 1948 I saw Paige pitch in the World Series for Cleveland; he was already a living legend in both black and white America. I wanted to know more about Gibson, who had already died at an untimely age. In 1969 I tracked down a few old players who had been his teammates—Buck Leonard, Cool Papa Bell, Jake Stephens, and Wilmer Fields—and others such as Paige, Frank Duncan, Buck O'Neil, and Verdell Mathis, who had been his opponents. I wrote the story and submitted it to the *Washington Post* magazine. The assistant editor protested that my history of Josh's eye-popping homers—he drove one over the roof of Yankee Stadium in 1930—couldn't be true.

The editor was eventually overruled by his boss, and the story made the cover. But I would encounter that attitude of disbelief, even hostility, many times in the 20 years since then. I still meet it.

I must hasten to say that I even rejected many of the stories I was told. They flew in the face of everything I had been taught about baseball. I firmly believed that blacks were good players on the semi-pro or perhaps minor league level, and that only one or two freaks like Paige or Gibson were indeed good enough to play in the "majors." Even Josh might hit the ball a mile, but not against major league curve balls, they said, and I believed them. I was convinced at the outset that I was merely probing a footnote to baseball history, a minor chapter akin to, say, the House of Davids or the Brooklyn Bushwicks of the 1930s.

> *It's not what you don't know that gets you into trouble, it's what you know for sure that isn't so.*
> Al Smith, Presidential candidate, 1928

My sixth grade teacher used to quote that to us, and today, almost five decades later, I think I understand what Al was saying. It's what Earl Weaver of the Orioles meant when he said, "It's what you learn after you know it all that counts."

For one thing, Paige and Gibson were not freaks. "There were many Satchels, there were many Joshes," Paige told the crowd at his own induction into Cooperstown. Nobody paid much attention to him when he said that, but I have become convinced that he was 100 percent right. In fact, when he repeated it at Cooperstown a few years later, an aide to Commissioner Bowie Kuhn told him to "sit down." Paige didn't sit down; instead he walked out of Cooperstown and never returned.

Ironically, it is the same generation of whites who kept Paige and the other talented blacks out of the white majors who are now the gatekeepers at Cooperstown, keeping most of them out of the Hall of Fame. Whites number 17 of the 20 members of the veterans committee, and so far they have opened the door only a crack to admit a token 11 blacks from the country of the Past. Compare that to about 150 whites of the same era who have been inducted into the shrine. The board of directors that appoints the committee is also almost all white—13 of its 15 members. The board sets the policy for the Hall and has relegated the black half of baseball history to a small portion in the corner of one room. Cooperstown clearly is a white memory bank and seemingly determined to remain that way.

Post-Jackie Robinson blacks—Hank Aaron, Willie Mays, Juan Marichal, Ernie Banks, Willie Stargell, etc.—as citizens of the country of the Present, are admitted without regard to race. But they entertained whites; the older players, from the country of the Past, entertained blacks mostly and have been largely excluded from the white man's Hall.

This bias seems to reflect baseball policy in general. Although every one of the 26 big league teams has two or three black stars on the roster, and most have a significant black population within a few miles of their parks, only about three percent of all major league tickets are bought by black fans. A few decades ago blacks filled stadia to see Negro league games and later lined up at ticket windows to see

Jackie Robinson and other blacks in the majors. Those black fans are gone today. For blacks, baseball is merely a way to escape from the ghetto by providing entertainment for whites. Black fans realize that baseball is not a black entertainment enterprise and have deserted the game they once loved. And baseball has undertaken no campaign to woo them back. Commissioner Peter Ueberroth in 1987 called for affirmative action to change the game's white complexion, but the 26 teams have made almost no significant progress in carrying it out.

Several years ago the ACLU opened negotiations with Commissioner Bowie Kuhn to admit more black vets to Cooperstown. It was told bluntly that the Hall of Fame is a private club, not subject to the civil rights laws or the interstate commerce clause of the Constitution, and answerable to no one regarding whom it admits and whom it rejects.

The mayor of Cooperstown sits on the board of the Hall. So does the town's wealthiest citizen, Stephen Clark, scion of the Singer Sewing Machine Company, which has endowed most of the buildings that house the Hall. Clark's family attorney, Edward Stack, is president of the board. They and other local residents once had the controlling majority on the board. In recent years, however, the baseball interests have gained a majority and can outvote the locals if they choose.

There is reason to believe that things are changing in the quiet village on the shores of James Fenimore Cooper's Lake Glimmerglass. For the first time, citizens of the country of the Present have moved into leadership roles in the government of the game. Both Ueberroth and the new commissioner, A. Bartlett Giamatti, were boys of seven or eight when Jackie Robinson made his debut, leading the way into the country of the Present. They have virtually no memories of seeing segregated baseball games or riding on segregated buses. They bring a new mindset to the game and its problems, unshackled by the shibboleths of the Past.

Likewise, the veterans committee is slowly but inexorably changing. Two members, Ted Williams and Stan Musial, hold dual citizenship in the countries of the Past and the Present. In the future more men of their generation will move onto the committee. They will be followed by the members of today's Baseball Writers Association, men now mostly in their 30s and 40s, who have done such a color-blind job of electing modern greats to the Hall. When that generational changeover is completed, the last bitter opposition to admitting black veterans will disappear, and these giants of the game will take their places beside the whites they played, and often beat. Unfortunately, by then they will be admitted posthumously.

The black half of baseball, while unknown to most white fans, was not unknown to white players of the Past. The two worlds met every autumn after the World Series and every winter in Cuba, California, Puerto Rico, and Mexico. I have collected more than 400 box scores pitting blacks against the best white players from 1886 to 1946— Cobb, Ruth, Mathewson, Johnson. The whites won 168, the blacks, 268.

Critics say the whites were loafing. But when I questioned the old-time white players about this game or that, they reacted with embarrassment. Lefty Grove looked me straight in the eye and said, "I never played against blacks." Yet I have box scores showing that he pitched and lost at least two games in the 1920s by scores of 9–3 and 6–1. If he was embarrassed about it half a century later, he was surely just as embarrassed when it happened on the field before a grand-stand full of quizzical fans, whether black or white.

Critics say 400 games are not enough for a valid statistical sam-pling. Yet batting championships and penants are awarded after 162 games, and world championships after only seven.

Still others protest that the blacks would not have done so well if they had played in the majors. Of course not. And the whites would not have been so heroic either if they had played in an integrated league, as today's players, white and black, must do. "I'd have taken a few points off those high batting averages," Paige said. Could Ty Cobb have hit .400? Could Walter Johnson have won 30 games? Could Joe DiMaggio have hit in 56 straight games?

Could Babe Ruth have hit 60 homers if black pitchers had been allowed in the American League in 1927? (Could he even have led the league if black sluggers had been allowed to compete with him?) When I asked this question in *The Sporting News* in 1977, the angry letters poured in. "You commie pinko bastard!" one fan began and continued in that vein for eight single-spaced pages.

I don't say this out of a sense of racial guilt. I'm proud when my race excels, when Roger Maris hits 61 homers, when Sandy Koufax or Nolan Ryan breaks strikeout records, when Ted Williams bats .406. But I also consider myself a historian, and I feel we should all unlearn any incorrect history we have absorbed and relearn the history that comes closer to the truth.

"If only you had the statistics," skeptical whites were always say-ing. So about 15 years ago I began the then lonely and still monumen-tal search for the missing numbers. Just how many home runs *did* Gibson hit? How many games did Paige really win? Can we build portraits in numbers that will define Willard Brown and Dave Barnhill just as today's Mike Schmidt or Orel Hershiser has his portrait painted by the old familiar numbers—HR, RBI, AB, IP, SO, W-L?

Dick Clark, chairman of SABR's Negro league committee, and dozens of other baseball "nuts" are pursuing the grail, squinting at thousands of box scores in dozens of papers, black and white. The task is ongoing, and the results, as of the time this book went to press, are found in the following pages. The totals are not yet complete, and many games will never be found, but we now know pretty much who were the .350 hitters, who were the .250 hitters, who were the biggest winners, and who hit the most home runs.

We are indebted to the many explorers who have blazed the trail back into the forgotten country of the Past, a country we all understand a little better today, thanks to their perseverance. Their names are: Terry Baxter, Dick Clark, Dick Cramer, Debbie Crawford, Paul Doherty, Troy Greene, Jim Holway, John Holway Jr., Tim Joyce, Merl Kleinknecht, Paul Kubicek, Neil Lanctot, Larry Lester, Jerry Malloy, Joe McGillen, Mona Peach, Bill Plott, Mike Stahl, A.D. Suehsdorf, Diane Walker, Edie Williams, and Charles Zarelli.

But as these dedicated fans enthusiastically agree, after all is said and done, the best argument for studying the history of the blackball leagues is that it is fun, as I hope the following pages will reveal. So hand in hand with the statistical research went the biographical research in the form of living autobiographies by the dozens of former players I tracked down across the country. The first group of these was published in 1975 as *Voices From the Great Black Baseball Leagues.* But the supply of new stories didn't end with that book, and my tape recorder continued to turn as the interviews continued. If anything, the stories got better because, as I grew more familiar with the subject, I was able to ask better questions.

Some of that research produced *Blackball Stars,* published in 1988, the stories of 26 greats, many of whom I never met, because death had reached them before I could. Their stories were pieced together from the written records and the memories of those who had known them.

Like the earlier books, the stories herein reveal history on two levels. First is the history on the field—the dramatic homers, the World Series victories, the all-star game thrills, etc. The second is the history of the larger field, the nation. We meet Dave Barnhill in zulu costume barnstorming with the Ethiopian Clowns, Buck O'Neil dodging bullets from a railroad cop in a hobo jungle, Gene Benson punching a soldier who ordered him out of a railroad car in Dixie, etc. These men all lived a moment of history that will never return, a history that can now be the heritage of us all.

Country Jake
PAUL "JAKE" STEPHENS

Peppery little Jake Stephens was the spitting image of Marty Feldman, who played bug-eyed Igor in Mel Brooks' Young Frankenstein. *He had the same hooked nose, the same merry twinkle in his eye, and the same slyly devilish grin. Jake was 70 years old when I first met him, and he bounced out of his living room easy chair to demonstrate how he gave a knee to a sliding runner or pulled the hidden ball trick some three decades earlier, when he covered shortstop for three different championship teams as one of the great glove men in America.*

He played on championship teams with Hilldale 1923–25, was traded to the Homestead Grays for Hall of Famer Martin Dihigo and sparked the Grays to the flag in 1930, then helped the Philadelphia Stars win in 1934.

While Jake's wife, a white woman, tried to keep their two-year-old son occupied, Stephens spun his stories. The memories had him doubling over with laughter, gasping, and crying, all at the same time. And when I met him later with his old teammate, Ted Page, the stories bubbled up faster than he could get them out of his lips.

"You were a good man to have on a team," Page told him. "You kept the spirits up. You were the life of the party."

"The peppiest players—Jake Stephens and Jimmy Crutchfield," said Buck Leonard. "Jake's got a lot of pep even now. Well, you can imagine how he was when he was playing shortstop. Jake kept things going a lot, telling jokes. Always when you would meet his team, he would jive you a little. He'd be beating you, and he'd be joking."

Stephens' fellow shortstops, Dick Seay and Sam Bankhead, admired him as an artist. "He couldn't hit a bull in the ass," Bankhead said, forgetting momentarily that he was on tape. "But he could field!"

Stephens' teammate on the great Philadelphia Hilldale champions of 1923–25, Scrip Lee, recalled him as "the smallest man on the club and the best glove man I know. If the ball hopped bad, he'd hop with it. Yes sir, he'd round those balls up and be in position to throw, where another man would be out of position."

The Chicago Defender *once called him "the human jumping jack."*

Hall of Famer Judy "Jing" Johnson, who played third base beside Jake, marveled that "a lot of times that ball was hit past third, it would go right past my head—whizz! He'd say, 'Duck, Jing,'" and throw the runner out.

1

He was "just a picture to watch going behind third base," whistled Page. "And he got his man. He was just like a little rabbit."

Page was also one of the black leagues' most infamous baserunners, many of whom filed their spikes. But as a fielder, "I don't think Stephens had any scars on him," Ted said. "I know I didn't put any on. He was too smart." ("How the hell you gonna hurt me when I'm going to right field" on the pivot? Jake chortled.)

Jake Stephens was also famous for "jiving" gullible runners off the base. "He'd sneak back in there, and the catcher would throw you out," recalled outfielder Crush Holloway. "We had a boy, Connie Day, they used to throw him out all the time. They used to catch him off that base every day! Stephens would talk him off it."

Clint Thomas, who played center field on the Hilldales when Jake was playing shortstop, smiled when he said that Stephens wasn't much of a hitter. "We were playing in Cuba one winter," Clint said, "and Jake had trouble hitting the curve ball. So, when the pitchers started curve balling him, he sent himself a wire saying his father had died and he had to go home. Later on we were playing in California, and they started curve balling him again, and he sent himself another telegram saying his father had died. I used to tease him, wondering how his father could have died twice."

But bunt! Seay and old-timer Bingo DeMoss were his only peers, and even Seay marveled at Jake's skill. "They used to say he could 'pick it out of the catcher's glove after it went by.' That's a lost art. Look at the big league games; you can count the ball players who do it."

Leonard says, "He was the only player I have ever seen who could bunt a ball, what we called, behind him. He'd be standing there like this, he'd tip his bat like that, actually behind him, bunt the ball down third base every time and run like I-don't-know-what. You don't find fellows can do that now. He was the only one I know could do it consistently."

Added pitcher Scrip Lee: "He'd go back with his bat like he was going to swing and then just turn it like that and tap the ball. And he was fast too."

While Jake was a delight to the fans and other players, he could drive his managers nuts. Patient Webster McDonald of the Philly Stars sighed: "Stephens was fast, aggressive, he could do a lot of things. But he was controversial, things upset him sometimes. The fans were 100 percent for that guy, but sometimes he'd burn you up the way he did it. Sometimes I'd roast him, because out of a clear blue sky he'd argue with the umpires. Jake was temperamental. He'd swear he was right. I'd say, 'Jake, look, all the umpires can't be wrong, some of them gotta be right.'"

Stephens broke in with Hilldale in 1921 after bombarding owner Ed Bolden with anonymous letters touting "the best shortstop to come out of York, Pennsylvania." Bolden was impressed and sent him a ticket to Philadelphia.

"We were the two youngsters on that team," Johnson recalled. "We were *pretty much in awe of all those players, particularly [Louis] Santop," the hard-hitting catcher.*

Stephens was indirectly responsible for one of the most famous misplays in blackball history, during the black World Series of 1924 against the Kansas City Monarchs. "Jake was so nervous, he was sitting in that dugout in Kansas City, and his shoes were going just like that—tap-tap-tap." So manager Frank Warfield moved Johnson to short, catcher Biz Mackey to third, and put the aging Santop behind the plate. That day Santop dropped a crucial foul tip, and Mackey let a hard grounder go through his legs, as the winning run scored.

So Jake was human, after all. But after the butterflies were gone, he sparked his teams to pennants.

In '30 Jake saved one of the finest pitching performances in blackball history, as the Grays' Smokey Joe Williams and the Monarchs' Chet Brewer hooked up in a 12-inning, 46-strikeout duel. Stephens snared a Texas leaguer that would have tied the game, as Williams finally won it 1–0. In the eastern playoff that year against Pop Lloyd's Lincoln Giants, Stephens won the fourth game on a walk, a steal, and an error in the tenth inning, 3–2.

Cum Posey picked Stephens for his authoritative all-star team in '34, writing that "Stephens was the backbone of the Stars. He was mixed up in all the rallies and played the same brand all season."

Three years later, when he was 37 and playing for the tail-end Black Yankees, Jake won the fans' vote for shortstop in the East-West game, defeating the famous Willie Wells. The following year, at the age of 38, he came in second in the vote.

After his retirement, Stephens was elected to the Pittsburgh Hall of Fame in Three Rivers Stadium, where he is now enshrined along with Honus Wagner, Paul Waner, Josh Gibson, Satchel Paige, Billy Conn, and Roberto Clemente.

On three of his teams, the Grays, Crawfords, and Stars, Stephens roomed with the husky, moody Jud "Boojum" Wilson as one of the great duos in baseball annals. Little Jake was virtually the only man who could tame the temperamental, quick-fisted Wilson. But sometimes even Jake couldn't tame Boojum. Judy Johnson, shaking with laughter, remembered:

> *We were sitting in a restaurant, and Boojum wasn't feeling too happy about being thrown out of the ball game that afternoon. I remember Stephens saying something like, "I hope they fine you $100, you big so-and-so." That did it! Boojum reached across the table, picked Paul up by the back of the coat and held him at arms' length, his feet kicking in mid-air. Boojum started shaking Stephens until I thought he would shake the life right out of him, and Stephens kept yelling, "Put me down!" You wouldn't believe how strong Wilson was.*

But years later, when Jud lay dying in a half coma, the only name he recognized was Jake's, according to Johnson. "He thought the world of Stephens."

Jake himself died in 1981.

They called me "Country Jake." They said my breath smelled like cordwood. Eventually they took off the "country" and just left "Jake." In those days they traveled by Pullmans, not in buses like they did later. In the berths you had a hammock for your clothes, but they told me it was to rest my arm in. So I rested my arm in it overnight, and it was so stiff next morning I couldn't throw for a week.

I played with Satchel Paige and Josh Gibson on the Pittsburgh Crawfords about 1931. They were wearing didies (diapers) when I broke in. Back then you had to be perfection or you didn't play. A young ball player had just as much chance of breaking into baseball as breaking into a bank. Unless he had real ability and was liked by the fans.

I played to win. I was lucky enough to be with Hilldale, Homestead Grays, Crawfords, Stars—all those ball clubs. We won pennants. Every one of them.

I was born in 1900 in York, Pennsylvania in a place called Pleasureville, or Coffeetown. My father had signed a fellow's note, and he didn't make good on it. They had a sheriff's sale. I was sleeping in a little baby crib then, and a friend bought it for 17 cents at the auction and gave it back to my mother. Here's my mother. She died when I was four years old. My father raised us. Here's the family. The one with the dress on is me. I was about four or five, and look what I had in my hand, a ball.

In the morning my father would give me to Mrs. Forest or Mrs. Lancaster to take care of me, and they'd put me in bed with their children. I was raised with them. And I went to church with them every Sunday, and there wasn't any such thing as a color line. I guess I was 14 or 15 before I *realized* I was a Negro. You just didn't have a color line. It was just one of those things, you didn't have it. It wasn't until about 1916 that we started associating with colored people. Over in Smoketown, that's where the colored people lived.

Near my house they had a street called Bullfrog Alley, nothing but gypsies and Germans. That was before they had cement paving. The bullfrogs would go "Grrump, grrump, grrump." You didn't cross that street there across the railroad track, because them gypsies and Germans just didn't allow it. Let's put it this way, you stayed in your own neighborhood, about three or four blocks.

So I'd make a few snowballs in the nighttime and soak them in water, and the first thing next morning I'd wake up and maybe I'd have ten or 12 or 15 kids, all waiting for Paulie Stephens and all worried about getting to school across Bullfrog Alley. And I'd take them on to school, because if I threw at you, I hit you. That's how I developed my good arm. They'd say, "Look out for that nigger, that nigger *hurts* you." I always threw at the middle. Others threw for the head, but I threw for the middle. So I became leader of this gang.

I worked for a horse dealer name of Sol along about 1919. I saw him buying horses for $25–$35 and selling them for $80–$90. So I got an idea. One day a fellow came in the stable with a horse, and instead of waiting to tell Sol, I said, "I'll give you $50." He said, "No, you won't, I'll take 70." I said, "I won't argue, you'll take 60 because I want to get back to my work." OK. Well, I took the horse over to the West End to sell him myself. Sol didn't know I was in business for myself over the West End. Well, when he found out, I knew he was going to come looking for me. So I made a hot fire and a bucket of water—hot water. About four o'clock that evening I saw him coming with a pitchfork. He came up on the steps and I threw a dipper of boiling water on his chest. He fell back and I can still see him screaming now.

In 1921 I went down to Philadelphia, to the Hilldales. Hilldale had become something big around 1918. Everybody told me, "Paul, you're too *little* to play big league baseball." Except one man, Jerry Hocksberger, a Jewish storekeeper. He said, "Paul, you have every-thing." He said, "You'll make it. Don't come back. If you can't make it playing baseball, don't come back to York."

I said, "Jerry, I won't. I'll never come back."

But my father didn't want me to play. So you know what I had to

Paul "Jake" Stephens. Photo courtesy of National Baseball Library, Coopers-town, N.Y.

do? A train left for Philadelphia at 11 o'clock that night, so I yawned and said, "Well, I think I'll go upstairs and go to bed." I went upstairs and climbed down the back balcony and hopped the train.

About 1918 the Hilldales had Dick Lundy, one of the greatest shortstops God put breath in. But Lundy jumped to the Bacharach Giants in 1920.

So then the Hilldales brought Scrappy Brown down there, and Scrappy was a flash. He could fly, he could do everything. He was just a hell of a good fellow, he enjoyed a good time. But he jumped to the Baltimore Black Sox. So they brought another young fellow, I disremember what his name was—one of the most graceful baseball players I ever saw. A college graduate. When he put a uniform on, it fit like a glove. He had grace, he had everything going for him. But the first time I saw him, I knew he would never make a ball player, because he'd watch his shadow. Glance down all the time and watch his own shadow. I knew he wasn't a ball player because, you know, you just don't watch your shadow.

At that time Bill Francis—we called him "Brody"—was manager of the ball club, one of the best third basemen you've ever seen. But Bill was washed up then. Judy Johnson was a rookie third baseman, and Brody knows he can't lick Judy, so he shoves Judy over to shortstop. That's my competition now—Judy Johnson. He was tough competition.

I called him Jing—"Jing-aling." Judy was a very conservative man. No alibis, always cool, lots of patience. He was a different type from me entirely. I was strong-willed and quick-tempered. He was a shortstop, and I was a shortstop, so one of us had to go. Judy is a better hitter than me. He was sure-handed, and his arm was truer. But the thing is, I covered so much more ground than Judy could. It wasn't long after that Frank Warfield became the manager, and he solved the problem. He put Judy on third and me on short, and that's where we stayed for the next eight years. Judy could hug third base, because I would protect him at short.

Him and Marcelle were the best third basemen ever were in baseball. You talk about Brooks Robinson, he couldn't carry their glove.

You've got to be able to protect third base, and you've got to be able to protect second base. On the fast ball, the batter's not going to pull it like you do a curve, so Judy would move over one or two steps, and I'd move over one or two steps, then I can protect Warfield over on the other side, at second. Many a time I went back over second base and got the ball.

I had long range in the field. But a poor hitter. I never will forget the first ball game I ever played, down in Wilmington, Delaware. First time at bat I hit a home run. I didn't hit any more the rest of the year. So they played me over in New York, and big Jeff Tesreau was pitching. He used to play for the New York Giants. And they had a mound made to order for him. It looked like I was down in a hole. That old man, he was way up there, and I felt like I was down in a hole. He just did this—pow—four straight times, and I never took the bat off my shoulder.

I never could hit that curve ball. They learned how to hug me with it, and I'd back away, turn my head, and fall away. That umpire would say, "How in hell you going to tell whether that ball curved if you're looking up in the grandstand?"

In 1922 they were talking about farming me out. I told them, "If I want to do any farming, I'll go back to York County, best farm country in America. You ain't gonna farm me no place." I jumped the club and went up and played in the New England states with Webster McDonald and Dan McClellan.

That winter I went out to California. I was sitting on the bench one day playing in the winter league out there, and I saw John Beckwith. There's one man they never mention. Ain't nobody hit a ball as far as that man! Listen, please believe me, no living human could hit as far. Beckwith was a slugger, but I saw him step in and just do that—drop it down the third base line. Well, it just shows what a slugger can teach a man who is inferior, I mean in batting ability. So I said to Frank Warfield, "Frank, get the ball bag, I want to do a little experiment." And that's how I learned to bunt, by trying to bunt the ball into the ball bag on the third base line.

You take a guy like Richie Allen playing third base. You know what I'd do on him? Bunt. Just keep bunting. Bunt, bunt, bunt.

Or take this fellow, was supposed to be such a hell of a good pitcher—Jim Bunning. Holy Christ, he's not in position to field a ball

Jake Stephens, lower right, with the 1924 champion Hilldales. Others include catcher Biz Mackey and pitcher Nip Winters (back, third and fourth from left); owner Ed Bolden, back, in overcoat; and catcher Louis Santop, back, far right.

after he pitches. The only thing to do is push that ball behind him. He can't field a bunt. Why try to hit that man? He's got a good curve ball. Even if you don't bunt, go through the motion, make him think you're going to bunt, make him come off the mound. Break up that timing. If he's got to be ready to come off that mound, he's a different kind of pitcher. I mean, that's what the smart ball players did, a fellow who was inferior like me. I had to get on base somehow or other.

So the infielders started to hug me—come in close on me. Now I got smart. I got me a big headed bat. Nobody else on that ball club could swing it. I couldn't swing it myself, the only thing I could do was punch with it. I became a right field hitter. I stopped worrying about that damn curve ball.

Another thing: I learned how to become a lead-off man. I'd pull my shirt tail out. Instead of falling back when the curve came, I'd twist back toward the umpire, and it would hit my shirt, it wouldn't hit me. Heck, these big leaguers today, they don't have sense. They fall back from a close pitch. They should pull that shirt out and run back to the umpire like this: "He hit me, he hit me!" Heck, that ball won't hurt you.

The main thing was, once I got on, I could trot, I could run.

There was one pitcher used to hate to see me come up: Jim Duffy, a white semipro pitcher. Listen, he was the toughest competitor. He cheated, he threw the emery ball, he threw the spit ball, he was mean, and they always saved him for some good colored ball club. He made more money, I guess, than the big leaguers. And he was the toughest competitor. When you licked Jim Duffy, you licked him 2-1, 3-2, or 1-0. Oscar Charleston, Beckwith, all those other fellows, he could take them in his hip pocket. But he hated to see me come up. Because I could push the ball. I could either push it over here or drop it down this other line. And when I got on, I watched Duffy's head. If it moved a little toward third base, I knew he was coming back at me with the ball. But if that big head of his would drop back toward second, I'd start a-running, because I knew he was going to throw home. That was the difference, just a slight movement of his head. So I'm running before he even delivers the ball. Because he can't change his motion. I never told nobody. That was *my* secret.

And then the club came up to New England and talked me into coming back: "We need you bad."

I said, "Ok, it's up to Dan and Mac."

They said, "Go on, Jake, it's your future, and I think you've got more future back there than you have here. You're just on a treadmill here." That's the kind of man Dan McClellan was.

You heard about the great John Henry Lloyd? They brought him over to replace me, but the old man couldn't do it. He was washed up. He could hit that ball, but you've got to cover territory. He didn't replace me; they retired *him!* Hell, within three weeks time, they set him on the bench.

Frank Warfield at second base was very sarcastic. Sometimes we didn't talk to each other for three of four weeks at a time. I said, "I can't play baseball with that man, he's sarcastic." He was a full grown ball player when I came up, I mean nationally known, and I was just a rookie. On a force play at second, he'd say, "Tag him, Jake, tag him." I said, "I know it's your turn to tag that man." He was talking about how he was going to punch me in the mouth. I said, "The day you do that is the day you sign your death warrant." Hell, he carried a knife. I didn't need a knife, but I said, "I'll get a shotgun and kill you." He was crazy.

Biz Mackey was our catcher. Of all the catchers, Mackey was the greatest, the smartest. Back in my day if they didn't throw the ball knee high, they weren't a catcher. Today they throw the ball too high: "pecker high"—belt-high, let's say.

Phil Cockrell was a great pitcher, but you hated to play behind him because he threw that spit ball and you'd get ahold of the god-damn spit sometimes. You just couldn't throw true. I never will forget this no-hit-no-run game one Sunday against the Paterson Silk Sox in New Jersey. They really had a good ball club. And I made a play out of this world. The following week they had a return bout, and we went along about the seventh or eighth inning 0–0, and with two men out and a man on second base, he threw the spit ball. I grabbed ahold of the spitty side and threw it into the dugout. The man scored and beat us, 1–0. Cockrell wouldn't talk to me for two weeks. If I'd been more experienced, I'd have thrown with three fingers.

Red Ryan was an entirely different ball player: "All right, you booted one, but they all do it." You felt like playing behind Red. You gave Red all you had.

We became the best of friends—everybody. We played like a team. There was so much cooperation; everybody knew his job. The main thing was to win ball games, regardless of how you did it. A winning club is something. Let's say a fellow hits a home run. We'd throw the towels down, give him the red carpet treatment: "Heh, great going," all that crap like that. The difference between a losing ball club and a winning one is like when we played Kansas City in the World Series in 1925. The guys in the hotel would whisper, "Heh, come here, look at this," and you'd bend down and peep through the keyhole, and wham! they'd hit you across the backside. Little jokes like that. That's what you call a winner, see? You wouldn't get mad, because you'd wait for somebody else to play it on. Good clean sport, something you could really enjoy because the others got the same treatment you got.

The Hilldales in the American league? Mmm. I don't think we'd have won the championship, but we'd have been a first division club. We beat the Athletics in 1925. We beat them three straight ball games: Eddie Rommel, Slim Harriss, Jimmy Dykes, Chick Galloway. We even beat them 18-3! That's when Judge Landis made a ruling that never would a big league ball club play a Negro baseball club intact again.

You just knew you were a better player than the major leaguers. Sometimes, when we had a day off, we'd go see them, and you just *knew* you were a better player. Like Chick Galloway of the Athletics and fellows like that. Why hell, Chick Galloway couldn't carry my glove. He couldn't move out of his tracks.

And see the way those major league ball players make that double play. They grab that ball and jump in the air; they're sitting ducks for a spiking. You take Crush Holloway, Jimmy Lyons, Bingo DeMoss— by God! You'd be committing hari-kari to get in the way of Crush Holloway and Jimmy Lyons. They'd cut you to death. I mean, they'd sharpen their spikes before they went out on the ball field, like Cobb.

What we used to do, particularly with a guy like Holloway: Throw it two or three steps high, so you had to jump to get it and come down with your knees in his throat just before he lets fly, just before he starts his slide. I guarantee you, if he wasn't shaken up after that! Then— the beautiful part about it—you'd trample on his feet and hands with your spikes, just grind your spikes into him, and then say, "Oh, excuse me." That'll teach him. But always say, "Oh, excuse me."

Mackey'd throw the ball so I had to jump up and come down on their face. They'd say, "That goddam Country Jake."

I used to catch the ball and take it out of my glove and tag with the glove. You weren't going to kick the ball out of *my* hand.

Why, I see those big league shortstops making double plays—they don't know any more about that double play than a 10-year-old child. The second baseman used to throw it to me letter high, and you've got to grab that ball as you went across second base. I'm going into right field, throwing that ball to first base. How in the world is that runner going to get me? You weren't no sitting duck standing there at second base. They don't even know how to *play* baseball today.

Take the old hidden ball play, for instance, something you don't see anymore. I used to stand behind the runner with the ball in my glove, get him off guard in a conversation: "Heh, man, you sure are hitting that ball . . . Excuse me, let me straighten that bag." You reach down to straighten the base, he'd step off. That's when you show him the ball. He'd cuss and yell: "That's a low-down dirty trick," and I'd wag my finger at him and say, "Uh-uh-uh, now you're using bad language." And the best part is, always say, "Excuse me" just before you put the ball on him.

They started me out at $150 a month, and after eight years I was making $200. But I knew I was worth more than that. We had the best Negro ball team in America, and I knew they could afford it. I was a halfway decent shortstop, and I knew I could get a job with another club. I told 'em if they didn't pay me more money, I'd go back to York County and farm, so they traded me to the Homestead Grays in 1929 for $350.

Depression? I didn't know what the Depression was. I lived high off the hog. You could get a haircut for 35 cents, a shave for 15 cents, and a pack of cigarettes for a dime.

I played for Cum Posey on the Homestead Grays in 1930. Every town he was in he had a woman. He was a great woman's man, but this one woman liked me. This night she was supposed to meet Cum Posey, but she met me. He called me over: "To start with, Stephens, my ball players don't monkey with my women. Or they don't play for me any more. Get the message?" I said, "I get the message, Mr. Posey."

Cum Posey didn't allow any gambling. You could play cards for fun, but no gambling in the clubhouse or hotel. So one night we were playing hearts. Every time a fellow would lose, he had to drink a quart of water. You could drink one quart okay, but the second and third one was hard. You drink that third quart, you've had it. Now Sam Streeter, our pitcher, was a little on the dark side. So was Lefty Williams. Every time Sam got that queen of spades he'd drop it on Lefty. You know what Lefty called him? "You black son of a bitch!"

Sometimes a ball player has a bad day, a really bad day. Well, one night Ted Page had one of them bad nights, everything he did was wrong—and Ted was a good ball player. I think he booted a couple out there, hit into a couple double plays. And we got licked, I think 4–3. Page ended the game by hitting into a double play. The bases were loaded. He would have to do that after booting a couple, letting a couple of runs in. So we changed at the YMCA that night and George Scales—I used to call him Tubby because he was a little on the portly side—Scales was stomping around: "Goddamn it" in that big deep voice of his. Now Page and Scales were roommates, they slept together. Page said, "George"—I knew he was talking too polite when he called him George instead of Tubby—"look, you're not captain of this ball club, why do you want to ride me?"

That's when Page busted him one. Knocked two of his teeth out. That's when George Britt came in. Britt could lick the whole ball club. He just grabbed both of them and said, "If you don't stop that, I'll beat both of you."

Well, I can't wait to get to Chicago, our next stop—I was the agitator, see? Man, I can't get in that hotel in Chicago fast enough.

Mule Suttles was waiting in the hotel there and I said, "Heh, ask Tubby where his two teeth are at." So Tubby came in, and Mule said, "Heh"—you know how you greet each other, even though you're going to play against each other, you're on friendly terms until you put that uniform on—"Heh, Tubby, where are them two teeth at?" Scales just said, "I spoke out of turn." Now, that night both of them, Scales and Page, got to sleep together. And both of them had knives, so both of them spent a sleepless night watching each other.

Sam Streeter—I used to let him break in my shoes. Sam's on the cheap side, and they hurt me, so I let him wear my shoes, give him a quarter to get them shined every week. He was a cheater though. When he got in a tight spot, he'd throw that spit ball. And threw strikes with it.

One time for two or three days you couldn't get me out. Everything I hit, a line drive. I called my bat "Bullet Joe." I told it, "Cool off, Joe " [talking to imaginary bat on the ground]. I said, "My *God,* that thing's ready!" And then for two weeks I couldn't get a base hit. Joe Williams said, "Your name's not "Bullet Joe," it's "Pullet Joe."

I jumped the Homestead Grays in '32, went over and played with the Crawfords. Oscar Charleston, the manager, drove to Montgomery, Alabama and picked up Satchel Paige and brought him back to the Crawfords' camp. Paige had to bask in the limelight of some of the older players, fellows like Jud Wilson and Charleston. He used to carry bats and balls into the park to get in.

You take Satchel and those, they were all southern boys. They lived a different life than we lived. We didn't even much associate with them off the ball field, because they were what you'd call clowns. They didn't dress the way we dressed, they didn't have the same mannerisms, the same speech.

And you have this other problem with southern boys. They've never been used to making money. Give them $150 a month, first thing you know they go all haywire, living on top of the world, walking in the restaurant with their baseball jackets on that say, "Pittsburgh Crawfords." The older fellows, we had neckties on when we went to dinner, I mean because that's how you're supposed to do. You're a gentleman, you're a big timer.

The ball club that, with a little supplementary pitching, would have been great was the Philadelphia Stars, about 1934. We didn't need but one or two runs, we had such a terrific defense. Peter Washington in center could run a country mile; Chaney White in left field could run a country mile. Rap Dixon in right. Boojum Wilson at first, Dick Seay second, I was shortstop—we covered a lot of ground; Dewey Creacy at third, Mackey catching, Slim Jones and Webster McDonald pitching. Hell, if we got three or four runs in a ball game, that was exceptional, 'cause we weren't a hitting club. We got one hit against Chicago one time and beat them 1-0. Pete Washington hit a home run. It must have been around 1934, because we won the championship of the league that year.

Boojum Wilson played first base or third base. There was never a meaner, nastier man than Boojum when he put his uniform on, but you couldn't find a nicer man when he took it off. And here's something funny: He loved me. All those fellows like Beckwith, Boojum Wilson—they loved me. Because I wasn't afraid. I took my licking. In Bullfrog Alley you took your licking. In order to be a man or a boy growing up, you had to take your licking, and nobody was going to help you, you were on your own.

You know what Wilson did to me one time? We were roommates, and we had played the all-star game out in Chicago. I came in about one or two o'clock in the morning, half juiced up. I said, "Get up! Tonight's the night." He grumbled, "Goddamn it, pipe down." I said, "Get up, get up!" So he got mad, he grabbed ahold of my leg and held me out the window 16 stories above the street. He said, "You goddamn midget." I said, "Oh, please, Willie, don't drop me." Those people looked like flies down there on the sidewalk. Then I started kicking, I said, "Turn me loose," and I was kicking his arm with my free leg. So he shifted hands on me, just like that—from one hand to the other—16 floors above the street. And I'm trying to shake loose. When they told me about it the next day and I saw that man's arm all scuffed up where I was kicking him, I couldn't believe it. For two days I couldn't walk. I just couldn't walk I got so scared. I'd try to walk and my legs would buckle.

I hadn't hit a home run all year, but one day in Baltimore against the Black Sox I got one past the outfielder. Wilson was coaching at third and waved me home, and I had my home run—I thought. The umpire said I didn't touch third, so naturally I got raving mad. Webster McDonald was our manager then, and he came running out of the dugout, and Wilson kept pushing me behind him, trying to keep me away from that umpire.

They were having one heck of an argument. Wilson was waving his arms around, and while his right arm was in the air, I reached around him and hit that umpire—pow!—right in the kisser.

The umpire turned around to Boojum: "He hit me!" So the cops charged Wilson, see? They put him in the patrol wagon and started working him over. The wagon started shaking, and here come three coppers out. And there was Boojum, they had hit him with a blackjack across the eye. When Boojum gets out of jail, he says, "I'm gonna kill that little midget. This time I'm gonna kill him. He's got me in trouble for the last time."

I hopped a train back to York, because I really thought he would kill me. Along around Wednesday I got a telegram, to come on back,

Boojum had cooled off. So I went back, but I kept my distance from that man for a while. Boojum says, "You little midget, you do something like that again, I'm gonna kill you."

Mac was always dignified, a perfect gentleman. The only time I heard Mac swear, we were playing in Philadelphia. I had a strawberry on my leg, and Mac gave me the sign to steal. I didn't go. He gave me the sign again; I still didn't go. The batter hit into a double play. So when Mac got back in the bus after the game, I never will forget. Rap Dixon and Chaney White had the time of their life. Mac said, "I ain't gonna call no names, but the next time I give a signal for a steal, there's one certain fella in here, if he don't steal, I'm gonna sock him right in the puss." And everybody knew who he was talking about. Only time I ever saw Mac get mad.

I've played against Lefty Grove, Rube Walberg, Grover Alexander. We played against Alexander eight or nine times. He was one of the greatest. He played with the House of David then. He'd only pitch three innings. We toured with them two or three weeks at a time twice a year.

Dizzy Dean and them were good guys. He was a hell of a pitcher. But he wasn't the kind of guy you'd want to introduce your sister to. Dean had a big mouth, like Satchel, ignorant. Didn't know right from wrong. Just a cotton picker, didn't have no education. When you contact people in the world, it gives you an education in itself. But I'll tell you the pitcher gave me the most trouble was Dean, 'cause he knocked you down. I was lead-off man and he'd throw at the back of my head. Trying to deprive me of my living.

At that time the pitchers would throw at you. This, across your chest, is just a brush-back. When they'd throw at the back of your head, that's when you knew you were being thrown at. That's what they called "sticking it in your ear." When Cannonball Dick Redding threw at you, you started to lean back and then dived forward. I mean, you left your hat in the air.

Did I ever tell you about the time I hung the Mule? Suttles was playing left field. He jumped up to catch that ball. There was a nail out there. The nail held him up there. They had to go down and unhook him. I got a home run. I hung him! That big spike held him up there. He couldn't get down, couldn't get up. Chaney White said, "Jake, you're the talk of the town. You hung the Mule tonight."

Now, I've played on a losing ball club too, the New York Black Yankees. What a difference between a winning club and a losing club. On a losing club they'd gamble, they'd drink, they ran after women. You have crap games and card games on a losing ball club. A man can't play baseball if he's losing money. How you going to lose your paycheck and play baseball?

And in the old days you rode by trains, you didn't have buses and all that stuff. But when night baseball came in, that's when the buses started. When they put those lights in and you played a double-header in the afternoon and a night game some other place, that's when they made sure they made money. Play a double-header Saturday afternoon, play a night game Saturday night, and a double-header Sunday, then go to Freeport or some other place—six games in two days. Does that make sense?

We stayed in any kind of hotel. Many's the night I've stayed at hotels so cold I wore my baseball uniform in bed. You took what came. In some towns they let the horses out of the stables, and we dressed in the damn stables! Up in Norristown we did that. I just got sick and tired of it.

I left baseball in 1937. I was a country boy, so I came home to York. I opened up a taproom and kept it for two years, but I didn't like it, because I had too many friends and they were getting hurt, so I sold out.

I was politically inclined and my friend was lieutenant governor, so I said, "Give me a job." He made me junior inspector in the Bureau of Motor Vehicles, and I stayed there from '39 to '55. Then the Democrats came in and they kicked me out. It was the best thing they ever did. I opened up a registry agency for car tags and driver's licenses. Everything you want here in Pennsylvania you got to go to Harrisburg to get it. I'd go up to Harrisburg and pick your tags up for you in 24 hours. I had the biggest business in York county, the cars used to line up around the block in front of my house, wanting me to get their tags.

One day I was up in Harrisburg counting all my money and putting it all in a sack. One-dollar bills I'd just shove in the desk drawer—they were too small to count. One Sunday night—I wasn't married then—I saw these fellows at this place and they said, "Come on, buy me a drink." I knew they didn't have any money, so I bought them a drink, took my change, and turned the dice loose. I came home, counted my money, and I had $115. So next Sunday I had about $900—I mean of my customers' money. And it was like a magnet drew me back to that place. I wasn't in there but half an hour, and when I walked out I didn't have a dime. A lot of people knew I'd been shooting, so I went to see this loan company, borrowed $300 here, $300 there, until I got the $900. Monday the people all were waiting for me: "Hi, Paul."

"Hi."

"Got our tags, Paul?"

"Oh, mmm-hmmm."

"They told me you lost all our money shooting."

"Are you kidding? Must be nuts. I was shooting my money, not your money"—they didn't know that. Last time I ever shot craps in my life. Looks like I could do some of the damn dumbest things.

My big problem is, I *know* too many people.

I'm a deputy sheriff now, part-time. You can't just sit around and do nothing, you get tired of living with yourself. I told them, "I'll never arrest anybody." Because you'd lose a friendship. "Once you arrest them and put them in jail, wherever you want me to take them, I'll take them." I've got too many friends. Dollars don't mean that much to me any more; I'd rather have friendship. I don't think I ever made an enemy intentionally. I'm running out of time. I just hope I don't make any now.

One thing, I own this house. Me and the bank don't own it—I do, me and my wife. I got married a few years ago for companionship. I'm 70 years old. After you hit that 60 mark, you slow up. You're supposed to live three score year and ten, so every year I live now, I've over-lived my time. I've got a little boy, two years old. He's a good little boy. My first son—my *only* child.

I'm the messenger boy around here now. My wife writes down a list of things for me to go out and get, and I better not forget, or I get my ears pinned back. My wife knows judo, and I don't want her to practice it on me.

See that gun on the wall, the old flintlock? That's been in my family for four generations. My father died when he was 94 years of age. His father had it before him, and his father's father had it before him.

I want you to come up the road with me. See that Lutheran church on the top of the hill? That's my church. That's where my seeds are. My father and mother are buried there. And my grandmother. She lived from 1809 to 1885. Sometimes when I'm feeling down, I go up there. There's a picnic area over on the other side of the cemetery, and I bring a sandwich and I sit there, and it just gives me a lift, you know. I guess we're all a little bit sentimental, aren't we?

I don't know where all the old fellows are now. You're bringing back a lot of memories. You tell those guys Jake Stephens said they're a big bunch of bums, I'll lick them all (every one of them could lick me). You tell those bunch of bums I'm going to learn a left hook, and the first thing, they're gonna get it. Tell them I'll give them a karate blow, that'll fix 'em. I'd just like to see them and sit down and talk. I wish some day we'd have a Roman holiday. Everybody, one grand meeting from Saturday to Monday.

Oh my goodness, it was wonderful knowing those fellows, though. You can't appreciate it, but nobody will know what a wonderful life I've lived. I've had the happiest life any man ever could.

Paul "Jake" Stephens

b: 2/10/00, Pleasureville, PA				d: 2/5/81, York, PA				BR TR		
Year	Team	PSN	G	AB	H	2B	3B	HR	BA	SB
1924	Philadelphia	SS	12	42	8	1	1	0	.191	1
1925	Philadelphia	SS	46	157	36	9	2	0	.229	7
1926	New England semi-pro									
1927	Philadelphia	SS	41	108	30	0	2	0	.278	7
1928	No record									
1929	No record									
1930	No record									
1931	Grays	SS	9	33	8	3	0	0	.242	0
1932	Grays, Crawfords	SS	28	116	31	2	0	0	.267	2
1933	Philadelphia	SS	12	47	15	0	0	1	.319	0
1934	Philadelphia	SS	19	77	17	—	—	—	.221	—
1935	Philadelphia	SS	27	64	14	0	0	0	.219	1
1936	New York	SS-2B	—	64	9	0	0	0	.141	0
1937	New York	SS	5	19	5	0	0	0	.263	0

Post-Season

1924	World Series	SS	1	2	0	0	0	0	.000	0
1925	World Series	SS	6	20	5	2	0	0	.250	1
1930	Playoffs	SS	9	37	10	1	0	0	.270	1
1934	Playoffs	SS	1	3	0	0	0	0	.000	0

Recap

	Negro league	SS	—	727	173	15	5	1	.238	18
	Post-Season	SS	17	62	15	3	0	0	.270	2
	East-West game	SS	1	6	2	0	0	0	.333	0
	Totals			795	190	18	5	1	.239	20

Papa Chet
CHET BREWER

If they ever have a Hall of Fame for great citizens, Chet Brewer will be one of the first ones in it. Before a series of accidents in 1987, Brewer, or "Papa Chet," as the kids in Los Angeles' Watts section call him, ran one of the most successful boys' baseball programs in America. Several of his kids made the major leagues—Dock Ellis, Reggie Smith, Bob Watson, Enos Cabell. But he was proudest of all of the boys he sent on to become good citizens like himself.

Chet's prospects for the Hall of Fame are hurt by the fact that he was overshadowed on the Monarchs' staff by, first, Bullet Rogan and later, Satchel Paige, plus a lingering reputation for cutting the ball, a charge that was also leveled at Whitey Ford, among others.

Catcher-pitcher Ted "Double Duty" Radcliffe recalled:

"Brewer was in the same league with Satchel and (Bullet Joe) Rogan. He and I started out the same time with Gilkerson's Union Giants—he and I and George Giles; we were all three good friends. Emory Osborne showed me and Brewer how to throw a scratched ball: didn't have to cut it, just scratch it a little. He just scratched it like I did."

"Brewer was a finesser," says his old teammate, Buck O'Neil. "Cut the ball? In the later years they say he roughed it up a bit, but during his prime he didn't have to cut it. Good curve ball, good control, spotted the ball."

Brewer may not have cut the ball, conceded outfielder Ted Page, but in the old days balls were not thrown out of play for every little smudge. Chet loved to see a foul ball glance off the grandstand. "He'd wait for that one to come back in play."

Added Willie Powell: "Brewer would throw a cut ball if someone else did the cutting for him. He didn't do the cutting—you didn't know who was cutting the ball. He threw everything but the kitchen stove. And he'd knock our hats off."

Even at the end of his career, Brewer "had a big old rainbow curve ball," says Wilmer Fields. "And good control, pitching them in and out."

He was "a dangerous sort of pitcher," Schoolboy Johnny Taylor said. "If a guy was hitting too good, Chet would say, 'Mmmmm-hmmmm.' The next thing you know, the guy is rubbing his back."

Above all, O'Neil recalls Brewer as "kind of a leader fella. Chet always was telling us the money wasn't enough: 'You should be making more money.' And I'm sure it wasn't."

When the fans chose their lineups for the first East-West game in 1933, Chet was the number-two pick for starting pitcher for the West. That year he also toured the Orient with the Monarchs, stopping in Japan and the Philippines to play.

In '34 the fans again picked him number-two for the East-West lineup, and Cum Posey named him to his all-black all-star team. Chet says he won 16 games in a row that year, undoubtedly including semipro opponents, since the Monarchs were not in the league. He and the Monarchs faced the House of Davids with Satchel Paige in the Denver *Post* national semipro tournament. Chet struck out 19 men in one game, a mark that was never broken (Satchel's high was 18 in the '36 tourney), though Paige beat Brewer 2–1 to take the crown.

That October Brewer faced an all-star team in Jamestown, North Dakota—Hall of Famers Jimmy Foxx (.333, 44 home runs), Heinie Manush (.349), and Ted Lyons (11–13), plus Pinky Higgins (.330) and Doc Cramer (.311). Chet gave them three hits and beat them 11–0. Foxx didn't get any hits, and Manush whiffed three times. (Chet admits, however, that Foxx "was filled up with some of that Canadian beer.")

One year later Brewer and Paige were teammates in the Wichita semipro tourney. Satch won three games and Chet four, as their club, Bismarck, North Dakota, breezed to victory undefeated.

Brewer went to Mexico in '38 and '39, the first American black to play there, and ran up a couple of no-hitters.

Brewer pitched and managed in the California winter league against many white major league and Pacific Coast league stars. Infielder Lou Dials says Chet approached Charlie Root, then managing Hollywood, about a job. "If I don't win 20 games, you don't have to pay me," Brewer said.

"I know you can do it," Root laughed, "but I just can't do anything."

Well over 40 years old in 1948, Chet joined the Cleveland Buckeyes, with youngsters like Sam Jethroe, and helped pitch them to the Negro league pennant while, across town, Paige was helping to hurl the Indians to the National League flag that same year. In 51 innings, Brewer walked four men. "Who is that guy?" demanded Indian General Manager Hank Greenberg. "He has better control than any pitcher on our club."

Brewer became a scout for the majors and began his program of working with boys, a mission that demanded both time and financial sacrifices. Major league baseball hasn't contributed to the program, but others have; Don Newcombe, for instance, contributed uniforms for the boys.

Mrs. Effa Manley, former owner of the Newark Eagles who retired to Los Angeles, also met Chet at that period. She wrote:

I am now busy trying to get something done that I feel is very worthwhile. Did you ever know Chet Brewer? Well, he has never been able to retire from baseball, so he has had a program going every Saturday and Sunday teaching young ball players. The games are staged in a playground park here. Chet's wife came and got me a couple months ago and took me to see one of the games. She and Chet pay all expenses—they have bought uniforms, the balls and bats, pay insurance—all expenses, and don't charge the kids anything. She wanted me to see the park and things that need to be done to put it in first-class shape. Well, I think I have made the proper contact, and I really feel things are going to materialize.

When I met Brewer at a reunion of Negro league vets in Ashland, Kentucky, he was still tall and erect and spoke in a slow, bass voice. SABR's Bob Hoie, who met him in Los Angeles in 1983, also reported that "he walks with a cane, but he still has that regal bearing."

I know I should be up there in that Hall of Fame. I played with Satchel Paige, and I beat him as many times as he beat me. My biggest thrill was when I beat Satchel a no-hitter in Santo Domingo in 1936. They made two scores on an error, and I beat them 4–2.

I played on the Kansas City Monarchs with Satchel. None of us got any publicity when Satchel was there, because he got all of it. I was unfortunate, because when I came up to the Monarchs in 1926, Bullet Joe Rogan got all the publicity. Then later Satchel got it. But I beat everyone the rest of them did.

I pitched against Satchel a lot of times. We just about broke even on wins. In Winnipeg we went 11 innings 0–0 until it got dark and we had to knock it off.

They always starred Satchel. He had all the billing. Several nights Satchel would pitch and come out, and Connie Johnson or I'd follow him. All of us were tall and black, and we were all throwing hard. The fans would say, "Which one of them niggers was Satchel?" They didn't know Satchel from the rest of us. It was awful the way the white people talked about us. We entertained them and beat the socks off them. We'd ignore their insults and just beat the pants off them.

I had a team out here in Los Angeles called the Kansas City Royals. The reason I named them that was because the players were from the Monarchs. Bob Feller would bring his all stars out here— Stan Musial, Bob Lemon, Mickey Vernon, Kenny Keltner, Johnny Sain, Mike Garcia, Jeff Heath. You know, we beat them guys as many times as they beat us.

Satchel pitched for me. Don Newcombe played for me. Jackie Robinson played on my team too before the Dodgers signed him. Sometimes Satchel didn't show up until we were taking infield practice. He'd come running down there tying his shoes. Had us all excited, because all the publicity was built around Satchel pitching, and if he didn't show up, we'd have to give all the money back.

Satchel did everything wrong. Just as wrong as he could be. And the public doesn't know it.

Satchel got his arm sore playing in the Dominican Republic. Mexico sent him money and a plane ticket—$2,000 a month, that was a lot of money. But he couldn't pitch. Those Mexicans found out he couldn't throw hard and just beat his brains out. They didn't want him there any more.

J. L. Wilkinson, the owner of the Kansas City Monarchs, took that man to the doctor, took him to the dentist, got him new teeth, then let him fool around, play first base. Finally, when his health got good, his arm came back and Wilkinson let him pitch. He'd hire him out on Sunday and take 15 percent off the top of the gate receipts, right after the government got their money.

But Satchel was always late getting to games, or he wouldn't get there at all. So Wilkinson put us to riding together. He figured I'd help Satchel.

One time in Three Rivers, Michigan, 200 miles to go, game starts at three o'clock; it's one now. Satchel in the middle of the floor shooting dice with some woman for pennies. They had won his pennies. I said, "Come on, Satchel, we're going to be late." He's still there. I said, "Come on, let's go."

"Oh, Dooflackem, you worry to much."

Satchel was driving this big Airflow Chrysler. We get in his car. He said, "If the red lights are going to make us late, I won't stop at any more." He's blowing his horn, going right through the red lights. Satchel was going so fast, we went about a block past the ball park— had to turn around. We walk in in the fifth inning, people going home, demanding their money back.

One time in Philadelphia, he had this white Lincoln Continental car then. We were late again. Down this street he went. "You can't go down the street! It's a one-way street!" Traffic coming at us, Satchel ducking in and out. Big motor cycle cop, siren: "Pull over there." Satchel pulled over. "Doggone, don't you see that's a one-way street?"

Satchel looked up at him so innocently: "I'm only going one way."

They took him to jail, fined him $50. "You're going to have to make court tomorrow at nine."

Satchel said, "Sir, we're going to leave at eight."

The judge said, "Another $50, you can go." Satchel paid. Just speeding again. We got to the ball park in the third inning. Late again!

Out here in California he broke every traffic law in Los Angeles, making U-turns, going through the safety zone with people standing in it. Out in Bakersfield on his way to 'Frisco to play, the cops were after Satchel, didn't catch him until he was in Oakland. He just said, "I wanted to see how fast I could go before you caught me."

They said, "Man, you can't drive out here." They took his California driver's license from him.

I told J. L.: "Now, instead of one pitcher being later, you got two late. I don't want to ride with Satchel any more. He's going to get both of us killed!"

In New York Satchel would pitch on Sunday when they had the big double headers in Yankee Stadium. You wouldn't see Satchel until the next Sunday. He was off in his big Cadillac, just having all his fun. Naturally he showed up the next Sunday and pitched one heck of a game, gets all the publicity, gets in his car, and gone again. The Monarchs put up with it, because they were making money off him. J. L. got rich on him.

Out here in Los Angeles we made $1,600, and that was good money for us. One night the park was full, and we got $300 a man just that one night.

Chet Brewer in Panama City in 1948.

Satchel was supposed to get 15 percent of the gross receipts. What they were doing, they were paying Satchel 15 percent of the net, after expenses. They didn't let me come up in their office. I didn't have the privilege, even though it was my team out here. But they gave me the government sheet of all the tickets they sold, and I saw they were paying Satchel 15 percent of the net. I said, "Satchel, Bob Feller owes you $2,400."

"Sure enough, Dooflackem?"

"Yeah."

"Come on, let's go." They didn't stop *him* from going up there in that office. Boy, Bob Feller hated me for a long time. I saw him once in the airport in Phoenix, and he didn't even speak to me. He hated to pay Satchel that $2,400.

Later we went down to Satchel's room in the hotel. He said, "Here, Dooflackem, here's $30."

I threw it back in his face. "I'm not hungry, you keep it."

Even when he got in the big leagues, he'd miss trains. He said, "I thought it was going to rain, I didn't think we were going to play." Lou Boudreau, manager of the Indians, covered up for him. They had Satchel on TV, "This Is Your Life." Boudreau was there praising him and everything. All he got was good publicity.

Satchel didn't really like me. All his wives threw me up to him: "Satchel, why don't you act like Chet? Why don't you dress like him? Look how Chet dresses, look how Chet acts." Boy, he didn't like that. His wife, Lucy Baby, out of Puerto Rico, she'd tell Satchel, "Why don't you act like Chet acts?" His last wife, Lahoma, would tell him the same thing. Naturally, Satchel is Mr. Big. He'd do just like he wants to do. He didn't like me.

All Satchel had to do was say a word, and I'd be in the Hall of Fame up there. But he didn't. He wrote a book and mentioned all the pitchers in there that couldn't even carry my glove, and he didn't even give me a mention. I said, "That's all right."

We were down in Ashland, Kentucky, at a Negro league reunion the year before he died. He was packing the car in the hotel parking lot. Lahoma was there and I went over with my wife to talk to her. She said, "Did Satchel come to see you?"

I said, "No."

"I told him to go say hello to you"—he was standing right on the other side of the car.

I said, "That's all right."

Well, Satchel's dead now, so let him rest in peace.

Now Jackie Robinson, he played for the Monarchs in '45 and for me in California that winter. He was just the opposite of Satchel—he was some kind of competitor! I had all the equipment, so I used to have to get to the clubhouse early. When I got there, Jackie was already sitting there half-dressed, shoes and socks on, supporter on.

Jackie had one of my uniforms when *Look* magazine interviewed him right after he signed with the Dodgers. I had that uniform made down in Mexico; it had ROYALS across the front. I have one of those old uniforms yet; I left Jackie's down in Ashland, for that black history museum there.

Jackie was playing shortstop for the Monarchs, but Jesse Williams [also of the Monarchs] was my shortstop, so I had Jackie play second. That's what started him playing second, because he was a better second baseman than a shortstop. And boy, could he play!

Jackie was an excellent choice [for the Dodgers] because of his intelligence. That, put together with his ability, made him a natural. A lot of other players would not have taken what Jackie did. Some of the other hot heads wouldn't have stood still for it. I don't know whether I could have or not.

I was born in Leavenworth, Kansas, in 1907. My father was a Methodist minister, but when I was a kid, I was a little so and so, a little hoodlum. I was mischievous. I didn't steal, anything like that. But in school I'd stick gum in the girls' hair. But my mother and father stayed on my case, and when I got older, I could see what they were trying to teach me. I was fortunate. I was reared in a Christian home, and I was given some good values to live by.

One time when I was 15 years old, the All Nations team came through Des Moines. That was J. L. Wilkinson's team; they had Negroes, whites, Cubans, a Chinese, even two girls. Dink Mothell, C. Bell, Jaybird Ray, those kinds of fellows.

I attended Western high school, played football and basketball there, ran track. They didn't have a baseball program so I slipped off in the summer time and played with a team called the Tennessee Rats. "Uncle Walt" ran it. I didn't know his name, just Uncle Walt.

Did you see the movie, *The Bingo Long Story?* It was on the same nature. Some of the modern day ball players say it was a come-down, a slap in the face, but this is what truly happened to us. We'd come to a town in our T-model Ford and go up and down the street with a megaphone—didn't have microphones then—and say, "Come out to the ball park," and slept in tents and played and clowned, just like Bingo Long. It was a way to make money. It was the only way we knew how to get the people to come. It was a tough life, but I see these big league ball players nowadays complaining. We couldn't eat in the restaurants or sleep in the better hotels, but we still entertained the people. Didn't make much money, but had a lot of fun playing, because we loved the game.

In 1924 I went with Gilkerson's Union Giants out of Joliet, near Chicago. Picked up players from the Negro leagues and toured the Northwest. It was more dignified than the Tennessee Rats. We had an old bus with long benches on each side. We all had to wear coveralls that fastened at the neck and around the bottom. When we got to a town, we'd take them off and hang them up and were well dressed. It was a classy outfit.

The driver couldn't stay on the highway five minutes. Had to be a lookout man up with him. One night we dropped down off a hill in Nashville, going to St. Louis. At a quarter after five the next morning someone woke up, said, "Where are we?"

"Nashville."

"You got to be kidding. We left Nashville last night!"

We used to ride three or four nights in that big bus and never see a bed. We'd play in one town at night and then after the game, shower in the shower room, get in that bus, ride all night to the next town and get out and go to some little hamburger joint and have some lunch, go to the ball park early, wash our underwear out, hang it up to dry, wash our socks and things. Then when the game was over, well, we were clean. We lived out of our shaving kits with our toothpaste and what-have-you.

I remember one night in Medford, Wisconsin, not anywhere near the South, in an old second-rate white hotel. They had a restaurant and the food was terrible. We wouldn't eat there, got a "Dutch lunch," sandwiches out of a grocery store. One cold morning in September this man came up at two o'clock in the morning with his pistol, made us get out of this hotel, said, "If my food's not good enough for you darkies to eat, my hotel isn't good enough for you to stay in." Had to get out and ride to the next town. And it was cold.

One time in Elkhart, Indiana, we went in the restaurant and ordered some hamburgers, about 36. The man had them on the grill. One of the fellows said, "I'll just sit down and have a piece of pie and a glass of milk while I'm waiting." The waitress said, "I'm sorry, we don't serve you like this, this is 'sack service.'" We said, "All right, since we can't eat here, you people have a good time eating all those hamburgers." We walked out and left them on the grill.

Another day, walking down the street: "Old dirty face, old dirty face. Mister, mister, your hands are all dirty. My father's hands get dirty, then he washes them and he's white and clean like I am." He hadn't been taught that all the soap and scrubbing isn't going to take that black off me.

All that stuff. We had to put up with everything. But we survived.

Just think of the life we had to live, paving the way for the guys who are making all this fabulous money. And not one of them thinks of doing anything for the old ball players. The only thing that's ever been done for us was those old-timers' reunions in Ashland. But these guys today, they never thought about getting up a fund, and some of the old-timers are in pretty bad shape, I understand. I'm just fortunate enough to have a scouting job and saved some of my money when I had it.

In 1925 the All Nations remembered me. They recommended me to Wilkinson's Kansas City Monarchs [Negro league champions of 1924 and '25]. When I got out of high school, the Monarchs sent for me.

I tell you, it was rough to be a rookie. The older fellows would give you a rough time: "Heh, rookie!" You were out there scared to death. William Bell, a pitcher, was the only one on that team that really encouraged me. Wade Johnson, an outfielder out of Ohio, was nice too. George Sweatt was another nice fellow.

Another baseball player who had class was Pat Patterson. I tried to pattern my way of living after Sweatt and Patterson. Of course education helps a lot. A lot of those old-time Monarchs weren't well educated. That's a hard thing to whip, ignorance. Two classes I just can't stand is ignorance and a drunk person. I hated a drunk worse than sin.

Bullet Joe Rogan was the manager and the star pitcher. I think Rogan was the best pitcher I ever saw, black or white, and I saw Bob Feller, Dizzy Dean, Satchel, Smokey Joe Williams. Who in the world had a curve ball like Rogan did? Jeepers, he could throw the curve ball faster than most pitchers could throw a fast ball. Cristobal Torriente was center field. He was Indian-colored brown, but he was considered a Negro. What a ball player he was! He could have been a super major leaguer. We had Dobie Moore, shortstop; Newt Allen, second; Newt Joseph, third; Frank Duncan catching. Some of those old-timers, it's a shame baseball wasn't open to them. Man oh man, we'd have rewritten the record book back in our prime.

Rube Currie of Chicago was a master pitcher. He kind of liked me, and when we'd go to Chicago, he'd say, "Come over here, let me tell you a few things about this game." Had good control, just a class pitcher. Looked like a professor out there on the mound, like a big-time teacher.

I threw an overhand curve ball, what we called a drop ball. It started about letter-high, then dropped down by the knees. Of course I could throw a screw ball and had a good, live, running fast ball. We'd play on those rough diamonds, when the ball hit the ground, it got roughed up. I could screw it real good then.

A cut ball? I got credit for that. If I picked up a rough one, I didn't throw it out of the game. I didn't exactly put the cuts on it myself, but I could pitch it.

Swede Risberg of the Chicago Black Sox was barnstorming against us in Winona, Wisconsin. You'd check a brand new ball right out of the box, and it was already scratched. We had to learn how to throw it too.

But with that curve ball I had, I could win without scratching the ball. When I learned the screw ball, they said, "Heck, he's scratching the ball," so I knew that I was getting on them. I'd face the outfield and rub the ball up, turn around, throw a screw ball: "Oh, he cut it!" But it was more a psychological thing.

They accused Don Sutton of the Dodgers of cutting the ball. And you know they undressed Don Drysdale and searched him. Robin Roberts of the Phils, I know he cut the ball in the winter. He was throwing that ball, and those guys were striking out. I was coaching first base, went out, picked up one of those balls, and it had a scratch the size of a half dollar. So those guys cheat in the major leagues, as well as throwing a spit ball in there some time. That's how it goes.

In 1926 Kansas City won the first half, the American Giants won the second half. We had a playoff to see who would go to Atlantic City

Chet Brewer (center) with the Kansas City Monarchs. Also shown are (from left) Charlie Beverly, Floyd Kranson, Maddison, and Andy Cooper.

to play the Bacharach Giants in the black World Series. I opened up Saturday and we beat them. William Bell pitched Sunday and beat them. They brought me back Monday and I beat them again 5–0. We went to Chicago leading three games to one, needing one more game.

You know, those guys beat us out.

They won Monday. It rained Tuesday. We had to play a double header Wednesday in order to make the train to Atlantic City. We had new uniforms and everything, because we just knew we were going.

Rogan was manager, and he lost the first game to Big Bill Foster of Chicago 1–0. I was warming up down in the bull pen, and I just knew I was going to pitch the second game. I had pitched like a dog all year [Brewer was 12–1]. It was getting dark, and I knew those guys didn't want to face me.

But Foster came back to pitch the second game for Chicago. When Rogan saw him, he said, "Well, if he's going back, so am I." They got three runs off him in the first inning and beat him 5–0.

In 1930 I lost to Smokey Joe [of the New York Lincolns] 1–0. They just had too much manpower for us. We had some young fellows, but those guys, the Homestead Grays, had Josh Gibson catching, Oscar Charleston first base, and Judy Johnson third base [all three are in the Hall of Fame]. Boy, what a team they had! I was glad to get down from that batter's box, because Joe could throw that ball harder than anyone I batted against. He struck out 27 people in 12 innings. I struck out 19.

We could have won that game in nine innings 1–0. Leroy Taylor was at bat, Newt Joseph at third. The count was 3–2, and Newt was running. The umpire called it a strike. If he had just called it ball four, we'd have won that ball game. Any other home umpire in the world would have called that a ball. In the 12th inning, they scored a run on a walk and an error. Little Jake Stephens was on. Chaney White hit the ball, and it hit the third base bag and went under the ropes around the portable lights. By the time Newt Joseph retrieved that ball, Jake Stephens scored the winning run. If that ball had just bounced into the infield, we would probably be playing yet.

I left the Monarchs in '31 and played up in Crookston, Minnesota. They were hiring colored players to play. Little Falls had John Donaldson [old-time left-hander of the Monarchs] and Hooks Foreman, a bow-legged catcher for the Monarchs—his real name was Sylvester Foreman. I pitched for Crookston; Johnny Vann was my catcher.

The first Sunday I was up there in Crookston, I said, "I'm going to see just what kind of people they are. I'm going to go to church." I've always been raised to go to church; in the colored league I would go to church. "I'm going to see what these people are going to do." I walked in, dressed nice, walked right down the middle, looked at the minister, sat there. When that minister finished his sermon, he almost ran to the door to get there ahead of me, shook my hand, told me how happy he was that I came to his service, invited me to Bible class. I was just like one of the citizens.

That was one of the most beautiful summers I lived. We were the only colored in town. I was staying in a hotel and eating in a restaurant with a big Norwegian woman. I told the hotel man I was going to send for my family and wanted to rent a house. He said, "There's a big house over there a couple doors from the mayor. They haven't kept it up. The grounds need work." So he said, "I tell you what: You can get things out of my store room—beds, and things." That hotel man and that restaurant owner, they furnished my house for me. About a day before my wife and kids were coming up there, a truck rolled out and those fellows started carrying groceries in there. A big kitchen, and they filled those shelves up with sugar, flour, meal, a couple slabs of bacon, all kind of canned goods. Looked like a grocery store. A German fellow ran the filling station. He said, "I have a car here, take the keys. You need gas, just pull up and fill up."

I went down to meet my wife and kids. You know how life is. Naturally, we were going to live down on the other side of the tracks. She said, "Well, I expected that."

I pulled up, said, "Let's stop in here a minute."

"OK, don't be long. I'm tired."

I said, "Come here a minute, I want you to meet some people." We got out, came in this big, spacious living room. "This is where we're going to live."

"Are you out of your mind? You got to be kidding!" She was so happy, tears came to her cheeks. The kids jumped up and hugged me. It was a big house, and when Vann's family came, we had room for them too. We had just the finest summer up there.

John Donaldson came through and beat me 2–1. He tried to get my job—there wasn't any brotherly love in my profession. But the man said, "If we get rid of Chet Brewer now, the way he's pitching, I'd have to leave town."

Dizzy Dean, he was a great pitcher. And he wanted us to make some money—he'd already made his. He would get out there and look at the crowd. He raised cain if he thought they were cheating us on our share of the receipts.

Paul Dean [Dizzy's brother] hurt his arm trying to beat the Monarchs one cold night. But Diz was throwing that fast ball by us.

We had George Giles playing first base for us. He said, "I can hit that fast ball." So Giles came up with the bases full. Dean stretched like he was reaching to the clouds, then boom! Threw that fast ball a little over Giles' letters. Giles held the bat way down on the end, couldn't come around fast enough.

So he choked up a little bit. Boom. Belt high. Giles took that strike.

He choked up some more. Had as much bat below his hands as he had above. The third pitch was knee-high. Giles bent over and smiled at it. He never did straighten up. Came right back to the dugout, still bent over. "Man, I couldn't get ready. The ball was by me before I could make up my mind to swing."

I told Dizzy, "I want one of those Cardinal jackets." We had jackets but not like that one. It was a beauty.

He said, "I'll give it to you when we quit playing." Wrigley Field, Los Angeles, he came in, said, "Here's a jacket, from one good pitcher to another."

He was one good ol' boy from the South.

Toughest hitter? Oh boy, there were so many of them. The toughest one for me to get out was Buck Leonard. I don't ever remember pitching a game against Buck he didn't get two hits off me. I could get Josh Gibson out, but by golly, that Buck Leonard hit me like he owned me. I played with him in Puerto Rico, and that sure was a pleasure.

The first time I saw Josh, 1930, he was a big rookie playing outside Pittsburgh. So I always figured him just a big rookie. I never was afraid of him. Our own pitchers were afraid of Josh, but I'd say, "What's wrong with you guys? He's human like anyone else."

Josh did something that a lot of pitchers didn't pick up on. When he crouched, you couldn't throw him anything low—he hit low balls like someone hitting a golf ball. And when he stood up straight, anything from the waist up, he'd hit that out of sight. So I'd pitch him high when he crouched and low when he stood up. Like Pete Rose: I don't think Rose would hit in our colored league, because when he crouched, our guys would throw it over his letters. By the time he straightened up, it would be by him.

Josh hit one home run off me. It was in Dyckman Oval, the ball park the New York Cubans had, not too far from the Polo Grounds. They had a nightclub right behind right field. Quite a deal. Right field was close, like Yankee Stadium, 200-some feet. Josh hit a home run off me over that short fence. Only one he hit off me.

I pitched against him in the all-star games and at Forbes Field. They said I was crazy. We all dressed in the same hotel and walked to the ball park. After the game, we'd walk back and bathe in the hotel. One day Josh and I were walking down the road. "See this bat, Chet Brewer? I'm going to wear you out on this."

I said, "The first time, if you get a hit on me, I'm going to hit you."

"You poor so-and-so, you couldn't hurt anybody."

"If a gnat gets in your eyes, it'll hurt you, and that's where I'm going to hit you." The first time, I got his cap bill—don't know how I missed his head. Down in the dirt he went. I walked halfway to home, "Missed you this time, but I'm going to get you the next time."

Mule Suttles, now there's a guy could hit that ball just as far as Josh or farther. He could hit anybody's curve ball but Rogan's—nobody could hit that successfully.

One day in St. Louis I threw Mule my overhand drop, broke down around his ankles. He golfed it right by my face, about six inches to the right of my face. Just kept on going up, up, up. He hit that ball over the top of that car barn in the outfield and so high, when it hit on the other side of the barn, the ball bounced back in the air. You could see it again. Ooh, if that ball had been six inches over, it would have killed me. Just think how hard it was hit! It just kept raising up, up, up and way away.

The next time I put the fear of God in him in that old frame ball park in St. Louis. That's when they served beer in bottles, and the fans were yelling, "Kick, Mule, kick!" I said to myself, "They don't know what's getting ready to happen." I shook the catcher off—no way for me to throw Mule a curve ball. Fast ball, about three feet outside, the catcher had to jump to catch it. The fans beat on the wood; they thought they had me all upset. The next pitch, out there again. Now it was bedlam then. Those fans were going crazy: "Kick, Mule, kick!"

Mule got out of the box, got moisture on his hands, got back in and dug in. And I hit Mule right side of the head. That ball bounced to the grandstand. That cat, Dick Kent [owner of the St. Louis Stars], sat in the corner of the stand with a megaphone; he'd holler to kids chasing balls over on Compton Avenue. That ball bounced over Dick Kent and onto Compton.

One guy got under Mule's arm, the other under his leg, and they carried him to the dugout.

After that, I just had to lean to third base, and back on his heels he went. Stepped in the bucket. I'd throw across his letters on him.

But if you let one slip out, that was it!

In Cuba, we had a little white pitcher named Acosta. We said, "Now, Acosta, we play against Mule every summer, so when he comes up, don't throw him any curve ball. Keep it letter-high, in on him." Acosta is white, he's not going to listen to any colored, figured we didn't know anything about baseball. Mule hit that ball 500-some feet down left field. Acosta just watched Mule go around the bases. When the inning was over, we said, "Acosta, what did you throw him?"

He said, "Oh, man, I never seen a ball hit so far in my life!"

We said, "We *know* that, Acosta, we could see where it went. What did you *throw* him?

He said, "I didn't believe any human being could hit a ball so far."
To this day he hasn't owned up that he threw that man a curve.

Down in Cuba, Jelly Gardner and Turkey Stearnes were on the
same team, and it was ungodly hot. Jelly had a habit, when he wanted
to get out of the game, about the fifth inning he'd single and stretch it
into a double and slide into second and fall out [faint]. The manager
would tell Turkey to take his place. One day it was so hot, you could
see the heat waves coming out of the ground. When Jelly slid in there
and fell out, Turkey fell out on the bench! Turkey was laying there,
they're fanning *him!* He said, "Shoot, man, I had enough of that
stuff."

In Santo Domingo, Satchel had Josh Gibson, Cool Papa Bell, Sam
Bankhead [older brother of Dodger pitcher Dan Bankhead]—boy,
what a player he was, one of the best ball players in our league.

We could have won that championship, but Trujillo, the dictator
there, was backing Satchel's team. He couldn't lose face by letting the
team he was backing lose. We were about tied up, but the Trujillo team
had three games left to play. Trujillo just took those games, said, "We'll
just forfeit those games to us."

When we wanted to socialize with the guys before the game, we
couldn't find them. They weren't at the hotel where they stayed. We
asked a little boy in the street, and he said, "They're down in the
carcel." Trujillo had put them in jail at night so he'd be sure they didn't
party. Boy, the police in those countries are something!

We had a lot of fun playing. Didn't make a lot of money, but we
did have some fun.

I spent two winters in Panama. The second year we won the
Caribbean Series. [Brewer pitched the victory in the final game.] It's
the only time Panama won the tourney. We were the poorest country
of all of them. The other players laughed at us when we lined up for
the pre-game ceremony. We looked like boys in knickers. But after the
victory, there were parades and parties all over Panama City.

In later years, about 1940, when the Monarchs had fellows like
Buck O'Neil, Ted Strong, Connie Johnson [who later pitched for the
White Sox and Orioles], Booker McDaniel, T. J. Young, it was fun.
Jeepers, it was fun playing with them.

During the war I was inspector for North American Aircraft. I
was their first Negro inspector. I worked my way up from janitor to
inspector. The army inspector was supposed to check after me, but
this young guy wanted to go out and play with some gals, so he gave
me his stamp: "Anything good enough for you, you just put my stamp
on there. I'll see you." Food was rationed, he'd give me his roasts and
steaks.

One Saturday he said, "I see all these colored girls say hi to you.

Let's get a couple of girls and we'll have a real party." I'm mad enough to kill him. I said, "I tell you what: I'll point you out to some of my friends. Meantime, you scout around and get a white girl for me. Not one I can pay ten dollars for, but the type you could take home to your sister." He's getting red in the face. I heard no more about that party.

The same year that Jackie signed with Brooklyn, Bakersfield, California, the farm club of the Cleveland Indians, wanted to sign me. I was 38. George Trautman, the minor league commissioner, okayed it, but Roger Peckinpaugh, the general manager of the Indians, shot it down.

I made the [Negro league] all-star team twice, two years in a row, 1947–48. I was 38 years old the last time. (I was 40, but they had my age as 38.) Fifty thousand people at the White Sox park in Chicago. The West beat the East 5–2 in '47. I pitched my three scoreless innings. Minnie Minoso played for the East that day.

We played the major leaguers in Oakland one night. When Luke Easter would come to bat, those big league outfielders would lean against the fence. One night he hit the ball on top of the lights. Three innings later a car went by and backfired, and the radio announcer said that was Luke Easter's home run coming down. He put the fear of God in those pitchers. And we made a lot of money.

I'm retired now. I got a pension from North American, and we get social security, so I'm one of the fortunate ones. I'm 77 years old, and I'm the busiest 77-year-old man you'll ever know.

I have this semipro baseball program for kids from 14 to 23 years of age. Every Sunday I run it as kind of a showcase for the major league scouting bureau. They send people out they want to get a good look at under game conditions. They honored me by naming that ball diamond Chet Brewer Field. I've been a Methodist all my life, so I go to church out here. I have to go to the 8:30 service, because I have to be at my ball park at ten o'clock.

A lot of ball players have left there under my tutelage. Joe Black [who pitched for the old Brooklyn Dodgers] was one of my protégés. Bobby Tolan, Reggie Smith, Willie Crawford, Enos Cabell, Ellis Valentine, Bob Watson in Atlanta—all those fellows came through my program. And I had any number of them that got in the minor leagues and didn't make it, but they turned out to be good citizens. I feel good when I see them staying out of trouble and doing something for themselves. That's kind of part of my life.

Dock Ellis was one of my first kids. Just before he signed with the Pirates, he and a buddy out of Fremont high school, Ray Jones—who was going to the Green Bay Packers—went out and stole an automobile. One morning about six o'clock Dock's mother called. "Mr.

Brewer, Dock is going to trial this morning at nine o'clock. I don't know what to do."

"What they do?"

"They say they stole an automobile."

"You go back to sleep, I'll go down there."

I walked in about 8:30. A big tall white fellow was coming out of the judge's office with a lot of books and papers in his hand. I introduced myself and told him I was there on behalf of a couple of young fellows. "I'd appreciate it if you'd get me in there to talk to the judge." He went back in and came out and beckoned me to come in.

I said, "Judge, your honor, I'm here on behalf of two fellows coming before you."

"Yes. This carries a five-year penalty."

I said, "Judge, I know you're going to have to find them guilty. But if there's any way within your good conscience you can help them and give them a chance to pursue their talents in their field of athletics, I think they would be good citizens. On the other hand, if you throw them in with hardened criminals, you would have two more criminals on the street when they come out."

He said, "You should be where I am, and I should be down where you are."

At the hearing, the judge ripped them up and down. He said, "But for the goodness of a man out there, you fellows would be on your way to the big house now, but I'm going to put you on two years probation. But if you break it, I'm going to throw the key away."

Dock went on to make $100,000 pitching for the Yankees and Dodgers. Won 19 games one season with the Yankees.

I had some kids in my backyard last night. They had been running loose in the street, so I organized a youth club, and they meet at my house. Yesterday I had a kind of cookout, hot dogs and things, punch and ice cream and cookies. I got a water container and set it up outside for them, because they're always thirsty. They think that's just fine: They got their own water cooler. I gave them a talk before the meeting: The purpose of this club is to let them have a better understanding of each other, their responsibility for each other, for the community, for their parents. They're really doing fine. My wife and I do this. We take up a collection. The treasurer keeps the books, and I keep the money for them. It's working out real well, because my wife helps me.

I'm just perfect for this job I'm doing with these kids, because I was a little so-and-so too. But I was fortunate. My mother and father stayed on my case all the time, and when I got older I could see what they were trying to teach me. Now these young kids try to pull something on me, I say, "Come here, son, I know just what you're thinking. When I was your age, I was a little hoodlum like you." It's like a slap in the face. They say, "Heh, here's an old man understands us. We can talk to him." So they come to me with troubles they should be taking to their parents.

They say, "Pops"—they call me Pops or Papa Chet—"you know one thing: You're like a father to us. You're better than our own father." That makes me feel real good that I'm doing something for the youth, keeping 15 to 20 young teenagers off the street. "An idle mind is the devil's workshop," the saying is.

George Hendricks was 17 at Fremont High. I had him in left field, and the very first ball hit to him, well, he dropped it. He came back to the bench with his head down, expecting me to get all over him; I guess that's what had happened in the past. I just told him to forget about it. I knew Clemente was his idol, and one day we went to Dodger Stadium, and I introduced the two in the clubhouse. Roberto gave him a bat, and that meant a lot to him. Now he's a star.

But there's a lot more than baseball going on here. Whether or not a kid makes it to the big leagues isn't the most important part of it. The main thing I stress is staying in school, getting that education. Baseball can only take you so far.

The other day I met someone who had played for me years ago. This guy had been a real bad actor. He walked up to me, shook my hand, and said, "Remember me?" He's teaching school now. He said, "I just want to thank you for straightening me out." That made me feel good, better than seeing a kid hit a home run or strike somebody out.

Heh, there's life after baseball. You just have to find it.

This has been my life. Fifty years I've been doing this, working with kids. And I have only lost one. He was a big 15-year-old boy, a catcher, had everything. Was going to be an outstanding catcher. But he was from a broken home and he missed practice two or three times. I told him, "You want to stay on my team, you gotta stay in school and get those grades. I'm not going to have you disrupting my team, have those other fellows running the streets like you do." It's a shame you have to do that, but you have to weed the bad ones out.

I couldn't keep up with him to counsel him. I went to his home and said, "Mrs. Stewart, I've come over here to talk to Charles."

"Mr. Brewer, I haven't seen Charles for four days."

He turned out to be a wino, laying around in the gutter. He's the only one I've lost in 50 years.

But you know, these big leaguers who came through my program, they don't ever think about it. They don't think enough to put a dime in the phone and say, "How you doin'? You like to have some tickets?" Watson gave me a dozen bats once. That's kind of typical of our race: "Hurray for me, and the heck with everyone else." Some of the white major leaguers are more sympathetic than our own Negro ball players.

One of the princes was this fellow with the Angels that got killed, Lyman Bostock. He was going to do wonders. Used to send a dozen bats and came by one day and gave me a check, a good-sized check. And don't let me forget Joe Black. Sent me a real sizeable check from Greyhound [Black was a vice-president of Greyhound].

I've got two broken hips, but I'm still around. I'm grateful to the Lord for letting me be able to do what I can.

They honored me at USC for 50 years in baseball. Rod Dedeaux and Bob Lemon were there. Lemon said, when he started out as an infielder, "this man here proved to me that I wasn't going to be the kind of hitter who makes it, so I started to be a pitcher." Dedeaux, the coach for the USC Trojans, put me on his all-time opponents team. I thought that was quite an honor.

When I started out, they didn't want you to play. They had this propaganda: They'd let a colored play if they found one who could play. But, shoot, they really didn't want you.

During the war they even let a one-armed white man play [Pete Gray of the Browns], but they wouldn't let a black man play. Shoot, the only thing a one-armed white man can do as good as a two-armed black man is scratch the side that itches.

I was managing a team up in Porterville, and this colored boy would come to the ball park and ask the white manager if he could play on his team. The manager said, "Go 'way, boy, I don't have no spot for no black boy."

Second day, same thing. The third night: "I've had it up to here with you. I'm going to have the police throw you out."

Next night the boy bought him a ticket right over the dugout. The ace relief pitcher in the league was pitching, a big six-foot-six pitcher, looked like he was throwing BBs, he threw so hard. Finally, the manager said, "Here's the time to show this black boy up. I'm going to embarrass him so he won't come back." He called that fellow down and put him in a uniform: "You pinch hit."

"Yes sir."

He grabbed the first bat he came to. The first pitch, he hit it up against the right center field fence, started tearing around the bases. That white manager jumped up, yelled, "Man, look at that Cuban go!"

Chet Brewer

b: 1/14/07, Leavenworth, KS		BR TR 6'4, 200	
Year	Team	W–L	Team Rank*
1925	Kansas City	1–0	1st
1926	Kansas City	12–1	1st
1927	Kansas City	8–6	2nd
1928	Kansas City	7–8	unknown
1929	Kansas City	16–3	1st
1930	Kansas City	8–5	3rd
	Cuba	2–2	
1931	Kansas City	2–2	unknown
1932	KC-Wash	5–1	unknown
1933	No record		
1934	Denver Post	4–0	
1935	Kansas City	0–1	unknown
	Denver Post	1–0	
1936	NY Cubans	6–6	4th
1937	Dominican Republic	2–3	
	Denver Post	0–2	
1938	Mexico	18–3	
1939	Mexico	12–7	
1940–45	Latin America		
1941	Kansas City-Phil	0–5	unknown
1946	Chi-Cleveland	4–3	unknown
1947	Cleveland	12–6	1st
1948	Cleveland	5–5	5th
1952	Riverside	6–5	
	Visalia	1–4	

Post-Season

1926	Playoffs	1–1	

*Overall won-lost percentage in a six-team league.

Chet Brewer vs. White Big Leaguers

Year	W-L	Score	IP	H	R	BB	SO	Players
1931	W	6-2	9	6	2	1	13	P. Waner, L. Waner, Kuhel
1936	W	11-0	9	3	0	—	—	Foxx, Manush, Higgins, Lyons

Recap

Negro league	88–60
Latin America	34–15
Minor leagues	7–9
Post-Season	1–1
vs. white major leaguers	2–0
Denver Post	5–2
Totals	137–87

An American Giant
ERNEST "WILLIE" POWELL

Willie Powell was the last surviving member of the great Chicago American Giants team that reigned as black baseball champions of the world 1926–27. Founded by the great Rube Foster, they were probably the strongest team in Chicago in the 1920s, when the Cubs and White Sox were "rebuilding," as they say. Many would like to have seen the Giants play the white champs of those years, the Yankees, Cardinals, and Pirates.

Though only 5'8" and weighing under 150 pounds, Powell was the Giants' money pitcher. He drew the pitching assignments in 12 post-season games—playoffs and black World Series—and won 10 of them.

He beat Kansas City in the 1926 playoffs, 2–1. In the World Series he lost the second game to the Bacharach Giants but came back to beat the Bacharachs' ace, Rats Henderson, 13–0, to tie the series four games each. Bill Foster then won the finale, 1–0, to give Chicago the crown.

The next year Powell defeated Satchel Paige and Birmingham twice in the playoff. He beat Paige and Harry Salmon in game two, 10–5, driving in one run with a single off Satch. In game four he defeated Sam Streeter and Paige, 6–2; both runs were unearned.

In the World Series that followed, Powell beat Atlantic City's Jesse Hubbard, 11–1, in the second game. He pitched a 1–1 tie in game five, then helped win the ninth and final game, 11–4.

In the '28 playoff, Powell beat St Louis' ace Ted Trent, 3–0, giving Cool Papa Bell, Mule Suttles, Willie Wells, and company just three hits.

And in the 1932 playoff Willie whipped New Orleans, 6–1, lost his next one, 5–4, and won his third one, 1–0.

"He had a fast ball that had a real hop on it," said his manager, Dave Malarcher, "and one of those fade-away curves that would come up like a fast ball and would just flutter away. Great."

Third baseman Alec Radcliff agreed.

> *He had a good change-of-pace curve ball and a sneaky fast ball that would take off, and he would mix it up on them. If that guy didn't get shot—his father-in-law shot him over the eye. . . . But he came back; it was amazing how he came back. He was still a masterful pitcher for about two more years. I think it was in 19*

and '32 or '3, he won 21 games and lost two. And they weren't by big scores. He
was a wonderful pitcher.*

*Radcliff recalled one 1932 double header against Josh Gibson and
Pittsburgh Crawfords. The Craws had scored three runs in the first inning
when Powell was rushed in with the bases loaded and nobody out. He got the
side out,*

> *Then—and this is remarkable, I think—he pitched the rest of the first game
> and we beat 'em 4–3, and he went to Malarcher and he said—I was surprised, it
> was hot, about 95 degrees—he said, "I want to change sweatshirts, Cap, let me
> pitch the second game." Foster was slated to pitch the second game. Malarcher
> said, "All right, if it's all right with Bill." Bill said, "All right, if he weakens, I'll go
> get him." So Powell started the second game and shut 'em out 3–0. He could give
> Josh the devil.*

*Powell retired to Three Rivers, Michigan, where he built a house literally
with his own hands. In 1985 a circulatory problem caused the amputation of
both legs, and a stroke left him without the use of his left arm. At the age of 84
Powell and his wife Virginia received SABR's Dick Clark and Marilyn Taylor
and me in his hospital room for separate interviews. Mrs. Powell's comments
are in italics.*

I played against Babe Ruth's All Stars, I think it was 1928, in the
American Giants park and in Kansas City. He hit a line drive on
me in Kansas City against that concrete wall in right field. That ball
was hit so hard, it bounced back to the infield. He almost got thrown
out at first base. Newt Allen, our second baseman, went out and got
that ball, and it was a close play. Ruth got one more single off me—he
got two hits. He hit one almost knocked Newt Allen out at second.
Good thing it wasn't hit straight at him, because he like to killed him.

It was dangerous to throw anything below his knees. Above the
knees, right across the letters, he wasn't so hot. But every time you
throw it low, look out; he could take you out with the low ball. I never
threw him another drop ball.

Lou Gehrig, now there was a hard man to pitch to: throw and
duck. He could hit everything you throw, pretty near. He got one hit
off me. They had Tony Lazzeri of the Yankees at second, Mickey
Cochrane of the Athletics catching, Art Shires of the White Sox, Tris
Speaker, and pitching was George Uhle of the Tigers. They loaded up
on us.

But it didn't help them none. We loaded up on them too. I
pitched all the way. We won it, I think it was 7–4. When I walked on
that mound, I felt like I was a lion and you were a titmouse.

---

*Presumably including semipro games.

He used to say, "I can strike that sucker out." He believed it too.

We played them seven games, and they won one. We beat them six out of seven games. Judge Landis, the commissioner, broke that up, cut down on the number of games they could play us.

It was pretty rough, to know what you could do but didn't get a chance. We didn't talk about it too much, but we couldn't help but think about it. When we played them big leaguers, we could beat them. One year Detroit stacked up with anybody and played us 11 games and won one.

Tommy Bridges [of the Tigers] was the best pitcher I ever saw. We had the best curve balls in either league. I pitched against him in the White Sox park, and we used to compare with each other. I forget the score, but it wasn't a big score, you can bet on that.

That was my main pitch, my curve ball. I had a good one too, if I do have to say so myself. I could put a bucket at home plate and drop my drop ball in it. I had a good curve ball and a good screw ball. Keep one outside and one right up under him: Keep it in on the hand and they can't do much with it. Ain't no one can hit a ball on the hand. That's the main thing: Keep it where he can't get no power to it.

When I wanted my curve ball to break away from you, I used sidearm. I could make it go down and out on the corner. Once they start chasing them, I got 'em, son.

We played Smead Jolley and Johnny Mostil of the White Sox over in the American Giants park. Lefty Sullivan, used to pitch for the White Sox, was pitching. Had 16–20,000 people out there. The park couldn't hold them all; they were standing everywhere—black and white.

They just laid down bunts against Sullivan. That's how they beat him—2–1 or something like that.

In 1932 we played Leo Durocher's All Stars in Cincinnati and Cleveland. I shut them out 3–0. Beat Jim Weaver of the Cubs—I didn't see how he was such a good pitcher.

We got along fine with the big leaguers. The Cubs used to come over quite a bit to talk to us at Tony's Book Store on 35th Street. The White Sox too. When the Yankees come to town, they used to come there and meet with us all the time. Every guy we played against, I liked to get tips from. I wanted to learn.

Sometimes I kinda think the owners didn't think the fans would like integration. I know the Cubs were like that. They were very uppity. The White Sox didn't mind us playing in their park. But the Cubs didn't want us.

Satchel Paige? Sure I beat him—name me somebody I didn't beat. I don't know of anyone we played that I didn't beat. We went to Birmingham in 1927, and the first day I got off the train, he pitched against me. He didn't know how to field a bunt, and that's how you beat him. You bunt and run, bunt and run, bunt and run.

Satchel was the fastest that's ever been in baseball. He was faster than Bob Feller, he was faster than Lefty Grove. But until he learned a curve ball, he was just a thrower. You know, you can't keep throwing that ball by people. I used to tell him that all the time. I says, "Satchel, you better learn how to throw a curve ball."

"Man, nobody can hit my fast ball."

I said, "You're right there. But they will learn how to hit it, because that's all they're looking for, and they will hit you." I took him aside—I called him my "bull" all the time—showed him how to grip it and how to spin it and let it go. Finally he learned him a good curve ball, and next thing you know he was with the Cleveland Indians.

But the best black pitcher was Dave Brown [American Giants' left-hander]. He had one of the best curve balls you want to look at and a

Ernest "Willie" Powell in the American Giants park during the 1927–28 season.

good drop ball. After Brown left, Bullet Joe Rogan of Kansas City was the king of the colored pitchers. I played on the same club with Satchel in 1928; we barnstormed in Memphis, Birmingham, Kansas City, St. Louis. I'd still take Rogan over Satchel.

I was born in Eutaw, Alabama, about 90 miles south of Birmingham, October 30, 1903. Larry Brown [who later caught for the Chicago American Giants] was our paper boy in Pratt City. We used to fight each other every day. He learned how to throw, throwing rocks at me. Pratt City had a good team. We used to beat all those little cities around there. We were the best; we could beat anybody.

You were chesty.

We were it, Mrs. Powell. We were the best thing out there.

I moved to Chicago in 1913. The Radcliff boys, Double Duty and Alec, went to school with me; they later played for the American Giants too. The American Giants were playing then out at 39th and Wentworth. I took me a knife and cut me a hole out in the fence back there with my name on it. When I came out there, I'd tell the other kids: "Let's move, fellows."

I saw Smokey Joe Williams pitch through that knothole. I remember he'd raise his foot way up.

Rube Foster was the American Giants' pitcher. Rube had a way to grip that ball, throw underhand, and he could hum that ball! Rube was a trick pitcher: He'd always try to trick you into doing something wrong. If you were a big enough fool to listen to him, he'd have you looking for something else and strike you out.

The first time I rode the Pullman with a ball club was with Joe Green of the Chicago Giants in 1922. I was 18. He gave me $25 to pitch a twilight game. They beat me 5–4 in 10 innings. Candy Jim Taylor kicked the ball out of the catcher's hands, scored, and that beat me. My curve ball was working that day.

We played Rube Foster's American Giants in exhibition games. We came out on the bad end of it, but we usually put up a good showing. They had more experience, that was the big thing. You had some good white teams around Chicago in the old Midwest league. Some awful good teams. There were the Duffy Florals, the Neeson Pies, the Logan Squares. A lot of guys went right out of there into the majors. And you had others, like Buck Weaver [of the infamous Chicago Black Sox] and Lefty Sullivan, who came out of the majors to play for those teams.

I stayed with Joe Green a year. We played in Wisconsin and up in Canada mostly. One time out in the country there was a barn out in the field and people sitting on the door of the barn. Joe Green stopped the game and told 'em to move the people out of the door, he didn't want to hurt anybody. Then he hit the ball right straight into that door. Nobody thought he could hit the ball that far. I like to fell out [fainted]. He was always pulling some stunt like that.

We were married in 1923.

Then I pitched for a semipro team in Evanston under Dick Lee, from the old Chicago Leland Giants, with Bobby Winston. It was $15 a game. Leroy Grant [first baseman for the American Giants] called me one day. He had told Rube about me; I think he got $25 for it.

Rube said to take me in the clubhouse and get me a uniform: "I want to see how you warm up." Rube called everybody darling. He said, "Darling, I'm going to give you a contract if you'll listen, but you got to listen. You watch me." Then he said: "You're pitching."

I pitched against Kansas City [Negro National League champions that year] seven innings and didn't give up nothing.

Rube called me over to the bench and said, "I want you to do what I say do." After every pitch he'd give me a sign what to throw. He told me who to throw a curve ball to and who to throw a fast ball to. Kansas City whipped my ass off in the eighth inning! After every pitch he'd give me a sign what to throw. And they hit it. He made me throw just what they wanted to hit. And I threw it too—I tried. They beat me 10–4.

After the game he called me over to the side, said, "You'll do." I got hit to death, but he said, "You know how to take orders." He didn't really want me to beat them. He said, "You know, if I'd left you alone, you'd have beat the great Kansas City Monarchs, then I'd never have been able to tell you nothing." You know, Rube had a whole lot of points. Later years I found out he was right. He was a smart man.

If you didn't listen to Rube, you didn't play. Whatever Rube said you were to do, you do it, or try to do it anyway. If you didn't, you were in trouble. In Kansas City one day he told Gisentaner to bunt. Gisentaner couldn't bunt, so he took a big swing and hit the ball out of the park. Cost him $50.

[Cristobal Torriente was the star Cuban center-fielder for the American Giants.] The first day me and Torriente had a little run-in. He and Padrone [Cuban pitcher] didn't want me on that team for nothing. I didn't know how to do anything right to suit them. They were talking about beating me because I was so little. John Beckwith was with the Giants then; that was their number-one slugger. Beckwith just came into the clubhouse and he says, "Now look—all you little guys can try him if you want to, and if you get away with it, all right. But don't none of you big guys fool with him. If you fool with him, you got to fool with me." That quieted them down.

You were 22; they thought you were 17. A ticket man figured I had to be that young too. I was calling him Jack. He said, "You should call me 'Mr. Jack.'"

They started calling me "Piggy," said I was the young, tender guy. They didn't know how tough I was. They found out though.

Later Bingo DeMoss [the Giants captain] told me I had to win the third-place money for the team. He told me if I lose the game, the American Giants don't get a cut of the World Series money; if I win, they get a cut. I won, and I think we got $107 apiece.

The ball club went to my side then; they thought I was a good ball player after that. Torriente, Jelly Gardner, all those guys went with me, because they thought I had the guts to pitch.

Jelly Gardner started calling him "Hoggy Baby," said he'd growed up.

We got $200 a month. But that wasn't anything, $200. Rube used to let Dick Lee borrow me two Sundays out of every month to pitch for the Progressives. Made $15–$25 a game.

The American Giants had Pullmans everywhere we traveled, had our own private cars. We played April through September. September was about it—a few exhibition games in October. We played against Tris Speaker in 1925. Judge Landis [the white baseball commissioner] made them cut it out.

Jim Brown, my catcher, was one of the best. Didn't forget a hitter.

Willie Powell (bottom row, third from left), with the 1926 world champion Chicago American Giants. Also shown are pitcher Willie Foster, outfielder Turkey Stearnes, third baseman Alec Radcliff (top row, fourth, fifth and sixth from left); manager Dave Malarcher (middle row, center); and outfielder Jimmy Lyons (bottom, second from right).

If you could hit something, Jim Brown knew about it; he wouldn't ask no pitcher to throw something a guy could hit. He used to curse me out a whole lot of times. I'd throw something, didn't get it where I wanted it, the guy would hit it. Jim Brown could cuss. Me and him got along though. It got so he schooled me quite a bit.

Jim Brown, now he used to play baseball for the fans. People would go out to see Jim Brown argue with the umpires. If he didn't argue, I could hear people on the street talking about it: "Man, I didn't enjoy that game; Jim Brown didn't even argue." Jim Brown wouldn't argue half the time; he made like he was arguing. He and the umpires talked it over before the game. He would jump off the bench and rush out to the umpire, but he be asking, "Where you goin' tonight? Come on out to 55th Street," things like that.

Later Pythias Russ replaced Brown, and I'd take Pythias Russ over all of them. He wasn't so much a better receiver, but he could remember the batters so good. That helps a pitcher out a whole lot, because a pitcher out there by himself on the mound is like a man on a desert without water. If a man comes up you ain't faced before, you're in trouble, because he might break your ball game up with one pitch.

I've seen Russ catch the ball before the batter could hit it.

He sat there snatching balls, I used to love that. And you could depend on him as a hitter—he was a great hitter. Pythias Russ could have become the greatest Negro hitter if he'd lived long enough. But he tried to work in the post office and play ball at the same time, and I think he died of pneumonia or something. I think he just worked himself to death.

The infield makes a good pitcher out of you. I loved the infield I had. They loved me, the way they played behind me.

For third base, Dave Malarcher, he's my man. I ain't seen any third baseman better than Dave Malarcher yet.

Charlie Williams at shortstop didn't look like he could move like he did, 'cause, oh man, he stayed fat all the time. We kept a rubber shirt on him. But he could move around.

Bingo DeMoss at second—that guy could pick up a ball and throw it behind him as good as he could throw it straight ahead.

Old Steel Arm Davis played first base. He was the savior of our ball club a lot of times yeah. In his younger days he was quite a pitcher; that's why they called him "Steel Arm," because he could throw so hard.

Jelly Gardner in the outfield could throw—boy, he could throw!

Jelly Gardner and Jimmy Lyons were Rube's bunt-and-run men. Rube Foster was smart: If they can't hit your pitcher, he knew what to do. Jimmy Lyons told me he didn't know what it was like to get up to bat and take his full swing, 'cause Rube always had him push it here, lay it down there. If you were a fast man, you had a chance with Rube; he was going to make you run.

They'd put on a triple act—three steals; one stole home. We had this happen more than one time.

Them were the guys could do it. You couldn't hesitate with none of them with the ball in your hand. If you hesitate, you were lost. Lyons was the fastest; I think Lyons was faster than Cool Papa Bell— and Bell could go around the bases so fast, give you pneumonia.

Willie Foster [Chicago pitcher] had Bell trapped off first one day, and Jim Brown couldn't get him out going to second. But I got so I could catch him. You know who told me how to pick him off? My wife.

Bell would hitch up his pants before he was going to steal.

That's just like Babe Ruth when he was pitching. He'd telegraph his curve ball by sticking his tongue out. I don't know if his wife ever told him about that or not.

Rube was trying to do too much, he was trying to do everything, trying to keep the league together, trying to take care of all the teams.

I'm quite sure that's what drove him off his mind. If you do things like that, it wrecks your brain.

Bullet Rogan started teaching me the screw ball when we first met, before the first game that I pitched, against Kansas City. All the Kansas City hitters—Newt Allen, Newt Joseph, Frank Duncan—they all got mad with him. But Rogan was a gentleman. He'd always try to help a youngster. Most old-timers didn't want you in there.

And I could use a cut ball too. Oh man, get me a cut ball, I could use it! Make it go in and up. You hold the cut side the way you want it to go, so the wind can get at it. A little scratch will do; doesn't have to be a big cut. I had a good curve ball anyhow. A cut ball moves so fast; it breaks real sharp, real quick. That's why you don't have a chance to move out of the way so good. Carl Mays of the Yankees killed Ray Chapman with one in 1920.

Bill Drake of the Monarchs always wanted to make like he was wild all the time. In practice he'd get a couple balls and throw over the catcher's head and up against the stand. He liked to holler, "Look out!" He had good control, but he liked to throw over a hitter's head for the fun of it. That was his idea of getting you scared of him. He was a big guy; he could throw hard too.

They wanted me to pitch against Kansas City, because if Bill Drake dusted off my players, I'm going to dust off theirs. Then our boys don't have to duck so much. Willie Foster wouldn't dust anybody off. I would.

Whenever the Kansas City Monarchs and Chicago were going to tangle up, the park would be just packed in.

They broke the gates down one time—the old White Sox park, 39th and Wentworth. Too many people in the stands. They had benches around the outfield. They could pack around 15,000 people in there, counting temporary seats. There's a housing project out there now. It was 406 feet to dead center field, and you had to hit the ball a long ways to get it out.

I had a friend went broke betting on Kansas City. I used to tell him all the time: "Man, you better save your money, you going to need it." I beat them most times I pitched against them. Then he'd get mad at me.

[Powell won one in the 1926 playoff. But the Giants still had to sweep the final double header to win.]

Kansas City had their bags all packed ready to go.

In the first game, Willie Foster beat Rogan, 1–0. I was supposed to pitch the second game, but Foster told me, "I'll go in and go as hard as I can as long as I can. You be ready to pick me up." I said, "Go ahead, I know you can take them. You take them and I'll stay ready." He shut 'em out again 5–0. The way he was pitching that day, there wasn't anybody who was going to beat him.

In the World Series, Atlantic City had Luther Farrell, an emery ball pitcher, a spitball pitcher, used to pitch for Gilkerson's Union Giants in Illinois. He hit Nat Rogers [Chicago outfielder] in the mouth with his emery ball, split his lip. Dave Malarcher taped the lip up and he went right on playing. Every time he come to bat, a line drive.

[Powell started the second game.]

I couldn't even pitch a strike; everything I threw was a ball. I never heard the umpire say strike. So Dave Malarcher took me out and put in Rube Currie. They called Currie "The Black Snake." He was kinda old and couldn't throw so hard then, but when he was young, Rube could throw hard as anybody you want to know. Rube Currie always knew what their weakness was: "You know what their weakness is? A fast ball between the eyes." He had a curve ball, a big one too, and it broke low. He threw the curve ball away from the plate and it would break over. Anyway, Rube Currie came in and threw nine balls and three men were out.

My second game I could have been better. Red Grier beat me 6-4. I lost my cool. Baby, you lose your head, and that's it. And that didn't please me a bit. It didn't please my ball players, and it didn't please my manager. Only somebody pleased was Atlantic City, 'cause those fans were sure riding me. A guy went up and down the street that night with a megaphone telling what the score was.

That winter I played in Cuba and we won the championship too.

Oscar Charleston [usually considered the best black player of all time] was my roommate. He used to wake me up throwing water on me.

Cuba had the slowest trains in the world. It'd take you four hours to go 50 miles. No kidding. We were in a little town to play a game, and a woman gave us a basket of green tomatoes. By the time we got back to Havana, the tomatoes were ripe.

I batted .412. Mike Gonzalez [St. Louis Cardinal coach] beat me out by two points. I used to brag about that a lot. You know how pitchers like to talk about their hitting. I was a pretty good hitter.

He thought he was.

I was. I was.

I used to pinch hit. Why not? I could get on base. I didn't hit the ball far, but I could hit it where I wanted to hit it a lot of times. If you hit between the infielders, you got something.

When you hit a home run in Cuba you got a case of beer. If I got that case of beer, Judy Johnson [great black third baseman] would come over to the house and drink it up with me. He put me out at third base one time when I was trying for a home run. He said, "I forgot about that case of beer."

I used to pride myself in running too. I thought I could move out a little bit, which I could.

I guess he should. It runs in the family. His uncle could run.

That guy could out-run a rabbit. He could out-run me—with his galoshes on. We were out in the pasture fixing the fence when a rain came up. That old man walked off and left me. And he was about 80 years old.

He was 70. Good grief, just to think about it!

He trained his boys how to run too. He used to get one of those buggy whips and get down on the end of it. You'd get as far as you could go, and he'd let you have it. He ain't going to let up on you either. The idea was to stay far enough ahead of him to keep from getting in the rear where he can hit you.

One time in St. Louis, I was stuck on third, and I've got to stay there until the ball goes through the infield. When Willie Wells started a double play, I started to take off for home. Mitch Murray was catching and he caught me about a yard from home plate. He dived on me and skint me from my ankles to my ears, and that was my buddy too. He stopped me from scoring and they had a triple play. And I was streaking too, baby.

I pitched a no-hit game against Memphis in 1927, three walks and no hits. I walked one man three straight times; I never will forget him.

[In 1927 the American Giants met Satchel Paige's Birmingham Black Barons in the playoff.]

Birmingham had four good pitchers—Satchel, Robert Poindexter, Harry Salmon, and Sam Streeter. Streeter didn't have no fast ball, but he sure had some good curve balls. But we could waltz through them like nothing.

You always thought you were it.

We were. We were.

They asked me, "Why do you think Chicago is going to win?"

"I'll tell you three good reasons—myself, George Harney, and Willie Foster—that's why Chicago is going to win." Just the three, that's all you need. What made it good, each man had different pitches: Harney had a spit ball, I had a curve ball; first you're looking at a left-hander [Foster], then a right-hander [Powell and Harney].

Old Steel Arm Davis was the savior of the ball club. He would get as many bats as he could carry and go in the Birmingham dugout and throw all those bats on the concrete in front of the dugout and holler, "Oh oh, the hooter man's in town!" [Davis got seven hits, including two home runs, as the Giants won four straight.]

When they played the American Giants park, the park would be all mixed, both black and white. But when they were away from home, the colored would hardly ever follow. When they would go on the road, maybe there would be only about 10–15 colored folks in the stands, that be mostly wives that would go with them. Evanston was mostly white. A few blacks, wouldn't be many, would come out to the games. But he didn't care nothing about them booing or saying anything. It didn't bother him.

I liked it, I liked it. Willie Foster was scared, and he'd tell you in a minute he was scared. Something would happen and he would cry, he wanted to go underground. He didn't like the crowds. I loved it, I loved it.

One time in Mississippi we stopped at a place coming back from Texas. Dave Malarcher bought us 16 hot dogs. The guy wanted to charge us for 18, told his help in there to lock the door. That's the only time I heard Dave Malarcher swear. Joe Little walked behind the guy, picked him up just like that, slammed him down on the floor, said, "You put your hand on the door again, I'm going to break your neck."

Now lots of colored would go to see games against the Duffy Florals. When Lefty Sullivan would pitch for Duffy Floral, the fans would go.

A left-handed spit ball pitcher. God, he was something! The Sox had him [in 1919], but he couldn't field bunts. He'd beat any team in the world, pretty near, if he could field bunts. We'd keep bunting it down the third base line most of the time. Something wrong with his inner ear. He'd lose his balance when he'd bend over and throw some of them away. But you didn't hit him too often. I never got a hit off him—I never got one hit off Lefty Sullivan.

And the Cubans—we played them a five-game series and the highest score was 3–2. Those guys could play your tongues out.

Wasn't it the Cubans had that funny ball? Who was it had the donkey riding?

The House of David. And Kansas City [beginning in 1930] had lights; they had trucks to carry the lights along with them.

When I started pitching, the kids didn't have to use a knothole. I'd go to the back gate and let them in. They would come in and scatter. Some of them knew they were going to get caught and put out, but once they scattered, you know, you can't catch them all.

When I got ready to leave after the game, I'd fill my pockets with balls, and every kid out there, I would throw him a ball. I gave away more balls. I met a whole lot of them kids later as young men, and they told me they remembered me.

Ed Rile of Detroit was a great big guy, weighed about 200 pounds, and he had a whole lot of pads on, made him look even bigger. Every time Ed Rile come to Chicago, Willie Foster would hide Ed Rile's bat. One time I told on him, and the first ball Foster pitched to Ed Rile, he hit it over the fence.

One time a ball was hit straight back at me. It hit me in the top of the head. All it did was knock my hat off, skidded off, and went into center field. I just let it rip. Didn't hurt; couldn't hardly feel it.

We lost the pennant in 1928 in a playoff with the St. Louis Stars. That was when I was in the shotgun accident. I had beaten Ted Trent 3-0 in the second game, and that night I was hurt. Chicago went to St. Louis, and they beat us down there. Willie Wells went wild in that last game.

Nineteen twenty-nine was a bad year for me. My arm was sore, and I could hardly throw. I think I only pitched in about four games. Chicago thought I was finished, and in 1930 they sold me to the Detroit Stars. Bingo DeMoss was manager.

You heard about Pepper Daniels, the catcher? Well, he was a good catcher, pretty smart, Daniels was. Now there's a man didn't come to the ball park without his chewing tobacco.

For 30 years he chewed tobacco. But at home, no tobacco.

Well, home was no place to chew tobacco. You ain't got no place to spit it out. But on the ball field, you got plenty of places to spit.

We like to starved to death over there in Detroit.

The Stars went broke—they were broke to start with. They never did pay off. Watson was one of our owners. You go down in the morning and catch him. He'd walk by and reach his hand in his pocket, and whatever he came up with, he'd give you. He came out with a five, he'd give you a five. And he ain't going to stop wallking, and he ain't going to talk to you. We'd stand on the corner and chew tobacco and spit. We couldn't get back home. Jelly Gardner had to get us back home; he knew someone he could borrow some money from.

[Powell returned to the American Giants in 1933.]

In '33 I had one of the best years of my life in baseball—well, all my years were good years, but I had a better team with me in '33. Our home grounds was Indianapolis. They turned our [Chicago] park into a dog track.

We played mostly on the road. We played a lot of games that year too. You'd play a game today, get into the bus, ride until the next day, and play somewhere else. Sometimes you'd play a day game and drive some place for another game that night. And there wasn't any way you could sleep on a bus. I'd get a little nap when the bus would stop.

Turkey Stearnes was my roommate. He could hit. One time when he was in Detroit, I struck him out four times in a row, and the fifth time up he hit a home run. After he came to Chicago, he'd talk about that homer all the time.

Our daughter was three years old. Bill "Bojangles" Robinson was out to the ball game one day, and was whistling and tap dancing, and my daughter would say, "Do it again." She just kept saying, "Do it again."

Bojangles was a good guy to get along with. He could run backwards faster than anyone on our team could run forwards. Yeah, he could.

The Pittsburgh Crawfords had the hardest hitting team in the league. Josh Gibson hit a home run off me through that tin fence in Greenlee Field in Pittsburgh. And it was a bad pitch. I knew what I was doing—or thought I knew. You couldn't pitch outside to him too much—a curve ball outside, Josh would kill it. And don't throw it inside, or he'll kill the third baseman. If you kept it low on Josh, you'd get away with it quite a bit. I wanted him to hit to right field. He was fooled on a curve ball, fell across the plate, and hit that ball through the tin fence. Hit a good curve ball too. I didn't believe anyone could reach out that far and hit it that far. Boy, he talked about that ball all the time we got together. I paid a guy $3 for that ball and then ended up losing it.

And I was having a good year too. That's the year I beat the Crawfords a double header, gave up two hits.

Red Parnell beat me in the playoff. I came in to relieve, and he hit a fly ball and beat me. A man on first, no out, I knew he was supposed to bunt the ball. Like a fool, I threw him one up high. He hit a fly ball, and Turkey Stearnes [in center field] didn't get in in time to get it, and that beat me. I didn't get bawled out for the pitch though. Dave Malarcher told me, "You pitched the right pitch. I would have done the same thing." You can't bunt a ball too good up high like that.

The next year they were going to trade me to Cleveland for a new team they were building. But it was too late in the game for me, and we didn't make any money then. I was working for the city, but I lost that job because of going to Indianapolis. No money, no nothing.

Dave Malarcher didn't believe me when I told him I wasn't going to play any more. They came by my house, wanted me in New York, brought me some money. I was in the bathtub taking a bath. I told them I wasn't going anywhere. So Dave Malarcher got Ted Trent to pitch instead, and Trent got left in New York.

I got me a job doing tannery work, buffing. I stayed on that job 30 years and learned to buff leather real good. I was doing piece work: If I made it, I made it; if I didn't, it was my fault. Some jobs have the money, and some jobs just have nothing.

Well, they just about paid you nothing.

Got a pension of $25 a month after 30 years. Can't go nowhere on that; can't cross the street. That's one thing we didn't fight hard enough for. And if you fight for it, you got nothing to fight with.

Back in 1933 each team had a big eater, and our big eater was Jack Marshall. One day a guy named Washington pitched this big lunch for us in Pittsburgh; his wife and her sister from New York cooked all day, getting ready. Now Jack Marshall and I had gone to Gus Greenlee's Grill to eat, and Jack had eaten a double order and drank two bottles of beer.

Then we went to the dinner party—three ball clubs: the Crawfords, the Homestead Grays, and the American Giants. They had a table twice as long as this room. We were the first ones to sit down, because we were the visitors from the West. Smokey Joe Williams was the Gray's champion eater. Jack Marshall was sitting straight across from him. They kept passing chicken down the table, and Jack ate and ate. When they'd pass the chicken, he'd take his fork and rake a whole lot of it into his bowl before he passed it.

They ate like that so long it was pitiful. Finally Jack got up and loosened his belt and belched. The he started eating again. They had one big bowl of chicken about that high. Jack had the bowl and was getting some more chicken, and Joe Williams says, "Pass the chicken," but Jack had raked the rest of it out on his plate. There was just an empty bowl. So Joe says, "I better go." He lit a cigar and walked away without saying good night and that's the last I seen of him.

Meanwhile, Jack's still eating, still eating. Jack ate that bowl of chicken up and went down and got another bowl at the other end of the table and ate some more.

But he had to stop that eating. He invited himself to our house one time, and I told him, "No, you can't come to my house to eat."

Ernest "Willie" Powell

b: 10/30/03, Eutaw, AL		d: 5/16/87, Three Rivers, MI	
Year	Team	W–L–Sv	Team Rank*
1925	Chicago	3–2	3rd
1926	Chicago	2–2	2nd
1927	Chicago	1–1	1st
	Cuba	3–7	
1928	Chicago	9–9–1	unknown
1929	Chicago	3–1	3rd
1930	Detroit	9–10–1	2nd
1931	Detroit	4–7	unknown
1932	Chicago	11–6	unknown
1933	Indianapolis	7–3–1	1st
1934	Cleveland	0–1	6th

Post-Season

1926	Playoffs	1–0
	World Series	1–1
1927	Playoffs	2–0
	World Series	1–0
1928	Playoffs	1–0
1930	Playoffs	2–0
1932	Playoffs	2–1
	Totals	10-2

Recap

	Negro league	49–42
	Cuban league	3–7
	Post-Season	10–2
	Totals	62–51

* Overall won-lost percentage in a six-team league.

The Black Terry
GEORGE GILES

George Giles (pron. Guiles) ranks with Buck Leonard and Ben Taylor as one of the three top first basemen in blackball annals, and at least one man, Double Duty Radcliffe, says he was the best of the three. Giles lacked the power of the better known Leonard, but he surpassed Buck in defense and speed.

Giles may be the greatest player ever to come out of Manhattan, Kansas, although his grandson, Brian, is better known, having played second base for the New York Mets 1981–83.

I met Giles at his laundromat-motel in his hometown and later at Cooperstown, where he was Cool Papa Bell's guest at Bell's induction.

(Parts of this interview are courtesy of Denise R. Harvey in the Manhattan Mercury *and the late John Coates in* Black Sports *magazine.)*

When I first came into the league, my goal was to become the best first baseman. I picked a guy played first base for Detroit—Edgar Wesley was his name—because he was supposed to have been the best at that time. Later on people began calling me the best, but I never cared for any fame or notoriety. Some players would hang around on street corners trying to be noticed, but on off days, I'd get up early and go down to the Loop in Chicago or some place and watch the movies.

But I'll tell you this: The first ball I caught when I went down to Kansas City and tried out with the Monarchs, Jose Mendez was managing the ball club, smart, very nice guy—called time. He said, "You don't know how to shift, do you?" I didn't know what he was talking about. Nobody out here in Kansas ever told me. He showed me. It don't take but a minute to learn. And that's the only time anyone ever told me about playing first base.

See, I was pretty fast. I had a way of running to first base and hitting the bag, and I'd be ready to shift either way. Even shift behind the line—that's the toughest shift for a first baseman to make. On that throw from third base, some time you got to shift behind the line and let the runner run between you and the ball. You catch the ball as he runs by you. Hank Greenberg got his arm broke in Detroit because he didn't shift behind and the guy ran into his arm. There's more to playing first base than just standing over there.

Joe Kuhel was a fancy dan too. He could dance around on first base. I played against him after he got in the big leagues. Joe Kuhel and I came to Kansas City the same year, 1927. He came from Springfield in the Three-Eye league to the Kansas City Blues, and I was with the Monarchs. We used the same ball park.

I've always played a deep first base, way back on the outfield grass. I think I played deeper than anyone. If the pitcher would cover first, why, it was kind of hard to hit a ball through there. I could protect that line. If a ball was hit to the second baseman, he'd call "Cover up," and I'd do a reverse and go back to the bag. We'd almost get everything coming down through there.

In 1930–31 I was hitting behind Cool Papa Bell. You know, they used to argue who went to first base the fastest, Cool or me. I always thought Cool could. When I hit behind Cool, nobody ever doubled us. Sometimes Cool'd be on second, and I'd lay the ball down the third baseline. Cool'd score, and they couldn't get me going to first.

All my life I played first base. I was playing with men when I was 12 years old, so I guess you could call it just a natural. I was born in Junction City, Kansas, May 2, 1909. Everybody around here said I was a real good player, but I wanted to find out for myself.

In 1925 the Monarchs were barnstorming through the area, and I was watching them play an exhibition in Manhattan. I was 15, a sophomore in high school. That night I went up to the desk at their hotel and talked to several of the guys. One of the guys I talked to was William Bell, the pitcher. I asked him, "How do you go about trying out with the Monarchs?"

He said, "Well, we're going to train in Kansas City next spring. Come on down."

Well my grandmother had raised me, and I talked to her about it. I didn't think it would take too much money, just enough for a round trip ticket and room and board at the YMCA. I figured inside of a week I should know something.

My grandmother was broad-minded, and in the spring she gave me the train fare to get to Kansas City. It cost $4.24. A train porter showed me where the Y in Kansas City was—it was the first time I'd been there—and I rented a room for the week. I think it cost $3.50. The Monarch headquarters was right around the corner there on 18th Street. You couldn't miss it, because there were two big posters of ball players in the window.

At that time, Muehlebach Field was the home of the Monarchs. The Kansas City Blues of the American association played there too. Jose Mendez was managing the club then. Some guy told Mendez about me, and he let me suit up and take batting practice with the rest of the team. I could whale the ball. That's what tickled those guys' eyes: They loved me because I could hit that ball and run like a deer. They look at you a second time if you can splatter that ball.

I was a slash hitter, hit where the ball was pitched. Sometimes I was lucky to hit one out, but I was mostly a line drive hitter. Pitch outside, I hit it outside, pitch inside, I hit it inside. You never try to pull the ball, you'll just pop it up. Just go the way he pitched.

There was a fellow name Piney Brown in the box seats that day, and he was going to take a ball club out that year. I guess I must have made some sort of impression on Mendez, because he told Piney, "You ought to take this boy out with you." For a year of seasoning, you know. I thought playing with the Monarchs was the end of the rainbow, so I just quit school. I made a mistake.

That team was called the Kansas City Royal Giants. We left Kansas City and took spring training down around Sepulpa, Oklahoma. We got back to Kansas City on May 2, that was my 16th birthday. Signed a contract for $125 a month. Still got the contract. We went to Minnesota and played at Hands Park, right outside of Fairmont, all summer.

In 1926 a guy named Bob Gilkerson from Spring Valley, Illinois came to Kansas City looking for ball players, and I went out with him. We didn't come back until late fall. We barnstormed through Canada,

George Giles.

the Dakotas, Minnesota. We played around the stockyards in Sioux City on the Missouri River. They had a dog out there; if you hit the ball in the river, the dog would go get the ball. I remember one day we hit so many over the fence, we almost drowned the dog.

In '27 I went to spring training with the Monarchs. I was 17. A white fellow named J. L. Wilkinson was the owner of the team.

Rogan was manager. Nobody ever says much about Rogan. I had never seen a drop before—it looked like it was falling off the table. Rogan had a tough fingernail. Two strikes, with men on base, why just look for that ball to do the dipsy doodle. All he wanted to do was pitch it one time, get him out of the hole. (If you knew how to combat it, why just cut it on the opposite side of the ball; it wouldn't do anything.) I'd rank Rogan right along there with Satch. He was smart. But Rogan wasn't too good a manager. He expected everybody to have as much ability as him.

Chet Brewer was pitching. He'd knock you down, he'd throw at you. A good emery ball pitcher.

Hurley McNair was a hell of a hitter. He gave me a few ideas about shifting, standing different on different pitchers. Some pitchers had great breaking curve balls.

Kansas City loved the Monarchs. At one time we outdrew the Kansas City Blues [of the American association].

I was the youngest, and all the other men were married. They traveled and sent money home to their families. They were a stable group of men. Those guys in those days didn't have much education, but they were natural ball players.

It was hard for a youngster to break into that lineup. You had to be pretty good. But I felt I was ready. My first year with the Monarchs I was trying to beat the regular first baseman out of his job. His name was Lemuel Hawkins. Now Hawkins was a good first baseman and a pretty good base runner, but he wasn't much of a hitter. I could do everything Hawk could do and more, and I moved him into the outfield pretty quick.

Hawkins and Rogan and Heavy Johnson and another guy, Dobie Moore, they come out of the 24th Infantry, so they were friends. That was pretty rough for me. Rogan wouldn't let me drink water for one summer. Every time I'd go towards the water barrel, he told me to put that stuff down. I put it down. I've seen ball players cry and go back home, they couldn't take that riding. All the other guys could go to the water barrel, but it looked like he rode me, to see how much guts I had, could I stay with them.

That winter the owner, Wilkinson, wrote me a letter and told me I was the regular first baseman. So the first thing I told Rogan when I saw him: "Rogan, I'm gonna drink water this summer."

He laughed. Surprised me, he laughed. And you know what his answer was? He said, "I was just going to see how much guts you had." He couldn't make me go home. I would have done anything just to play with the Monarchs. Like I told my grandson: Just three things you have to have—be in condition, guts, hustle. If you have those three things, you'll stay up there awhile. If you don't have guts, they'll run you home to momma.

We played an exhibition in Manhattan. A lot of people had taken to me as a hometown boy. I remember all the colored people out to the ball park, just as quiet. I guess they were waiting for me to do something, I hadn't done anything all day. The ball game went up to the ninth inning, two men out. Rogan was hitting ahead of me, I was hitting clean-up. I told him to save me a bat. Sure enough, he got on. There used to be a little creek over in back of the ball park. I hit the ball there, and those fans came alive!

Satchel Paige and I came in the league the same year, 1927. He was with Birmingham. When he first came in the league, he could throw awfully hard, but that was all. No curve ball, no change-up. He just threw the ball by you. But he had wonderful control. You never had to worry about Satch hitting you. Later years Satch got smart, started throwing hoopy-doopies—curve balls, change of pace, and all that. I always stood flatfooted, choked up on the bat, and tried to punch the ball. I'd have been foolish to have swung for the fences, because he'd have overpowered me. Didn't have to worry about him throwing curve balls. Fast ball straight in. Straight, right down the alley. It didn't take off like Rogan's fast ball. Straight as an arrow. Fast too. Don't hold your bat at the end and swing, because you ain't going to get around.

In the league conditions were pretty good. But we played so many exhibition games. Sometimes out in western Kansas they'd make the ball park the day we got in town—some pasture.

We couldn't stay in white hotels, we couldn't eat in restaurants. In cities there were usually Negro hotels. In those small towns we would stay in family houses, two players here, two players there. Sometimes they'd fix us a meal in the colored church, or we'd bring out food from the grocery store in a paper sack. If we were in Nebraska, we'd ride all night to Lincoln or Omaha. In some of those small towns we couldn't stay, and sometimes we'd just ride all night and sleep in the bus. Then we'd have to play ball the next day. A lot of times we couldn't take a bath after the ball game. I remember once in Colby, Kansas we set tubs of water out in the sun to get them warm so we could take a bath.

I never could understand this racial thing. It was kind of disgusting. When we were barnstorming, the white teams would stay in a hotel, and we'd be changing clothes in a farmer's barn. We've been in towns where they wouldn't even sell us sandwiches to take out: Shelby, Montana, where Dempsey fought Tommy Gibbons.

We had our own private Pullman car on the Missouri-Pacific, and we were some place in Texas. The owner, Wilkinson, came back to our car and told us, "Say now, when you get to this next town, pull your curtains down." See, I experienced all of that. Nothing you could do about it, you couldn't fight the issue.

And my home state was the worst. Abilene! Never will forget it. Went out to play an exhibition game, and I never heard the expression nigger used so much in my life. It was "nigger this" and "nigger that," and "look at that nigger run." I told the manager, "Man, let's hurry up and get this game over with so we can get out of town, 'cause I'm tired of hearing this word nigger." We played all through the South and everywhere, but that was the worst. And it was all white people in the town, maybe one or two black families. But it was just one of those things you learn to accept. You just roll with the punches. That was the way it was all over the country. See, we played all the states. Colorado was just as bad as Mississippi. New York was just as bad as Alabama. It was all the same.

George Giles (third from left) with the Kansas City Monarchs. Also pictured are (from left) Newt Allen, Frank Duncan, and Quincy Trouppe.

The next year I was a 20-year-old holdout. I got married in January 1929, and when spring training came, I thought I needed more money than what the Monarchs were paying me, so I asked for a raise in salary. The reply I got from the owner was, he could go to Louisiana and get three ball players for what I wanted. In the meantime I'd heard from the Gilkerson Union Giants. They wanted me back for the same salary the Monarchs were paying me, plus a round trip ticket and all my expenses. So I had an ace in the hole, and I went back with Gilkerson's Union Giants.

In 1930 Double Duty Radcliffe, who was catching and pitching for the St. Louis Stars, came out to get me, because they needed a first baseman. Mule Suttles had been playing first, but he left to go out East somewhere.

Owners were Dick Kent, had a taxi line there, and Dr. Keyes. A little dark guy named Johnny Reese was managing the club; he had been a pinch runner for Rube Foster, and I guess he could outrun the word God. Oh, we had a good ball club!

Ted Trent, Eggie Hensley, Leroy Matlock, Roosevelt Davis, and [William] Nagadoches Ross, from down in Texas some damn place, made up the pitching staff. Trent was the mainstay. Nobody ever says anything about Trent. He had a curve ball would go around this building. And a good fast ball. And when he threw a drop ball—forget it. He was hard to beat. Didn't get too much publicity. Satchel got more publicity than anybody. I think Trent died young. Death is taking its toll from all the guys.

We had Quincy Trouppe too; he couldn't have been over 16 or 17 years old. He could play the outfield and catch; I think he also fought in the Golden Gloves.

Dewey Creacy on third; he was slow, but he could hit. Wells shortstop—I don't see how they can miss Wells for the Hall of Fame! John Russell playing second base—Pistol Pete, they called him. Good ground ball man, couldn't hit too much; him and Wells making those double plays.

Russell's brother, Branch, played right field—Pop Russell—he came out of the army, hit the ball real good.

Bell center field. The Stars played all their home games at Compton and Market Streets. The streetcar barns ran along the left field fence. That was only about 260 feet for a right-handed hitter. Center field was deep, and Cool Papa used to catch anything that stayed in the park out there. We always looked to Cool and Wells when things got rough. Cool Papa could outrun that ball. I'd have to take Cool over Oscar Charleston as far as running the ball. Charleston was probably a longer ball hitter, but Cool was going to get on base. He was always a threat. And a good guy too. You never did have to worry about him being in condition, he was always ready to play. That Cool was what you'd call a ball player's ball player.

Bell was a threat to any ball club, because when Bell would get on base, why he'd worry a pitcher to death.

I was hitting behind Bell, Wells was hitting behind me. When Mule came back, they put him in left field, and he hit behind Wells. We'd get runs.

I could bunt. It worked beautifully. If I knew Cool was running, I'd get as far back in the batter's box as I could and lean back in the catcher's arms. That'd keep the catcher back. Swing that bat. That makes him get back even further. He'd have two or three more feet he'd have to throw the ball. All those tricks. You gotta have teamwork. They called that unorthodox, but the main thing, we was winning. I don't know if the other guys on the Dodgers helped Maury Wills or not.

But Cool got all the publicity. Didn't make any difference to me, as long as we won the ball games. I took my grandson and introduced him to Cool. He was tickled to death. Cool was always a gentleman. Never did hear him curse, never saw him taking a drink either.

They used to say I could do it all. I don't know when I ever was throwed out going to second base. Very, very seldom. Because you steal on the pitcher, that's who you steal on. I would steal when I wanted to. Pick my chances. They didn't tell me when to steal. Just turned you loose. They don't turn all ball players loose. I remember one time Pepper Martin was playing third base. I was lucky enough to get a hit off Dizzy Dean and stole third. Pepper said, "Why did you steal third, George? You could go home from second on a hit."

I said, "Shoot, who's going to hit Dizzy? Now I can go home on a fly." And that's what I did. T. J. Young hit a fly, and that's all the run we needed, because whoever was pitching for us didn't give up nothing, and Dizzy didn't give up nothing else. So that's what an extra base means.

That was a team, I'm telling you! Those guys came from the old school and made a study of the game. And you had to be in condition too. That's the name of the game: Hustle and condition. In my day if you weren't in condition, you just didn't play. A lot of running. We'd go to spring training and run, go to the hotel or restaurant to eat lunch, go back out there and run some more. The main thing was to get your legs in shape. You had to be in the hotel at 12 o'clock. And they checked on you.

We won the Negro National league pennant in 1930. Won 32 games in a row. I remember when Josh Gibson first started, the Grays came through St. Louis, played a five-game series. Didn't win a game.

We left St. Louis, needed to win a series in Chicago, one in Detroit. We had to win eight of nine games to win the doggone pennant. We beat Chicago five straight. Over to Detroit, won the first three. They won the fourth. Damn if they didn't have us beat in the ninth inning by three runs in the fifth game. Hensley was pitching, a nothing pitcher—slow, slower, and slower. But he never was known to hit that ball. Reese got so disgusted, he let Hensley hit. Somehow or other, the guy singled. Cool Papa followed with a single. I doubled. Wells hit. Mule hit one out of the stadium, and we beat 'em.

I hated for the season to come to an end, because the guys were so together. It was a pleasure to play on that ball club; everybody got along good. They acted like they didn't care who they played, all they wanted to know was what time they had to be at the ball park. Those guys could play! My, my. And they were good guys on the field or off the field, because I think their idea was that conduct off the field meant as much as it does on the field.

We played the Dean boys, the Waner boys, Billy Herman, Ruth, Gehrig, Waite Hoyt, Herb Pennock, Steve Swetonic, Max Carey, Pepper Martin, Jim Bottomley, Lefty Grove, Schoolboy Rowe, Tommy Bridges, George Earnshaw, Lefty O'Doul. Those games would go down to the wire. They were toss-ups, could go either way. We could beat them; they could beat us. Two good ball clubs get together, just a matter of who gets the breaks.

The thing the big leaguers had on us: They had more good pitchers. We had two pretty good pitchers, two fair. But the big leaguers carried more ball players, guys who could fill in. It made a difference.

I remember one time we were playing Bill Terry's All Stars—the Waner brothers, Heinie Meine, Babe Herman. Trent shot 'em down like clay pigeons. He struck out Terry about four times one night. That was the year the Cardinals and Philadelphia A's played in the World Series. We had lights in our park—that was before they had lights in the major league parks. We'd go out and watch the World Series during the daytime, and they'd come watch us at night. I don't recall if they beat us at all in that series.* We could hold our own. I do remember one night Babe Herman hit one over my head, and I don't know where that baby wound up—probably down at Union Station!

Best ball player I saw in the big leagues was that doggone Charlie Gehringer. He was a finished ball player. Frankie Frisch would be standing on his head catching a ball; Charlie made it look like an easy chance.

---

*The Stars beat Meine 10–8 and the Giants' Bill Walker 18–1.

In those days we never talked about a black player going to the majors. But there was a lot of wishing.

I used to be out at Sportsmen's Park in St. Louis when they wouldn't have 500 people there. I told guys then that they ought to put one solid colored team into the National or American League. There were enough Negroes in towns like Detroit and Chicago to fill a ball park, but a lot of white people came to see our games too. When people want to see a good ball game, they don't care who's playing.

A lot of Negro ball players used to play in Cuba during the winter too. We'd get round-trip tickets, all expenses, salary. That way we could make ends meet. Send your salary back home, and your family could live fairly decently. We'd take a train down to Key West and then a boat to the island. It was only about 90 miles to Havana. Bell, Wells, Suttles, Frank Duncan, and I all played on the same team down there. Mike Gonzalez and Dolph Luque of the major leagues were down every year to manage. Those Cubans took their baseball seriously too. The policemen wore soldiers' uniforms, and they were around that ball park all the time.

You didn't have those problems like riding on the train or the bus, none of those kinds of things. It was different than in the United States. But the American tourists is what messed up things. They saw how those people treated us. Then the American tourists come and say, "We don't treat 'em like that in the United States." After that black Cubans sat on one side of the park, white Cubans on the other side of the park.

Canada used to be sweet. Then one time we were up there in Winnipeg. They had a big convention up there. Next year we went back and couldn't even stay in the same hotel. American tourists. Those countries liked that American tourist money, so they went along with the program.

The Stars won again in '31.

In 1932 the Stars broke up. What happened was that they sold the ball park to the city and made a playground out of it. This was during the Depression, and there was no league at all that year. So I went east to the Homestead Grays.

The Homestead Grays played so many ball games! Oh, they'd travel, those Homestead Grays. There were nine of us riding in one big Buick. Slept in those Buicks. I called 'em "Hotel Buicks." We'd have a double header in Pittsburgh, ride all night to Buffalo, play a game there, ride back to Detroit for another double header, and then come back to Pittsburgh the next day. All we took along was a toothbrush. We got so we could sleep on each other's shoulders. Somebody'd say, "Swing," during the night, and we'd lean the other way.

By June Newt Allen, Wells, and I came back to Kansas City. The

Monarchs had another good club that year, and we knew we'd be paid every two weeks. Anyway, we wound up in Mexico.

Mexico City had written Wilkinson and asked him to bring a good ball club down there. Rogers Hornsby, Lon Warneke, and a bunch of those big league guys had been there ahead of us. I don't know if they made too good a showing though. I think we played one or two games against them. Spoony Palm pinch-hit against Warneke, hit it out the stadium. Palm was from Texas. At the bullfight, Palm's sitting with the president of Mexico and his family. People down there are something else! We'd play a ball game Sunday morning and go to the bullfights in the afternoon. We had a wonderful time in Mexico. That's one place I'd like to go back to.

We used to barnstorm with Dizzy Dean, Larry French, and the Waner brothers. I never will forget Dizzy. He was something else. He was a lot of fun. He never did take anything serious. Most times he'd come to the ball park late. He'd miss the train. Did I hit him? Not too much. Paul Dean was easy. His ball looked like this: looked like a volleyball. He wasn't a Dizzy. Those games would go down to the wire. Dizzy and Lefty Grove were tough. Grove, he was liable to beat us, because he was pretty stingy.

House of David was a team out of Benton Harbor, Michigan. That was a colony up there, a religious group. Tucker and Talley and all those guys. They were good. But their religion wouldn't let them cut their hair or let them go to the big leagues. They had to stay in their colony.

In 1934 we played in the Denver semipro tournament against the House of David with Paige, Bill Perkins, Grover Alexander. We split the money, didn't matter who won it.

We were playing in Columbus, Ohio, an exhibition game, in 1934. I told Tex Burnett, "Man, I want to play ball in New York before I quit playing."

He said, "As soon as anything comes up, I'll let you know." That winter he called me; the Brooklyn Eagles wanted a first baseman. The money was right, so I met them down in Jacksonville. Abe Manley, the owner, was an easy-going fellow, let Mrs. Manley run the whole show. She was like Charlie Finley or George Steinbrenner. They're not good for baseball. You're supposed to have some kind of class, dignity, when you get to the big leagues. But she was very intelligent, she knew how to wear her clothes.

Ben Taylor, the old first baseman, was managing the Eagles club. I guess he was partial to first basemen, because he appointed me team captain. He went to the old-fashioned bunting game. But the ball was too damn lively. On opening day, Ebbetts Field, a big crowd, Mayor LaGuardia threw out the first ball. The Homestead Grays damn near killed us! Josh hit a couple home runs with people on. Couldn't hardly get 'em out. Those Homestead Grays *still* makin' runs! Those people almost drove us out of the ball park! Mrs. Manley left. When she was displeased, the world come to an end. She'd stop traffic. Mrs. Manley didn't like a loser.

Taylor had some good players, but he wasn't playing them right. We had Ray Dandridge, Leon Day, Fats Jenkins, Rap Dixon. Those guys could *run*. Harry Williams could bunt like hell. You can play hit-and-run, all that kind of stuff; you don't play for one run! Unless it's the late innings. But Taylor hadn't utilized their speed. He played too conservatively. He played for one run, like years ago when the ball was dead. One run wasn't no good with the lively ball.

And frankly I never thought the players there took baseball as seriously as we did in the Midwest. Out here we studied it. If we lost a ball game in Kansas City or St. Louis, we'd discuss it and get on guys. We had skull practice: Why this and why that? I've seen guys come in the clubhouse after losing a tight ball game, they'd be sick about it. In the East, after a game was over, everybody forgot about it. Those guys would lose a ball game, wouldn't say anything about it. If they won a ball game, OK; if they lost it, OK. But I wasn't brought up that way.

Mrs. Manley loved baseball, but she couldn't stand to lose. I was a pretty hard loser myself, but I think she'd take it more seriously than anybody. Manley met me in his apartment and offered me the manager's job. Manley's wife had been talking all over New York about me. She thought I was the last word. He said, "My wife wants you to manage the ball club." He didn't say he wanted me; he said "my wife" wanted me. We made a deal, and he let Taylor go.

She was proud of her ball team and proud of her players. Everywhere she went she was talking about the first baseman. I got some pretty good write-ups there—Dan Parker in the *American,* Ed Sullivan had a column in the *News.* Just through her. My wife used to keep a scrapbook. The only clippings I had, and pictures, I sent back to the Hall of Fame. That's when they were calling me "the black Bill Terry." They'd say, "Mrs. Manley sure likes your ball playing."

When I took the ball club over, I think we were close to the bottom. I tried to utilize what I had. I concentrated on speed and hustle. I remember one time Fats Jenkins loafed after a foul ball in the outfield. I guess he thought it was going into the stands, but it didn't. So after the inning was over, I told him, "I think you better take a shower, 'cause you act like you're tired." Fats usually did hustle; he was a star basketball player for the Renaissance in the winter. He sat out a day or two and then asked me when could he get back into the lineup, and I let him in. A manager can't just run roughshod over guys, but you've got to have some discipline. We ended up around third place.

With a couple more good pitchers, I think we would have given the Homestead Grays a run for the championship. My salary was $450, the top salary I ever made. I was managing and playing.

The next year they moved the franchise to Newark and played in the Bears' stadium over there. I never did like Jersey. Hell, I didn't want to leave New York and go to New Jersey.

I always wanted to play ball in New York. Yankee Stadium. So I stayed and played with the Black Yankees. The Black Yankees were an independent club. We played in Yankee Stadium and the Polo Grounds when the Yankees and Giants were on the road. They used to hold those four-team double headers up there on Sundays. Maybe the Baltimore Elites would play the Black Yankees, and the Pittsburgh Crawfords would play the Philadelphia Stars. Pretty good crowd too. There'd be 30 or 40,000 people out there.

We were good for 200 ball games a year or more. The big leagues played 154. Every holiday and Sunday we were good for four games on that day. We'd have a game at 11 o'clock, there'd be a double header somewhere that afternoon, and we'd go out to Long Island that night.

We had a lot of good first basemen then. Buck Leonard could bust that ball, baby. I wouldn't say he was a finished first baseman, 'cause he wasn't too fast, but he'd walk up with that stick and bust it.

Showboat Thomas: A fancy dan. He looked good out there on first base. But that's about as far as it went; he couldn't hit too much.

Jim West with Baltimore: Slow. But you know, Jim West developed into a pretty good hitter. He used to be our automatic out. And he could catch a ball at first base, stretch out there and catch it.

I wasn't as quick any more, so I had to cheat a little and play in closer to the bag.

In 1939 I went back to the Monarchs and finished out. Got tired of running all over the country. We were playing in Nebraska, Dizzy Dean's All Stars. We changed clothes in the jail house. I didn't mind that, but there wasn't any place to take a bath. Dizzy Dean's All Stars were changing clothes in a hotel right across the alley. We had to ride all night to Lincoln, Nebraska. So the next morning I told the owner of the ball club, "I'm tired of riding all night, eating out of these grocery store sacks. I'm just tired. I'm going home, be with my family, get on welfare." Been home ever since.

The kids got to have a father around, put them on the right track, pass your experience on to them. I opened up a barbecue place. Some friends loaned me some money, I opened this tavern I got, then built a little four-unit motel. That'll keep you alive, put a couple girls through college. Two sons, one retiring from the army, one from the air force. Ain't nothing wrong with me that a porterhouse steak and a hundred-dollar bill won't cure. Out in the country, breathing good, fresh air.

People lose track of me because I'm out here in the woods. When you're out here in the wilderness, they don't know anything about you, think we still got cowboys and Indians running up and down these hills.

You talk about pioneering! We slept in hotels where they had chinches and bedbugs. We'd leave the light on at night so the cockroaches wouldn't come out. So you had to love the game. You made a little money, and you got to travel and see the country, meet people you never would have met if you hadn't been playing baseball. In the big leagues, all you had to do was play ball and not worry about anything. I could have played forever in the big leagues.

These guys today, they're in heaven. They're enjoying life. This is the greatest thing could ever happen to them, but they don't realize it. I'm not much of a baseball fan now. When basketball rolls around and football, I'm right there in front of that TV. But I don't see the hustle in baseball that I think should be there. They don't run out plays like they should, they don't put forth that extra effort. I went down to Kansas City one time, I think I left the game about the fifth inning. They don't have the push, they don't have the desire. Something's missing. From my viewpoint, they're not hustling for the money and the conditions—the wonderful conditions—they play under. Why, they live like kings!

Did segregation anger me? Naw, it's just the American way of life. I remember once or twice my kids came home from school. My youngest boy, he played basketball, football a lot. He asked about why he couldn't go here, go there. I said, "Well, that's the American way of life. Accept it. I experienced it, now you experience it." I said, "Maybe it will change, it's getting better all the time. See, you have to have patience."

Would I do it again? Whew, a hundred times over! With the situation like it is now? That's a ball player's dream.

If I hadn't played baseball, I'd probably have been in Manhattan all my life. So you see, it was an opportunity. I think opportunity comes to everybody once, maybe twice, in life, if you're smart enough to recognize it. Baseball made it possible.

George Giles

b: 5/2/09, Junction City, KS   BL TR   6'1'', 175

Year	Team	PSN	G	AB	H	2B	3B	HR	BA	SB
1927	Kansas City	1B	49	163	48	8	5	9	.294	1
1928	Kansas City	1B	62	234	72	11	7	1	.308	4
1929	Gilkersons (semi-pro)									
1930	St. Louis	1B	54	223	76	14	4	3	.341	6
	Cuba	1B	—	50	13	0	0	0	.260	—
1931	St. Louis	1B	11	48	9	1	1	0	.187	3
1932	Grays-KC	1B	26	103	31	3	0	0	.301	6
	Mexico	No record								
1933	KC-Baltimore	1B	1	3	2	1	0	0	.667	0
1934		No record								
1935	Brooklyn	1B	44	181	65	9	3	3	.360	8
1936	New York	1B	—	68	19	1	1	0	.277	0
	Puerto Rico	No record								
1937	New York	1B	—	33	10	0	1	0	.303	0
1938	Phil-Craw	1B	30	129	35	0	1	0	.271	2
1939	Kansas City	No record								

Post-Season

1930	Playoffs	1B	4	11	4	3	0	0	.364	1
1938	Playoffs	1B	1	3	1	0	0	0	.333	0

Recap

	Negro league	1B	—	1235	380	48	23	16	.309	30
	Cuba	1B	—	50	13	0	0	0	.260	0
	Post-Season	—	5	14	5	3	0	0	.357	0
	East-West game	—	1	5	0	0	0	0	.000	1
	Totals			1304	398	51	23	16	.302	31

Black Star of Philadelphia
GENE BENSON

*In addition to being a fine hitter and outfielder, Gene Benson is one of the great
living resources of black baseball history.*

*"Benny was a hell of a hitter," says Bill "Ready" Cash, his old teammate
on the Philadelphia Stars of 40 years ago.*

*"I never did figure out how to get Benson out," says Buck O'Neil, shaking
his head.*

*"Benson was a solid hitter, hit line drives," Stars pitcher Webster
McDonald said. "A very peculiar stance, looked like he wasn't ready—that
would fool a lot of pitchers."*

*Roy Campanella's strategy was, "Let him hit to left field and play him that
way." Unfortunately, however, "he would still get his hit."*

*"And," adds Monte Irvin, "he could hit left-handers." The best chance to
get him out was after he hit the ball. "When he ran, he'd kind of waddle."*

*Today Gene Benson is a cherubic storyteller and oral history resource on
the Negro leagues, spinning his stories with a cheerful and quiet conviction.
He has held audiences rapt and entertained for hours.*

You know Willie Mays had that "basket catch" he used on the New
York Giants? Well, I used that same catch when I was with the
Philadelphia Stars in the old Negro leagues. We were playing in
Birmingham one night against the Birmingham Black Barons. Willie
Mays was just a kid then, playing on the playground, and they were
talking about him, and they said that he was going to be a good ball
player. I think he was out there peeking through the hole in the fence,
you know, watching us play. Now I don't know where he got that catch
from, but I was the only one in the Negro leagues that used it.

One year we played Jimmy Foxx's All Stars in an exhibition. He
had George McQuinn on first, Walter Masterson of the Washington
Senators pitching. Masterson could throw hard. Maybe I had an
unorthodox stance at the plate; I didn't look like I was ready, and I
didn't swing hard. Jimmy Foxx kept telling Masterson to throw fast
balls on my hands. After the game, Jimmy Foxx looked me up in the
showers, wanted to know who I was. He said, "You're not supposed to
hit inside pitches."

I said, "I'm not?"

He said, "You must have real good reflexes." But they weren't paying attention to how I was striding. I'd go with the pitch. If they threw inside to me, I'd pull it. I was hoping they'd keep throwing it there, because that's where my power was. Hitting is a natural thing, and we were all so unorthodox. I taught myself to hit. They went by the book.

I would make Satchel Paige so mad. Satchel didn't do nothing but just throw hard, and I was a slap hitter. He'd say, "If you'd swing at the ball, you wouldn't hit so good." That's how I got on his all-star team to play against Bob Feller in 1946. He said, "Now maybe you can hit those other people like you hit me."

Feller had a big year that year; that's the year he won 26 games and struck out 348. He had three 20-game winners—Feller, Spud Chandler [20–8], and Johnny Sain [20–14]. He also had Bob Lemon [4–5] and Dutch Leonard [10–10]. I don't rightly know which was the toughest to hit, because I didn't have too much trouble hitting any of them, really. I guess I was a natural hitter; I never had any trouble with anybody.

Feller started calling me "Cousin." He said, "You have to be a relative in my family, as hard as you hit me. I can't get anything by you. What is it? Am I telegraphing my pitches?"

I said, "No, physically you're not."

He said, "You know what I'm gonna throw?"

I said, "I'm not gonna tell you." I had him puzzled. What I did: I sat on the bench and watched him with men on bases, and I found out something about him. You know what it was? Everybody talked about how hard he could throw. But you know, when he got men on base, he had more confidence in his curve ball. He would throw more curve balls. So I went up to hit his curve ball. If he had thrown fast balls, I would have been the All-American Out.

After the tour he looked me up in the hotel and said, "Now you can tell me." When I told him, he jumped straight up in the air. "I'll be doggone. How'd you figure that out?" He told me, "As long as I have been in the majors, nobody ever discovered this but you." I saw him in 1979 at a reunion down in Kentucky. He told everybody, "There's the guy that hit me so hard."

So as far as the competition, I could see no difference in the major leagues and our leagues, as far as hitting against the different pitchers. When we played head-to-head, it was nip-and-tuck. They won some and we won some.* The white ball players knew it. They respected us. They considered us equals.

What we had to hit at was much worse in our league than in the

---

*The Fellers won seven; the Paiges, six.

major leagues. In the majors you didn't have to worry about being thrown at, you didn't have to worry about anybody cuttin' the ball or sailin' the ball or throwin' spit balls, or deliberately throwin' at you. I've had balls come in on the heart of the plate; when I'd swing it would be over my head! Now *no* ball jumps that much unless it's cut. And you couldn't get a toe-hold at the plate. You see those batters today dig a hole with their toe. You couldn't dig in on those guys in our league. They would *leave* you there. But in the majors you didn't have to worry about all that. All you had to do was concentrate on hittin' the ball.

In 1945 we went down to Venezuela with an all-star team. We took Jackie Robinson with us. Jackie had just been signed by the Dodgers, but he hadn't been in our league too long. He was playing with Kansas City, but he didn't have too much confidence in his ability as a player, simply because I don't guess he had played enough or had enough experience. See, Jackie came up as a shortstop, but Kansas City had a boy over there, Jesse Williams, playing shortstop, and Jackie was just filling in. He couldn't beat Williams out for a job.

So naturally when we went to Venezuela, his confidence wasn't too high, and he wasn't even doing much playing over there. So, by he and I being roommates, we talked a lot. Sat up till all hours of the night, talking baseball. I'd been out there a long time, and he was just new. And I was trying to give him some confidence. I would tell him, "You can't just judge yourself by what you're doing down here." Because it's a known fact that everybody can't play in those Latin countries. Some people don't acclimate to those climates. I guess you don't remember, but there was a time when they had a fellow in Mexico named Jorge Pasquel; he was robbing the major leagues and the black leagues of ball players. A lot of the major leaguers went down there and couldn't make it. They couldn't play under those conditions, the climate and everything.

So I would try to tell Jackie, I said, "Jackie," I said, "you think you can't make it in the major leagues because you feel as though you haven't proven anything here." But I said, "Baseball is baseball; it doesn't make any difference whether it's the major league, black league, or whatever it is. If you can play, you can play."

I told Jackie how many times we'd played against the major leaguers while we were barnstorming. I told him about the year we played against Bob Feller, when he'd already had four 20-game winning years, and we hit him just the same as we did the guys in our league, guys like Satchel Paige. I never saw anything they did that we couldn't do. Commissioner Landis stopped us from playing them because we were winning too many games.

Jackie sat straight up in bed. He said, "Is that right?"

I said, "Jackie, always remember: Where you're goin' ain't half as tough as where you been."

After he went to the major leagues, he told me, "You were right. It was a whole lot easier playing there than in the Negro leagues."

Jackie was a heck of a guy. I do believe though, if Jackie hadn't gone to the majors, I think he'd still be living. I think baseball killed him. You would have to know him to appreciate what he did. You see, he was a high-spirited guy, would fight at the drop of a hat. He had no patience. There were a lot of ball players had better tempers than Jackie's. He fought just about everybody he could fight. I know at least three fights he had while he was in our league, with different ball players. Another time Jackie jumped up and knocked the umpire out cold—knocked him out. But they hushed that up.

I think that's why he's dead today; he destroyed himself.

It was by accident that I became a ball player. Fighting was my

Gene Benson.

game. My stepfather was a prize-fighter, and I'd spar with him. He fought Tiger Flowers to a draw.

Another thing: I was a piano plucker. That's right. And a pretty good piano player. I started out, I was going to be a musician. I started taking music when I was quite young in Moundsville, West Virginia. I had a German teacher, and I finished 10 music books with her. I was playing operas and concertos, I was playing *anything*. Heck, I was playing in the movie theater when I must have been about eight or nine years old. When they would have stage shows, I would play the piano. My teacher told my mother I was one of the best pupils she ever had. My father was a musician, so I think it was more or less an inherited talent with me.

But I gave it up for baseball.

I moved to Philadelphia when I was 14 and went to West Philly High and played a little baseball around the playgrounds, just for the fun of it. A friend of mine, Chester Buchanan, asked me to go away with him one year to Brooklyn to play with the Brooklyn Royals. I told him I didn't want to mess with baseball.

A lot of the fellows on the playground, they tried to talk you out of it. You know how people are. They'd say, "You can't do this," and "You can't do that." Well, that just made me a little more determined. Because I could play. So I went to New York. I must have been 18–19, something like that. Around 1933.

Buck Leonard and I kind of started together. I was a first baseman, Buck was a first baseman, and a fellow named Highpockets Hudspeth *was* the first baseman. He must have been seven foot tall. I knew I didn't have any chance playing first.

The manager, Dick Redding, comes up to me one day, says, "Kid, I sure like the way you can hit that ball. I'd like to keep you on the team, but I don't know where to play you. I've got a first baseman. Can you play outfield?"

I said, "Sure"—I'd never played outfield in my life. So I opened up in left field and was the lead-off man all year. And that's how I started out as a ball player.

I went to Boston one year, up playing with Burlin White and Pud Flournoy. Flournoy was a left-hand pitcher; he was before my time, they say he struck Babe Ruth out just about every time. I attribute my hitting to him. I was a left-hander, and naturally, like any other left-hander, I had a tendency to bail out when left-handers threw me a curve ball. Flournoy took a liking to me. One day Flournoy said to me, "Come on, Kid, I'm gonna teach you how to hit left-handers."

He took me out and he told me to get the bat, stand at the plate. He said, "I'm gonna throw you curve balls, and don't move. Just stand there and watch it. Don't swing, and don't move!" Well, I guess maybe the first two or three he threw up there, I couldn't stay there, you

know. But he kept telling me, "Don't move, I'm not gonna hit you."
He threw curve ball after curve ball at me until I got so I could stand
there and watch that ball coming at me and breaking away from me.

He told me, "Now—start swinging." And I started hitting those
curve balls. He used to take me out different times and do that.
Finally, one day he told me, "You're ready. You can hit 'em." And you
know, from that day on, I never moved from the lineup, no matter
who pitched. In fact, some of my teammates said I hit the left-handers
better than I hit the right-handers.

Buck Leonard would cry every time he saw a left-hander. A lot of
left-handed hitters don't even know what a strike is, because they're
not standing up there to see it; they're ducking. But to me, it didn't
make any difference. I even pinch-hit against left-handers. I was
hitting that ball on the line.

I think it would do a lot more good for a ball player if somebody
gave him confidence like that. Tell him he *can* do something instead of
telling him he can't. If somebody tells you often enough you can't do
something, you'll start to believe it. That's what's happening in the
major leagues today with the platoon system.

I stayed with the Boston Royals for a year. We kind of got
stranded out in Kalamazoo, Michigan, so Chester Buchanan and I
wrote to Otto Briggs, who was managing the Bacharach Giants at that
time, and he sent for us.

Pay day came. Wasn't much, but I was looking for what I had
coming. But Briggs took out my transportation from Kalamazoo.
That was just about all I had! They had the money spread out over the
table. I reached in there and took out the exact amount of money they
owed me. Briggs didn't say anything.

Then the other fellows told me, "Otto Briggs is carrying a gun for
you. He's got a gun in his bag. He's scared of you." We used to dress at
the Olympic Hotel at Broad Street in Philadelphia. One day I walked
up to Briggs and took his gun. You never heard such pleading in all
your life! After that he was all right. Come to find out, the owners
didn't tell him to take that money from me.

Finally I got with the Philadelphia Stars in the Negro big leagues.
Another left-hander was the reason for me coming with the Stars—
Slim Jones. Slim Jones was pitching for the Stars, I was playing with
the Bacharachs. We were sort of their farm club, and they always
played us one game a year. By them being the parent club and the
champions of Philadelphia, they didn't want us to beat 'em. They took
no chances, so they would always pitch Slim Jones. They thought he
was the best in the world. They say he threw as hard as anybody in
baseball. He had a good running fast ball, and he had a good curve
ball. By me being a left-hand hitter, I guess maybe they thought I
wasn't supposed to hit him. But I did. So the next year they came to

get me to play with the Stars. They said, "Well, you can play with us, because any time you hit Slim Jones, you can hit anybody!"

I never *will* forget the first time I came with the Stars. I hadn't had any spring training, and they took me to their stadium at 44th and Parkside and played me a double header. Hadn't even had a ball in my hands. Naturally I didn't do too much. I didn't get no hits—I'm lucky I didn't *get* hit. I heard Jud Wilson whisper, "He's all right for the Bacharachs, but he can't play this kind of ball"—he's talking this around the owner. The old ball players were mean, they felt they had to do that to keep their jobs. A lot of them resented young players, and they were harder on you, because you were a threat to them. If they could talk you out of there, they'd do it. When you couldn't perform in our league, they let you know real fast, the owners got rid of us fast. You had to produce.

But I didn't come there on a tryout, I had a contract. I made up my mind: "Once I get in shape, I'll show 'em." When I messed around a week and got in condition, it was a different story. Then they came on *my* side: "Youngster, you sure can pick on that ball!" I didn't even look at 'em.

One thing I think: You gain respect by producin'. But until then they're gonna try to run you out. If they *can*.

After that, Wilson and I got along fine. Never had another argument with him. A lot of those guys were bullies, but I could take care of myself. I let him know I didn't have any fear of him. He understood, and we got along fine after that. No problem. But I had to straighten him out first.

Like the first time I went to Homestead and played the Homestead Grays. The pitchers on the Homestead Grays made a regular procession by where I was sitting. They would walk around and come up to you: "I understand you're the youngster that hits that ball so hard over there in Philadelphia." I didn't say anything to 'em, I would just look at them and laugh. The next thing they'd say to me: "Well, let's see how good you hit layin' down today."

And they weren't kidding! They threw at you—and some of those guys could throw *hard*. They would knock you down. You'd look around at the ump, you know what he'd tell you? "Get in there and bat."

I think our league was actually harder than the major leagues. It's much easier to go to bat and don't worry about getting out of the way. In our league, nothing was outlawed. Throwing at us was part of the game.

You had to have a lot of courage to keep playing. They threw at you like you were a reindeer. Until they found out it didn't work. Because if they knocked me down, I'd get right back up and hit a line drive, maybe hit one back at 'em, 'cause I hit a lot of balls through the box and I hit a lot of pitchers. I used to laugh at them. So after they found out I didn't scare, they'd lighten up off me.

When I first came in the league, I was a power hitter, could hit the ball out of any ball park. Like all power hitters, I struck out a lot. I found out I could be more valuable to my team not striking out a lot. I told the batting practice pitchers, "Now I don't want you to tell me what you're going to throw, just throw it." This was to stop me being a guess-hitter. They'd throw me fastballs, curve balls, change-ups. Hank Aaron said, "See the ball and hit it," and that was my theory.

I used to hit most of my balls to left field. When the umpires started to call strikes on inside pitches, I said, "I got to learn to hit to right field."

And I could hit bad pitches better than I could good pitches. Bill Byrd, an old spit baller, told me, "We just decided at Baltimore we weren't going to try to trick you."

And Josh Gibson told Buck Leonard he never could distract me.

Gene Benson.

Connie Rector, they told him to walk me with two on base. Connie threw one of those hard balls, up here, and I hit it over the center-field fence. He tore up everything, like to have a fit.

One day Leroy Matlock was pitching. They walked Red Parnell to get to me, because I was a left-hander. I hit the ball against the right-field fence. They said, "There's something wrong here, because no left-hander hit Matlock like that." Maybe that was just luck. I was new in the league, I didn't know Matlock from anyone else. I was just up there swinging. I hit the ball through the box next time. Jimmy Crutchfield of the Crawfords said, "None of us ever got over that." But you know, I didn't hit him no more. Once you find out who he is, you psych yourself out.

Those of us who played baseball then, we know quite a few pitchers who were better than Satchel. He wasn't a better pitcher than Webster McDonald here in Philadelphia, for instance, when you're talking about consistency. And Satchel had a player on his same team, the Kansas City Monarchs, who was over him—Hilton Smith. I would much rather hit at Satchel than hit at Smith. But Satchel was a drawing card, you know.

Some of those other pitchers that weren't rated high would get me out! Luis Tiant, Sr., the father of the pitcher that's with the Yankees, he could get me out. He had a left-handed screw ball. The way that ball would break to a left-handed hitter, it seemed I just couldn't get a hit.

When I first came in the league, you know what they got mad at me for? They got on my neck because I wouldn't cut anybody going into the bases; I wouldn't knock anybody down. We had fellows in our league—this is no lie—I walk in the clubhouse, there's 12–13 guys with files in their hands, sharpening their spikes. This is how mean those guys were. But that wasn't my style. Finally they let me alone.

The first time I played with the Stars I think my pay was $125 a month. You used to borrow part of next year's pay from the owner. If you could borrow enough money, you knew you had a job the next year. As years went by, the pay went up: $5–600 a month. We made more money playing in the Latin countries than we did here. Most of the times your expenses were paid, and you could take your wife with you. It was real nice.

'Course, back in those days the major leagues weren't making *too* much either. I can remember certain teams like the Bay Parkways and the Brooklyn Bushwicks and those teams around Philly and New York. They had major league caliber ball clubs, but the players wouldn't go to the major league, because they could do better where they were, playing on weekends. They all had good jobs, and they had this weekend money coming in, and they wouldn't *go* to the major leagues. They tried to get them to the majors, but they wouldn't go.

And the major league ball players, when they got so they couldn't play in the majors, they came to the Bushwicks and played—George Earnshaw, Rube Walberg and those fellows. We played against those fellows.

In fact, I can remember a time, right at 44th and Parkside, we outdrew the Phillies. Our park held maybe 7–8–9,000. When the Phillies were playing in Baker Bowl, we had more people in the park than they did! And not only the black fans, but a lot of the whites came to see us. Because we were good.

There was a roundhouse past the center-field wall. Every time you come to bat, looked like the engines stirred up that smoke and soot on you. You had to stop a little while until the smoke cleared away.

We had a tennis court in center field. Josh Gibson used to say I hid a ball in my pocket. He said I'd go back in the dark and nobody could see me, "and you just take one out of your pocket and throw the ball." Nobody could tell him any different.

Oscar Charleston taught me how to play center field. In the Negro league you had to turn your back on the ball and take your eye off it. He'd hit the ball over my head and tell me to go get it. You learned to judge the ball and turn around and find yourself in front of the ball all the time. A lot of balls missed today should be caught easy. Today they "trail" the ball, they watch it all the way. Very few can take their eyes off the ball and go back to the fence. DiMaggio did it, Terry Moore of the Cardinals could do it, Jimmy Piersall could do it, Willie Mays. But most got to run and look at the same time.

There was no foolishness, no clowning. Some of us were approached [to clown], but we all turned it down. We had a team called the Clowns, but that wasn't in our [Negro National] league. We were ball players, we had some principles. We weren't clown ball players; we played *baseball*.

We only had 13-14 players at most. The fellows on the bench wanted to play, but in those days eight players played every day. Unless somebody broke a leg or died, you just didn't get in there. I even had a ball player to steal my glove one night so he could play. Back in those days you worked out in the outfield, you'd leave your glove there. One night I went back out, the glove wasn't there. The someone that got it was another player on my team who hadn't gotten a chance to get in the line-up, so he stole my glove!

A lot of times we would play a game, maybe you'd see one of the sports writers on one of the black papers, and he would ask us who we played and how we made out. And sometimes we would tell him lies— he'd put it in the paper the next day!

We used to play prison teams—they had some good ball players in prison. Everyone knew me, they'd come out shaking hands. My teammates all thought I'd been in jail, but they were all guys from around the corner in my neighborhood.

We went everywhere on the bus. I can sit in a chair today and get my rest, because I was the look-out man on the bus. If I saw the driver start picking on his ears [getting sleepy], I'd say, "OK, pull over."

It must have been 1937 or '38. We were on the way to Cleveland to play a double header that day. A car hit the bus and turned the bus over. Killed both of them in the car, I understand. Our bus was a complete wreck. Some of the fellows got broken ribs. One player punched out the glass window so we could get out.

We called the owner. He asked how many were dead. We told him no one was dead. The next thing he said was, "Play the ball game"— they had 8–9,000 people in the stands. I had stitches in my leg and ran them out playing the double header.

But we survived. I don't know how we survived, but we loved the game so well we overlooked some things. But now, looking back, you wonder how you made it. We just went on and had fun playing.

In 1938 I was traded to the Pittsburgh Crawfords. The Crawfords gave up three or four guys for me: Cy Perkins, the catcher, used to catch Satchel; George Giles; a couple of other guys.

When I got to Pittsburgh, the Crawfords were out of town. The Homestead Grays were in town, and they got me to play with them until my team came back. When my team came back, they had an awful fight about keepin' me. But I had to go to the Crawfords. Gus Greenlee was owner of the Crawfords. I guess maybe his numbers business was a little bad, and Gus wasn't payin' off. So you know *I* was disgusted, 'cause in Philadelphia I got paid.

One day we came to Philly and played the Stars. I practically beat the Stars myself that day, I had a terrific day. Oscar Charleston was manager of Philadelphia then. He came to me and said, "Benson," he said, "I know you're not satisfied over there. I understand that they're not payin' off, one thing and another. You're not used to that." He said, "I'm gonna see if I can get you back with the Stars." And that's where I stayed.

I went to Puerto Rico in 1939. Spoony Palm played on our team, San Juan. He used to mail letters in the "basura" [trash can]. He came home one day, said, " 'Hoy' [today] must be a good movie, it's playing all over town."

Orlando Cepeda's father, Perucho, was playing down there. He was a better hitter than Orlando. He was bigger than his son too.

They took their baseball seriously. If you lost a ball game, you could go in town, nobody would speak to you; everyone was looking at you mean.

I was the first one started taking wives there. I made them give us an apartment, furnished it. [Pitcher] Raymond Brown and his wife, and my wife and I stayed together in an apartment in San Juan. We always had the other ball players over to dinner to eat American food.

We played Satchel's team for the championship. Satchel and them beat us out of the series. They said in the paper we didn't try our hardest. I hit .450, [Roy] Partlow pitched 27 or 28 scoreless innings. The ball game was lost from the native ball players booting the ball away.

When we got back to the States, Brown tells people I never got base hits off him. That wasn't true. I got hits, and he got me out, that's the way it is in baseball. One night, I said, "Ray, I'm not a talking man, I never brag, but I'll tell you something: The way you're running your mouth, from here on in, whenever you pick up that ball, you better be right." They say I ran him out of baseball, because I hit him so hard. I never hit him hard before that.

I went to Mexico when Jorge Pasquel was giving all that money away. I jumped and went too.

We were going to Mexico, the wife and I and our little baby. Back in those days they segregated you. The porter hadn't put us in the right car, and after we left St. Louis they stopped in Arkansas, and we were in the wrong car.

I was sleepy, and these soldiers were getting on the car. One of the soldiers looked at me, said, "All right, Nigger, this is the Mason-Dixon line, you know what you're supposed to do." I did what I was

Gene Benson (front, second from right) with the 1940 Philadelphia Stars. Also shown are Oscar Charleston (standing, far right) and the owner Ed Bolden (standing, center). Catcher Bill Cash kneels at right.

supposed to do: I knocked him over three rows of seats. Sometimes when you get angry, you lose your sense to a certain extent.

As the other soldiers were coming on the train, they see this soldier laying over the seats, wanted to know what happened. One of the others said, "He's had too much to drink, I'll take care of him," and winked his eye at me. He didn't want to see any trouble.

I took my time getting in the other car, I was so angry. I sat down in a seat alone away from my wife and baby. After a while she came over to me and said, "Why don't you sit with us?" and I was sitting there crying, I was just so angry.

Had this soldier not said what he did, they would have killed me, because I didn't have no help. I couldn't whip an army. I'm glad that was the only real incident I got into.

Even though I was born and raised up in West Virginia, we didn't run into a whole lot of things in West Virginia.

Being out on the road, we had to have things to eat, go places to have a sandwich. I used to detest it when the restaurants had those sliding doors, raise it up and ask you what you wanted, and slam it down in your face. I like to starved to death. The other guys said, "You'll get all of us killed." But I just wasn't used to being treated like that, so it went a little hard with me. Eventually I got used to it; I was able to endure like the rest of them. You figured you were just as much a man as anybody else and people should respect you. But I got through that too.

Remember in 1986 when Oil Can Boyd was having trouble in the hospital and they couldn't figure out what was wrong with him? I knew what was wrong with him.

Oil Can Boyd was born and raised in Meridian, Mississippi. One night we played there. The park we were supposed to play in, something happened. They did let us play in the white park, but they didn't let us dress there. We had to go to colored families and dress. When we left to dress, there were colored people in the stands watching us. When we got back, there were no colored people in the stands. I asked, "Where are all the colored people in this town?" They said they had a curfew on them; if they were out after hours, they were locked up. So you figure a boy brought up like that, going to Boston and finding things just the same, he blows up. That's what happened to the boy. It wasn't drugs, thank goodness.

The first time I went to Mexico City, I was always in good physical condition—so I thought. One of my friends was living in a hotel there. I went up to see him and trotted up the steps, ran up two–three flights of steps, and I had to lay down when I got upstairs. See, it's the altitude. They laughed at me. That's the reason why, if you're the visiting team, going to Mexico City, you try to get there four or five days ahead of time, so you can work out and kind of adjust. The major leaguers couldn't adjust; they played very bad baseball down there.

I was with Torreon, Martin Dihigo was managing. Come to find out, I was making more money than Dihigo, and Martin found out what I was making. We were supposed to play Monterrey the first game. You remember Barney Morris, a knuckle ball pitcher? I had a lot of trouble with him in the States. I hadn't had a ball in my hand for two weeks, and I'm on a team the manager don't want me. I said to myself, "I'm in a bad fix. I got to go out and hit against a guy I couldn't get any hits off in the States. I don't know what my chances are tonight." I told my wife, "If there wasn't bad luck, I wouldn't have any luck at all."

I think I got five-for-five that night! I must have driven in 8–10 runs. They were going to give me half the city. Seems like I always could rise to the occasion.

I played in Puerto Rico, Mexico, Cuba, Panama, South America.

Maracaibo, Venezuela: They called it hell. If you played the outfield, the heat burns up through your shoes. You have to keep continually moving. You couldn't play a double header: One game in the morning, go home, then come back and play the second game.

They had an election there, bullets zinging all over the walls. From what I hear, they're still doing it.

That was the first time I was away from home without a round-trip ticket. The guy we were playing for bet all his money on the other team. But we won the game, and before we got back to the hotel, he was dead. Blew his brains out. They were *serious* about baseball.

I said, "We'll go to the American consul," but it didn't do any good, so we decided to go to the inquest. But everybody there was broke too. After that I made sure I never went anywhere without transportation.

Johnny Berardino played second base on that Bob Feller tour in '46. He's a television star now [ABC's "General Hospital"]. I'm the one put him in the soap operas. What happened: Dutch Leonard threw me a knuckle ball, and I hit it straight at Berardino. The ball ducked and hit him in the knee cap. The guy never played regular after that. He's been with "General Hospital" ever since. I made him a rich guy. So I think I should go see him. I think he owes me something for getting him out of baseball.

That was quite a tour. It was a toss-up which team was better.* Of course you know we got gypped out of a lot of money. We started out

---

*Feller also had batting champions Stan Musial and Mickey Vernon, plus Phil Rizzuto, Jeff Heath, Ken Keltner, Charlie Keller.

in Pittsburgh. I think we got something like 300-and-some dollars a man. Then after that the crowds got bigger, and the money got smaller. The "ducks" got into it, you know—that's what we called the deductions. We made a complaint about it, but they just as good as told us if we weren't satisfied, we didn't have to play. So you know, you weren't going to turn down that money. That was as much money as we ever made in our life. I think in about two weeks time, shoot, I bought a house!

So there was no difference in the caliber of baseball that was played back then, comparing the white and black leagues. If you're a ball player, makes no difference what color you are. I couldn't see anything they did that we couldn't do.

The white ball players knew we could play, but the top people didn't want it too much. Landis figured we were having too much success, so he stopped it. But by that time we found out we could play with them.

Most of the time we got robbed. We used to play the Bushwicks. What they would do, they used to put the balls in the ice box and freeze 'em before the game. When we came to bat, they'd use the frozen balls.

We used to play the white teams with their portable lights. When we came to bat, it seemed like they could always find a way the motor wouldn't run so good, the lights would dim. We had 15-16 strikeouts one night.

We sent Bobby Shantz to the major leagues. He was pitching for a team named Mayfair in Philadelphia. We had a fellow by the name of Miller, beat him 2–1. But if you could play well against a colored team, you could go to the major leagues. He went to the majors the next day.

When Suitcase Simpson first came to the Stars, he didn't know how to do too much. One day Goose Curry, the manager, came to me, said, "Benson, I'm going to give Harry to you. Tell him how to play outfield and how to hit left-handers." And you know, Suitcase Simpson made good with the Cleveland Indians. I'm proud of that.

If we had played according to the money we made, I guess none of us would have been ball players long. We loved the game. And we were playing just as hard for nothing as we would for money. But today I think there's not too much desire out there like there used to be. All the money they're making takes the desire out of it. If you pay a guy $500,000 or $600,000 a year and give him a contract for five or six years, he don't care whether he plays or not. I think eventually they're going to price themselves out of baseball.

And another thing they can't do well today—bunt. You didn't see a ball player come along when we did, who couldn't bunt. We were playing the Bushwicks one Sunday. Oscar Charleston was the manager. The game was tied up 3–3, something like that. We were in overtime, 11th or 12th inning, and we got a man as far as third with two men out. They had two strikes on me. Oscar Charleston gave me the bunt signal with two men out and two strikes. I looked at him, said, "There's something wrong here." But I had to do it. I laid it down.

Oscar Charleston always thought I could bunt.

Jim Duffy used to pitch for a white semipro team, a heck of a pitcher, but he had a belly that stuck out. We finally found out how to beat him. Just bunt. After three or four innings he wasn't able to go get them.

We didn't steal so many bases. We stole bases when necessary, but we didn't make a habit of it like they do today. Cool Papa Bell would do most of his running taking extra bases when somebody got a hit. Didn't just steal a base.

We'd go from first to third on a bunt. The infielders were all in, so we'd just keep running. We'd get four hits and six runs, and the big leaguers couldn't understand it. But you can get runs without hitting the ball out of the park. Pow—that's where the money is now. Of course the money is everywhere now, sitting on the bench even.

I left baseball in 1949 and opened a billiard parlor for 12 years. Then I drove a supply truck for the board of education in Philadelphia. I'm retired now. Maybe I'll take up the piano again. I'm going to have to do something, because it's no good to retire and just sit down. I wouldn't last no time if I did that.

I belong to Concerned Black Men. We put essay contests in the schools; the winners, we give bonds. We had a banquet for them. I'm on the bond committee, picked up over $5,000 worth of bonds. That's to give them some incentive. We always read about the bad kids, but there's some good kids out there too, so we try to give them some kind of recognition.

Last Saturday we went to Newark to dedicate Ray Dandridge field. Ray felt so happy he cried. There were about 300 kids. They have an incentive program too. They call it Achievers; they work hard in school. The counselors said, "Here's the living proof" of the Negro leagues. The kids got a chance to see us Saturday.

So I have no regrets. It was just one of those things.

We never thought about the major leagues. We never thought it would happen. We never dreamed that it would come true. But I know we were the pioneers. Without our league, where would Robinson have been drafted from? If we weren't out there suffering and struggling, they wouldn't have any blacks in there now.

I think baseball has done one thing: It's taught me how to win and how to lose. That's important in life. Life is ups and downs. You win and you lose. And you have to take it all in stride if you're gonna make it. So baseball, if you play it, you *will* learn how to win and lose. So you can carry this same thing over to life. Sometimes things might break bad for you. Things I can't do nothin' about, why worry about them? I think that's a good thing for everybody to learn. Because we can all win, but a lot of us can't lose. That's when the trouble comes in, when the losin' comes up. But it's all a part of the game, a part of life. Like, heck, today it might rain all day long, tomorrow is sunshine.

My wife says, "Nothing bothers you."

I said, "Well, after playing in the Negro league, I've done my worrying already."

Chet Brewer (far left) and George Giles (third from left) next to owner J. L. Wilkinson of the Kansas City Monarchs. Bullet Joe Rogan is seated behind them.

Gene Benson

b: 10/2/13, Pittsburgh, PA				BL TL 5'8", 180					
Year	Team	PSN	G	AB	H	2B	3B	HR	BA	SB
1936	Bacharachs	CF	2	8	2	0	0	0	.250	0
1937	Philadelphia	CF	—	103	27	2	0	3	.262	2
1938	Phil-Craw	CF	21	84	24	0	0	1	.286	1
1939	Philadelphia	CF	—	200	64	8	1	3	.320	0
1940	Philadelphia	CF	—	259	69	5	4	6	.266	0
1941	Philadelphia	CF	—	58	25	5	0	0	.258	0
1942	Philadelphia	CF	—	90	16	1	0	0	.178	0
1943	Philadelphia	CF	—	139	49	5	4	0	.350	1
1944	Philadelphia	CF	43	168	55	7	7	1	.327	4
1945	Philadelphia	CF	38	154	57	8	3	2	.370	2
	Venezuela	—	—	59	16	—	—	—	.271	—
1946	Philadelphia	CF	54	213	72	12	4	0	.338	1
1947	Philadelphia	CF	—	217	62	12	0	1	.286	4
	Cuba	OF	—	239	57	9	2	1	.238	5

Post-Season

1939	Playoffs	OF	3	10	4	0	1	0	.400	0

Gene Benson vs. White Big Leaguers

Year	AB	H	2B	3B	HR	Pitcher
1946	4	1	1	0	0	Feller (26-15), Sain (20-14), Lemon (4-5)
	4	1	0	0	0	Feller, Chandler (20-8)
	4	1	0	0	0	Chandler, Feller
	4	1	0	0	0	Feller, Leonard (10-10)
	4	1	1	0	0	Feller, Sain
	4	1	0	0	0	Feller, Lemon
	4	0	0	0	0	Feller, Sain
	4	1	0	0	0	Feller
Totals	32	7	2	0	0	Average: .219

Note: No box scores have been found of 1938–39 series.

Recap

	PSN	G	AB	H	2B	3B	HR	BA	SB
Negro league	OF	—	1693	522	65	23	17	.308	15
Winter leagues	OF	—	298	73	9	2	1	.245	5
White big leagues	OF	7	32	7	2	0	0	.219	0
East-West games	OF	4	12	3	1	0	1	.250	0
Post-Season	OF	3	10	4	0	1	0	.400	0
Totals			2045	609	77	26	19	.298	20

An American Monarch
JOHN "BUCK" O'NEIL

The first black coach in the major leagues, Buck O'Neil, was also the scout who signed Ernie Banks and Lou Brock for the Cubs. And before that, he was a long-time first baseman for the Kansas City Monarchs and played a key role in their black championships of 1942 and '46.

"A very knowledgeable man," said Richard Wilkinson, son of the Monarchs' owner. "It's a shame he couldn't have been a manager in the major leagues. I think he was qualified, both emotionally and everything else."

I met O'Neil several times, at Cooperstown, where he serves on the veterans' committee, and at old-timers' reunions. He speaks softly, thoughtfully, slowly, melodiously. His head has turned a curly white, but his chest and stomach are still as tight and hard as when he was playing for the Monarchs half a century ago.

In 1935 we picked up some guys from around Sarasota, my home town, plus Ollie Marcelle* and Bill Riggins of the New York Black Yankees, and made up a team and went west. Wayne Carr, our manager, got a little backing from somebody out east, and actually I put in some of the money—I wanted to get out of those celery fields there so bad. We got two old seven-passenger Cadillacs; they were giving them away if you had any money, just to get them off the lot.

Let's go!

We played our way into Louisiana, but we didn't do so hot; there wasn't much money. The Monarchs and the Pittsburgh Crawfords were training in Monroe. The Monarchs had a good club—Hilton Smith, Leroy Morney. And this was the first time I saw the Crawfords. That's when I saw Josh Gibson. Outstanding! I just loved looking at them.

We lost one of our cars in Monroe; the lady there kept it because we couldn't pay our room rent. The coach of Grambling college, Ralph Jones, later was president of the college, had umpired some of the games for the Crawfords. He said, "Come up here and play me a ball game." We were going to eat breakfast, lunch, and dinner there,

---

*One of the top three black third basemen of all time.

and they weren't charging anything. Well, there wasn't but 12 of us, so we piled into the second car and moved on up the road to Grambling. Two buildings on the campus was all they had—two buildings and a ball field.

We were going to play in Wichita Falls June 19 against the Black Spudders—it was potato country out there. June 19 is Emancipation Day, when the slaves out there found out they were free. That's a big day in Texas for blacks—a big celebration, barbeque and all that. I imagine they still do it. But the river came out of the bank, had a little flood, and we couldn't get to Wichita Falls, so we spent the 19th of June without a game. Didn't have any money. But I was a pretty good pool player, played 10-cent nine-ball. I picked up a dollar or two, bought a lot of beans and white pork and meal to make some bread. We did all right. We did all right.

The Black Spudders out of Mineola, Texas were going out to the Denver *Post* Semipro tournament. The tournament people wanted another black team, so the Spudders said, "Why don't you guys go out there too?"

But we had lost our other car. The man took it because we owed him bills for gas, said we could get it when we got back. The Spudders took six of our ball players along with their team, and five of us hoboed on a freight train from Wichita Falls to Denver.

We stopped at a hobo jungle. A hobo jungle is where the hoboes would stop, usually outside a railroad terminal, where the freight is running slow enough for them to get on and off. They hang pots and pans on trees, and it's near some water so you can clean up the pans and hang them back up for the next people. That night there wasn't anyone there but us. It was right beside a corn field, and we got some corn and were boiling it.

We could hear the railroad dicks [cops] walking the cars and knocking on the doors of the cars to get the hoboes out. But we weren't worried, we didn't think they'd bother us. But this guy got off the car, came over and asked what we were doing there. He asked me did my father own a railroad. I said, "No sir," [laughs].

He said, "If your father don't own a railroad, you got no business here." He shot in the can I was boiling the corn in, and all the water came out. Then he started shooting at the ground, and we started running. I think he wanted to frighten us—and he did. I guess we ran about a mile. I wish we'd had some timing on that, we just might have set a record. We ran down through the outskirts of a little town and came back to the tracks about a mile away. We caught another freight and went on to Denver.

I remember getting into Denver early one morning, went to a

rest room and washed up, then got in the soup line to eat. After we got our stomachs full, Wayne Carr went to meet Mr. Joe Alperts, who owned a clothing store and wanted a ball club to represent his store. He put us up in a house in Denver, gave us money for food and cleaned us up, and we played in the tournament in Denver and made a little money.

We wanted to go to the tournament in Wichita, Kansas next, so Wayne Carr talked to a guy who had a Graham Page car, kind of a sport-minded fellow, and he said all of us could go down there in his car. We jumped in the car and went down.

Satchel Paige was down there with the Bismarck North Dakota team—Hilton Smith, Chet Brewer, Quincy Trouppe, Double Duty Radcliffe. They had a pretty good ball club, had four of five white boys like Moose Johnson, a big home run hitter. Satchel and them won it. But we came out with $100. We could take $50 and get an old automobile. They said, "Foots (they called me Foots because I had big hands and feet), we going to give the money to you. You keep it for us."

This was Kansas City Monarch territory, they were great favorites out there, and they were coming to Wichita to play the winner of the tournament—Satchel and them. Riggins and the older guys knew the fellows from the Monarchs—Bullet Rogan, Newt Allen, Newt Joseph—and they went out with the Monarchs on the town.

That night I was at the rooming house. Around 9-10:00, maybe later than that, they'd come back: "Heh, Foots, give me my cut." After I got through giving, didn't anybody have anything left but me. I must have had $5 at the most. I got to buy some food again for us to eat on.

Next we went up to Goodling, Kansas to play, make enough money and get our car back. But listen—it was snowing! We couldn't play.

I decided to go back to Sarasota with another guy, Dobey Major, so I called Papa. He said, "OK, we'll send you some money." But our parents sent us train tickets, nothing else. I think I had 75 cents. The lady in Wichita who had the rooming house was Mrs. Jacobs. We didn't have any money to give her, but I told her I'd pay her one day.

We got on the train and rode. Right near the station in Chattanooga was a bakery with day-old bread, so I stocked up on black donuts and sweet rolls and got back on the train. That was the only food we had on the entire trip—that's all.

I knew we had to change trains at Jacksonville, my old stomping grounds. I knew all the redcaps there, I used to play ball with them, and I knew I've got to see some of them. So I took my suit off, put on some slacks, and folded the suit up under the train seat to get the wrinkles out. Then I went back in the rest room, cleaned up, and put on my suit just before we got to Jacksonville.

"Heh, Foots, man, where you been?"

I told them.

"Man, you're looking good."

Dobey wanted me to ask them for some money so we could get some more food, but I was too proud, I didn't want them to know we'd had a bad time. So we didn't get any food, because I wouldn't ask for it.

When I got home, I ate so much, my Momma cried. And I slept for two days. I said, "Well, Momma, that's it. I'm not going any more."

But next spring, when the birds started singing, when they started throwing that ball, I was ready to go again.

I got started playing baseball in Sarasota. I was born Nov. 13, 1911 in Carrabelle, Florida on the Gulf coast, 50 miles southwest of Tallahassee. My daddy was a saw-miller. We left there and went to

John "Buck" O'Neil.

Sarasota when I was 12 years old, but there wasn't a sawmill around Sarasota, mostly palm trees then, so my father was working in the sawmills in west Florida and southern Georgia. Got home about once a month. After he got his big toe cut off in the sawmill, he worked as a foreman out in the celery fields around Sarasota. That's where my first baseball was.

I got very interested in baseball, because at the time the New York Giants were training there. Mr. Mack and the Philadelphia Athletics were down in Fort Myer. So I saw a lot of baseball. A hell of a lot of it was sitting on the fence, but that was all right—I saw it.

My daddy took me down to Palm Beach to see some black guys playing. These guys were representing the Royal Ponciana Hotel and the Breakers Hotel. They would work as waiters and bell hops for the rich folk. It was actually outstanding baseball, that's why they were down there. I saw Rube Foster* in Palm Beach. He was an amazing character! Quite a student of the game. He was like a Whitey Herzog, built his team around speed. Used his noggin very well. My daddy wanted me to see those folks, because I'd been reading about them in the *Amsterdam News* and the Chicago *Defender*.

In school everyone was fond of Marian Anderson and everything she did. My teacher would talk about what a wonderful person she was. It meant a lot to us.

That was in the 'twenties, when I was in grammar school. The highest we went was eighth grade, because there was no black high school in Sarasota. The closest black high school was Tampa. In the state of Florida, the only black high schools were Tampa and Jacksonville. All the smaller cities, the highest you could go was eighth grade; that was it. I'd walk past the white high school and tell my mother, "It's kinda bad I can't go there."

She said, "You learn just as much in 8 grades as they do in 12."

I shined shoes, and Mr. Roth, a German Jew, a very fine man, I thought, was going to teach me a trade making shoes, and I was doing a pretty fair job of it. Then when the celery season would come, I would work in the field and carry the boxes. They called me a box boy. I could carry four boxes in one hand.

During lunch time one day, the older folk were on one side of the crates and I was by myself on the other side. I said, "Damn, there's got to be something better than this!"

I didn't know my father had heard me. But that night when we got off the truck, a block and a half from our house, he said, "Jay"— my name was John Jordan, or J.J., and everyone called me Jay—"I

---

*Owner of the Chicago American Giants and founder of the Negro National league in 1920.

heard what you said during lunch time." He had never heard me curse; I thought that was what he was talking about.

But he said, "There *is* something better than this, but, you know, it's not here. You'll just have to go and try to get it. You just have to get out of here. You can't get it here." I had a friend, Maisley Lloyd, who went to Edward Waters College in Jacksonville, a little AME [African Methodist Episcopal] college. So I went four years in high school there and two years in college. But I played baseball all six years, because I was a big kid and they didn't have so many students.

Some of the guys who played ball in the Negro league would come down to Jacksonville and play on the Red Caps. The great shortstop, Dick Lundy, worked as a redcap and picked up pretty good change. Lundy would sit and talk to us for hours about Pop Lloyd, Smokey Joe Williams, Rube Foster. Outstanding!

In 19 and '34 I went down to Miami and played with the Miami Giants. Johnny Pierce and Buck O'Neal owned the team; they were bootleggers and business partners. O'Neal had played baseball around Waycross, Georgia. That's where I got my nickname, Buck, after him. Syd Pollock was the booking agent. We played all over the East, all the way up into northern New York, but there wasn't too much money we could make up there. When we came back South, you know, everybody stopped at the Woodmont Hotel in New York, and Riggins and Marcelle wanted to go some place warm for the winter, so we picked them up with us. We played in Miami all winter, twice a week—Thursday, the maids' day off, and Sunday afternoon.

Charlie Henry brought the Zulu Giants to Miami to play us. These were the guys that played in straw dresses and wore makeup like we'd see in the Tarzan movies; they would paint their faces like they had a ring in their nose; a lot of them wore wigs, but they wore baseball shoes and socks. That was when Mussolini was giving Haile Selassie so much hell down there in Ethiopia, and Ethiopia was so popular. Charlie Henry was "Haile Selassi," and he named the players all African names. There was Rojo, Limpopo, Sheba, Bebop—a midget—King Tut. Dave Barnhill was Impo—he married Johnny Pierce's daughter. Some of those guys that could really run ran with a straw dress in the outfield. Saturday they paraded up and down Second Avenue, a big avenue for blacks in Miami, and that Sunday we packed that little ball park there. The people took to 'em so they stayed in Miami all year.

This is where Syd Pollock got the idea for the Clowns. Johnny Pierce died, and Syd paid his widow some money, and it was his ball club. He named the Miami Giants the Ethiopian Clowns, put them in different clowning uniforms, and they always had a couple of comedians in straw dresses. He took the team up North, to New York and all the way into Canada. He had a pretty fair ball club.

They went to the Denver *Post* tournament and won it. But some of the black people were squawking about the name, Ethiopian Clowns, they thought it was degrading, so they changed it to the Cincinnati Clowns, then the Indianapolis Clowns.*

Wingfield Welch, who had the Shreveport Acme Giants, had seen me play when I came to Shreveport and said, "Next year, come play with me." So in '36 I got a letter from him, waiting at the store. I gave it to Poppa to read.

"When you going?"

"You know what Momma will say."

"You got to go. You can't stay here. This is your opportunity. Go ahead and take it."

We talked Momma into it. It wasn't as hard as I thought it was going to be.

J. L. Wilkinson, who owned the Monarchs, was kind of sponsoring the Acme Giants, he was using the team as a farm team for the Monarchs. Dunsieth, North Dakota, up in the wheat country, also sponsored us. We played out of that little town, up into Canada and all around, and played our way back down to Shreveport.

We played the Black Spudders. Klingerman, the owner, was a German and a fine man. He got the best ball players off both these teams to go to Mexico. We couldn't take our bus into Mexico, so the Mexican people picked us up. When we got ready, our bus was going to come back and pick us up. But when we got to the border, there was nobody there! I didn't have any money, but this time I was too ashamed to call Momma.

John Markham, a pitcher, lived in Shreveport, so John and I went hoboing from Laredo to Shreveport, and I spent that winter with John.

We were picking up any job we could to make a dime. One guy worked at the hotel, the biggest hotel; he'd make a buck or two and leave us off a dollar to get some groceries. Willard Brown came home from Mexico, had two or three suits, looked good. He'd help us out. We got along: Ate all winter, went to a movie every once in a while.

Next spring, 1937, the Kansas City Monarchs came to Shreveport to train and get a chance to look at our ball players. The Memphis Red Sox came through and picked me up and took me with them—Larry Brown, Goose Curry, Nat Rogers. We went to Chicago to play, and I

*Hank Aaron got his professional start as a shortstop with the Indianapolis Clowns.

ran into Charlie Henry, the guy with the Zulu Giants. After the ball game, Charlie said, "Man, you better come with us, make some money"—I believe with the Memphis Red Sox I was making $90 a month—"we going to Canada." Charlie gave me $50 that night.

I wore that straw skirt. We played shadow ball in the infield, without a ball, and pepper ball, throwing behind your back, like that. King Tut did most of the clowning. This is when I met Abe Saperstein, who was sponsoring Charlie Henry. He had the Globe Trotters basketball club and a baseball team.

'Thirty-eight was when I first came to the Monarchs. Stayed with them through 1955, until I went to the Cubs.

This was the height for me, a great feeling—a *great* feeling. I was looking at some of the old pictures today. We had some pretty good ball players.

Willard Brown was a home run hitter.

Newt Allen at second base had a tremendous arm. He could stand in center field and throw the ball over the grandstand behind home plate. I've never seen anyone could throw that far.

Ted Strong hit with power from both sides. And had an arm like Clemente. I would have liked to see him play major league baseball. And an outstanding basketball player; played with the Harlem Globe Trotters in the winter.

Hilton Smith was unbeatable there for a spell, from '38 to '42. Unbeatable! He had more natural stuff, a good rising fast ball and an excellent curve ball with good control. My land! He would have been a 20-game winner in the major leagues with the stuff he had. We played against an all-star team the year Stan Musial came up, 1941. Satchel Paige and Bob Feller pitched three innings. Musial hit a home run on Satchel on the roof of that stadium. But Musial and John Mize said they'd never seen a curve ball like Hilton's curve ball.

Satchel Paige had hurt his arm in '37 in South America. Wilkie brought him up to the Monarchs. We had got another ball club playing the Northwest, all the way to Canada and all the way to the Coast, playing mostly with the House of Davids. And Wilkie sent Satchel there with Jewbaby Floyd [a masseur] to work on his arm. One day Satchel says, "Don't have to save my arm; it's loose." He struck out nine men that night, said, "I'm ready."

We started building Satchel up. Satchel was our franchise—Satchel was a *lot* of franchises. If Memphis needed to make a payroll, Wilkie would rent Satchel out, and Satchel would pitch three innings for them. He was making payrolls for the entire league. Babe Ruth made the payroll for a lot of clubs in the white leagues.

Satchel was the first black that got the publicity. They put a beautiful article about Satchel in *The Saturday Evening Post*. Wilkie's son was a captain in the air force, and they bought a plane to take Satchel to the different towns. From there his career really jumped off, and Satchel became very, very popular. The Monarchs were getting a percentage of the gate where he played. Satchel played darn near every night somewhere and was getting 15 percent off of the gate. So Satchel was making more than the major leaguers were getting. Satchel's first year in the major leagues [1948], actually he lost money.

Satchel was more or less of a prankster. He'd pitch pennies to the line. He was deadly with a half dollar, because it's heavier. But we said no half dollars, you have to pitch with a quarter or less. He got deadly with the quarter, so we dropped it to a dime, then a nickel, then pennies, because they were the hardest to throw because they were the lightest. He played cards, whist. He just loved it. He loved it!

John "Buck" O'Neil with the Chicago Cubs.

He was a fun person to be around. He was always cracking some kind of joke. He liked to sing on the ukulele; he'd strum on that, and we'd sing. On the road, we see his car waiting up in front of us. We'd stop. "I thought about this song," he'd say. "I want to sing."

Everybody had a nickname. I was Nancy. The way I got it was one night he had a girl in one room and an Indian girl in the other room. He's knocking on one door, whispering, "Nancy? Nancy?" Then the first girl opens her door, says, "What's going on? Who's this Nancy?" Just then I came out of my door. I says, "Yeah, Satch, what you want?" So that's how I got my nickname Nancy.

Satchel would take infield practice right along with the third baseman. He would *flip* it over to first. He liked for us to hit it in close, so he could run in and flip it over. He had more fun than the fans did. The people would come to see us take infield practice. We'd go months without anyone juggling the ball. We'd put on a show!

We played a lot of ball out of the league. The Northwest was our territory. The early Monarchs had a couple of trailers, eight men to a trailer, with bunks on the side you could let up and down. We played a lot with the House of David into Canada and back into the league.

The House of David were out there to make money. Win or lose didn't mean that much. We weren't going to run them, and they weren't going to run us. We were there to entertain people. Long before the Clowns, the House of David were clowning too, raising money for their church. And trying to convert me. Maybe three of the guys were from the cult; all the other guys were fill-ins, would grow whiskers and long beards and hair down their backs. Big John Tucker and Doc Talley were great. The first portable lights I saw, the House of David brought to Miami.

The Monarchs had their own lights.* They had two guys with the truck who drove the dynamos around, but the ball players helped set the lights up. There was a pole behind home plate, a pole behind first base, one behind third base, and in the outfield maybe three poles.

Most crowds we played for were white crowds in the Northwest, a few Indians, but no blacks. You'd get a mixed crowd in Des Moines or Omaha, a few blacks in Sioux City because of the packing houses. We were treated wonderful. Any town that couldn't house us, we wouldn't play. We'd know just where we were going to stay. Might stay in Yakima three nights, or Seattle a week, and play the surrounding areas, then on into the Canadian provinces, to Montreal and back to Vancouver. We had no problems. A lot of times we slept in houses in

---

*In April 1930 the Monarchs had pioneered professional night baseball with a historic game in Enid, Oklahoma, the same night that Independence, Kansas played the first night game in organized baseball.

the small towns. I've slept in funeral homes. Usually the undertaker would have space, and they would put down cots. I've done it more than once, mostly in the southern cities.

We trained and played all through the South, but we knew the places to go. We'd go to a filling station, and the guy would lock the rest room. But after traveling so long, we knew the stations we could stop at.

Some white players might say, "I ain't going to play with that nigger." But if they did play us, they wouldn't say that. So we never had any friction whatsoever.

Everyone had a quartet, like the Ink Spots. You tried to catch a cold so you could sound like Louis Armstrong.

But the movies, like *Bingo Long,* never tell it right. They turn it into burlesque. We didn't cake walk into town before the game. We didn't have to. We were *Monarchs.* We were an institution. This was Kansas City, this was our town.

Wilkinson hand-picked the players. A Monarch never had a fight on the street. A Monarch never cut anybody. You couldn't shoot craps on our bus. This was the only way to open the door [of the major leagues].

Those were pretty good years for me. I'm learning all the time how to play. I think the most help I got was when Dizzy Dismukes came over to our ball club.* Dismukes was our traveling secretary. He taught me a lot of things I needed to know.

I batted around the sixth spot. I've hit fourth at times, but when I hit fourth, Willard Brown and Ted Strong were in Mexico. My best spot in the line up was second, because I could move the ball around, hit behind the runners; I could do a lot of things with the bat. I hit quite a bit to right field. My power was to right-center. I was more of a team player, I remember more about the other guys than about me. I thought more about managing than about playing.

Wilkinson was more or less a pushover. He'd let the ball players have money in the winter season or before pay day. So Wilkie was a great guy to them.

Tom Baird, the co-owner, was kind of the opposite. He would try to get you not to draw your money until pay day, because he realized you'd need the money come winter. The older ball players would go to town, and Baird wouldn't let them have the money. They would call Wilkinson, and he would tell Tom to give them the money. I liked Tom. The house I own now, Tom bought it; I got the money from him. No note whatsoever. My wife was a schoolteacher. She wanted a

---

*Former underhand pitcher with Rube Foster on the Philadelphia X-Giants of the 1906 era.

job, and Tom called a good friend of the superintendent in Kansas City, Kansas; Tom got the job for her.

In 1942 we beat the Homestead Grays four straight in the World Series. We had great pitching in that series, with Smith and Satchel.

The Clowns came in the league in 1943. Bebop painted himself up and would dance with King Tut. Goose Tatum be looking some place else, and the ball would come, and he'd catch it. It was more like a minstrel show. Our players didn't like it so much. We were playing strong baseball, we had Satchel for a good draw. We didn't want the Clowns in the league, but they were such a good draw, everyone else wanted them; everyone wanted our ball club and the Clowns. Syd wanted us to make it like the Globe Trotters did, they'd never lose. We didn't mind them clowning, but we wanted to win.

The war started up, and I was a U.S. Navy CB [Construction Battalion]. I did most of my time in Subic Bay in the Philippines, in a stevedore battalion. We helped build up that place. Didn't play ball; I didn't have time. I worked in the Service.

[While O'Neil was in the Pacific, a Monarch rookie, Jackie Robinson, was signed by the Brooklyn Dodgers.]

We all thought, "Great! Great! The door is open."

In 1946, the year I came out of the Service, I hit .350, and we won again. Newark* beat us out in the World Series. I hit a home run in the sixth game, hit the ball straight over that center-field fence in that Newark ball park. I thought I had hit another. The right-field stands came around like a bowl, and you'd hit the ball in that stands for a home run. I missed the stands but hit it far enough over Leon Day's head; I was sure it was gone. Leon Day ran that ball down and caught it over his shoulder. He could play center-field! [Newark won the game 9–7.]

We would have won that series, but the guys from Puerto Rico came and gave Ted Strong a lot of money to go to Puerto Rico, and he left before the series was over, so we played the last three games without him. That weakened our ball club. And we didn't have Satchel in the last game either. They were trying to dicker with Satchel to go barnstorming with Bob Feller instead. Gave him a $2,000–$3,000 bonus to go. That's the only reason they beat us.

We used to play in the Dallas, Texas league ball park quite a bit. Hank Thompson‡ was batboy for the Dallas club and would take batting practice, you know how kids do, and we signed him.

I tell you the kind of guy Hank Thompson was: I'd come by Sunday morning, say, "Come on, let's go to Sunday school."

---

*Newark starred future big leaguers Larry Doby and Monte Irvin.
‡Thompson played with the New York Giants 1949–55.

"OK, let's go."

But if someone else said, "Let's go visit the dives," he'd go there.

We were going to spring training and stopped in Dallas. Some man was abusing Hank's sister, and Hank shot the man; he killed the man. They took Hank to jail, and we went on to San Antonio. The police called us and said the guy that Hank killed had been a murderer himself, a trouble maker. So they sent Hank on to us two or three days later.

After that, you could see a change in Hank. He started drinking a lot more, and I'm sure the killing worried him. I think all the things Hank did later was because of that.

In 1954 Alvin Dark of the New York Giants told me: "You take care of Hank Thompson, and we'll win the Series [against the Cleveland Indians]." I stayed at Hank's home. We'd have a cocktail after the game, went to bed early. And he had a great Series.*

The winter of '47 Wilkinson sold out to Tom, and that's the year I took over as manager. I managed them until 1955.

I'd send our rookies to a tailor named Meyers on 18th Street, and he'd fit them for a suit on credit. Pay day, I'd ask each of them, "How is Mr. Meyers? Have you taken care of Mr. Meyers?"

I saw Willie Mays when he first played in '48, before he finished high school. Man on second, the batter hit a line drive to right-center field. The runner tagged up. Willie Mays a right-hander, toughest play in baseball. He did something, the first time I had ever seen it. He caught the ball, pivoted around, and threw the guy out at home plate. I said, "This guy can throw!" Next time someone hit one to center field, I said, "Don't run; the guy's got a shotgun!"

Satchel couldn't hit, but he had a lot of fun. When I was managing, I left him in a ball game to hit, over in East Chicago. Satchel said, "Nancy, I can hit this guy," and he hit the ball over the center-fielder's head. Anyone else would have made a home run, but he laughed all the way to second base, said, "You can take me out now." He talked about that till the day he died.

How did I manage Satchel? I don't think anybody ever managed Satchel. He was a very agreeable fellow, a fun-loving man. You just had to let him have the reins. The little things you really wanted him to do, you could kid him into doing. But just putting down a demand—that would never be met.

"We want you to be on time." You say that, he's never on time. But you say, "I bet you we'll be in Cleveland before you get there; I'll bet you a dollar."

I signed Ernie Banks two times, once in Dallas to a Monarchs'

---

*Thompson batted .364, as the Giants swept Cleveland four straight.

contract, once in Wrigley Field to a Cubs' contract. I didn't find Ernie; who found Ernie Banks was Cool Papa Bell. He was running our second team. Cool saw Ernie play and called and said, "I saw a kid, and I thought he could help our ball club." That winter Tom Baird sent me down to Dallas to sign him to a contract. He played with us in 1950, then he went in the Service, 1951–52. He was a shy kid, though, he was very shy—until he got on the field: those soft hands he had, and that quick bat.

In 1953 the White Sox and Cubs were after Ernie. I thought the White Sox were going to get Ernie, because John Donaldson [old-time Monarch pitcher and later a White Sox scout] was following us for about a month. At the East-West, or All-Star, game in '53, Ernie had a good day with the bat. Baird called me, said, "Take Banks to the Cubs' ball park Monday. I'm going to sell him." Wendell Smith, writer for the Chicago *Defender*—he'd been with Jackie on the Dodgers, re-member?—picked us up and took us to Wrigley Field. Wid Mathews, the general manager, said, "Buck, your baseball is about over, because the major leagues going to take all these stars. Whenever you get ready, I want you to work for the Cubs."

In '55 the Philadelphia A's came in to Kansas City, and we knew that was the death knell for us. They just killed us as far as the draw was concerned. Baird sold the team to a numbers man out of Grand Rapids, Michigan. That winter, 1956, Wid Mathews signed me to a contract with the Cubs scouting.

Lou Brock wasn't hard to sign. I was covering all black colleges, and Lou Brock was attending Southern College at Baton Rouge. LSU was the white state university, and Southern was the black state univer-sity—this is the way it was at that time. A scout might see a couple innings at Southern, then go to LSU; they just didn't look at these black kids enough. I saw Brock his freshman year. He couldn't play that good, but he was quick, fast, had a pretty good arm. I liked Lou Brock. He made a lot of mistakes in the outfield, but he was so fast he could make up for them. There's no substitute for speed, really.

He had an *outstanding* sophomore year. I think he was one of the best hitters as far as the record was concerned, in college baseball that year. That was the first year any black team went to the National Intercollegiate Athletic tournament. Southern won, which was a sur-prise to everyone. The scouts saw him and liked him.

The following year a lot of scouts came to Southern to see Lou Brock. But Lou had a bad junior year, so a lot of people got off of Lou Brock, because they hadn't seen him much. This is why I didn't have that much competition. I had the run of the black belt.

Lou had promised me he wanted to sign that year. He came to Chicago to work out with the White Sox, but he said, "Well, Buck, I won't sign; I'm going to give you the last shot," which was the position I wanted. Whatever the White Sox offered him, I could give him a little bit more, so I had the hole card. The next day he came out to the Cub ball park, and I signed him in the office that day.

He named his son Emory O'Neil Brock—the assistant coach at Southern was Emory Hines. I've got a beautiful picture of both his boys.

I've signed Ernie Banks and Lou Brock. But I like to think I haven't signed the best prospect yet. I do believe the athlete now is greater than I ever was: stronger, quicker. Back then, in basketball, George Mikan, or Tarzan Cooper of the [New York] Rens were big guys who could move. Now they come up with these other big guys who can outmove *them*. It used to be little guys would run all over them. But not any more. Not any more. And the equipment is so much better. Mmmm. The guys in baseball today catch with one hand. We caught with two; the gloves were so small, you needed two hands to catch the ball. Something else they do that we didn't do as much: dive for the ball. I know a lot of balls that we passed up, these kids knock down. It's been quite a revolution. Baseball as I knew it will never be back again.

I'm fortunate I lived long enough to see financial justice in baseball. After the Black Sox scandal, here came Babe Ruth. After Babe Ruth, baseball slacked off a little. Then came lights; I saw that change. Then when things were kind of slowing off, there comes Jackie Robinson. He made a difference in the draw. Do you think that Branch Rickey took Jackie Robinson in the major league because he thought, "Well, it's time to put a black guy in baseball"? No. He thought Jackie was going to be a good ball player and what Jackie would do to that gate. And he did just what Rickey thought; he was an outstanding draw. It was a bonanza. I often say I believe in the '50s and '60s baseball was at its best, because we had the best white athletes in the world and the best black athletes in the world playing baseball.

The Jackies and the Ernies changed things around; they changed the pattern for the black man. I think sports, and baseball, did more for integration than anything did. Public accommodations were changed back with Jackie; Jackie was the cause of the change. One day he decided he wasn't going [to a black hotel] any more, so they had to set him down at the Chase.

But in other phases of life, one man thinks he's superior. He just might be, because he's had the advantage, but when you get on that field, it's just you—you got to do it yourself. All men are equal in sports.

I coached for the Cubs in '62. That made me the first black coach in the major leagues. I got a letter from the commissioner to be in the

All-Star Game as a coach. I told him I'd rather wear my Monarch uniform. He said, "That's a good idea." I coached in my old uniform.

Now I'm on the veterans committee of the Hall of Fame. Quite a few Negro league veterans left I think should be in there. Hilton Smith would have to be one. Smokey Joe Williams. Bullet Joe [Rogan] would have to go. Willie Foster. Willie Wells should be in there. Ozzie Smith with St. Louis could have played with Wells—but he couldn't have hit with Wells.

But don't feel sorry for any of us. Because no matter how high George Brett goes, these old fellows have already been there; they've experienced all these things. We know that we could play as well as anyone that ever played. There is nothing greater for a human being than to get his body to react to all the things one does on a ball field. It's as good as sex; it's as good as music. It fills you up.

Born too soon? Forget it. You forget that. Waste no tears for me. I had a beautiful life. I played with the greatest ball players in the world, and I played against the best ball players in the world. I saw this country and a lot of other countries, and I met some wonderful people. They say, "Buck, you were born at the wrong time." I say, "No, I was born *right* on time."

That's what surprises people about me. I'm not bitter. No. I don't have the bitter story. If I was going to be bitter about anything, it wouldn't be about baseball but about education. I have no idea what I could have been. Suppose I could have gone to Sarasota High School, the University of Florida. All these things I'll never know, about what kind of man I could have been.

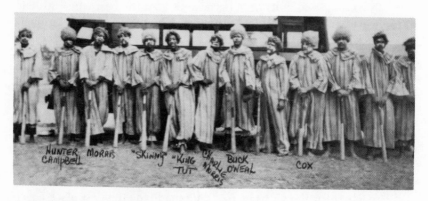

The Ethiopian Clowns baseball club.

John "Buck" O'Neil

b: 11/13/11, Carrabelle, FL   BR TR   6'2", 190

Year	Team	PSN	G	AB	H	2B	3B	HR	BA	SB
1936	Memphis	2B	2	8	1	0	0	0	.125	0
1937	Memphis		3	11	1	0	0	0	.091	0
1938	Kansas City	1B	—	79	20	5	2	0	.253	7
1939	Kansas City	1B	—	101	26	7	2	2*	.257	3
1940	Kansas City	1B	—	88	32	5	3	0	.364	2
1941	Kansas City	1B	—	85	22	4	1	0	.259	3
1942	Kansas City	1B	—	176	44	6	1	1	.250	0
1943	Kansas City	1B	—	92	20	0	1	2	.213	1
1944	U.S. Navy									
1945	U.S. Navy									
1946	Kansas City	1B	58	197	69	—	—	1	.350*	12
	Cuba	1B	—	116	25	3	1	0	.216	2
1947		No record								
1948	Kansas City	1B	27	162	41	6	1	1	.253	
1953	Kansas City		15	21	10	0	0	0	.476	
1954	Kansas City		27	68	23	2	0	1	.338	

Post-Season

Year	Team	PSN	G	AB	H	2B	3B	HR	BA	SB
1942	World Series	1B	1	3	1	0	0	0	.333	0
1946	World Series	1B	3	13	6	0	0	2	.461	0

* Led league.

John "Buck" O'Neil vs. White Big Leaguers

Year	AB	H	2B	3B	HR	Pitcher
1941	4	1	0	0	0	Feller (25-13), Heintzelman (11-11)
1942	4	1	0	0	0	Grodzicki*, Piechota*, (Dean)
1946	4	1	0	0	0	Feller (26-15), Bob Lemon (4-5)
	2	2	0	1	0	Feller, John Sain (20-14), Lemon
	3	1	0	0	0	Chandler (20-8), Feller
	4	2	0	0	0	Feller, Leonard (10-10)
Totals	25	9	0	1	0	Average: .360

Recap

	PSN	G	AB	H	2B	3B	HR	BA	SB
Negro league	1B	—	1006	280	33	11	7	.278	30
Cuban league	1B	—	116	25	3	1	0	.216	2
vs. white big leaguers	1B	3	21	8	0	1	0	.381	0
Post-Season	1B	—	16	7	0	0	2	.438	0
East-West games	1B	3	7	0	0	0	0	.000	0
Totals			1168	320	36	13	9	.274	32

* In service.

Ese Hombre
WILLARD "HOME RUN" BROWN

Latins called him Ese Hombre—*That Man.*

"Brown was the big bomb," said shortstop Tom "Pee Wee" Butts. "Every time he'd come to bat, they'd say, Ese Hombre! *They just knew he was going to hit a home run."*

In Puerto Rico in 1948 Brown smashed 27 homers in 115 at bats to erase Josh Gibson's previous record, 13. The mark still stands. Number two is Reggie Jackson with 20.

Throughout their careers, Brown of the Monarchs and Gibson of the Grays waged some titanic contests for the title of king of the black sluggers in America. Could Brown hit them farther than the fabled Josh?

"No," says Buck Leonard, Gibson's teammate on the Grays.

"Yes," says Cool Papa Bell, another Gibson teammate. "He could hit as far as anybody, but not as constantly as Josh Gibson."

"My first choice for the Hall of Fame is Willard Brown," says pitcher Wilmer Fields of the Grays. "There were no fences too far for him to reach. I know, because he hit a couple off me. You generally remember those who hurt you. Willard Brown was the best right-handed hitter then. He was **strong.** *God knows how good he could have been. In Puerto Rico he wasn't even thinking about it, and he put a* hole *in the ball. Didn't make any difference what field it was either. And he hit everybody." But Willard was lackadaisical. "He would read* Reader's Digest *in center field. Then he'd hit the ball 10 miles."*

Brown's teammate, Hilton Smith, considered Brown a better player than Jackie Robinson. "He was," Smith insisted. "He was a better hitter, he was faster. People thought Jackie was fast: Jackie was smart and studied how to run bases, but he wasn't that fast. And he had a poor arm. Brown had a real good arm.

"And his power! Oh man, I've seen guys try to waste a pitch, Brown [a right-hander] would hit it over the right-field fence. I've seen that guy hit one of the longest home runs I've ever seen right out here at this ball park in Kansas City off Satchel Paige in 1937. Brown hit the ball clear over everything, almost down to 18th Street. Man, that ball just sailed *over the fence. It was still going when it went over the fence. That particular time this ball park [Muehlebach] was much larger than it is now. Oh yeah, it was around 440 to center field."*

"The best ball player we ever had, could run like a deer," says Othello "Chico" Renfroe, Monarch catcher and now an Atlanta sportscaster. "Willard Brown could outrun anybody in our league. But he'd only play hard on Sunday, he'd loaf the rest of the time. He was a very lazy, stubborn ball player. When the crowd was big, you got a performance from him. But he just didn't have that drive."

"Brown was just a mass of muscle," recalled Richard Wilkinson, son of the Monarch owner. "A big strong boy, not very tall, and just wonderful timing. He would have been a great one had he had the desire to play."

Buck O'Neil, Brown's teammate and later manager, thinks Willard was so talented that he didn't look as if he was hustling:

Willard Brown stole bases standing up; he didn't slide because he didn't have to. He'd get there just in time to beat the throw; that's enough, that was all he needed.

Willard Brown could do all the things in baseball—hit, run, field, throw, and hit for power. He could also bunt, and sometimes would pass up a perfect home run pitch in order to bunt and give the fans a show beating it out. But Willard was like Hank Aaron, you always thought he could do a little more. Both Brown and Aaron were so talented, they didn't look as if they were hustling. Everything looked so easy for them. You were always saying, "Come on, Willard, come on, Willard." This was the difference between Willard Brown and Jackie Robinson. Jackie Robinson looked like he was doing; Willie Mays looked like he was doing. Hank never did. And this was Willard. Everything came so easy for him.

Look at Pete Rose. Pete Rose hasn't stolen that many bases. He has to hustle, he doesn't have as much natural ability as Brown.

Brown ran when he had to run. And he could relax. That's why he was a good hitter. Brown was the last guy to trot off the field: "What's the use of me wasting this energy flying off the field? I'll use it when I need it." A tremendous player for 20 years with Kansas City and in the Texas league. That's why—he saved his strength.

Brown "had an attitude," added pitcher Bob Harvey. If the pitcher made a mistake, and an opponent hit the ball over Brown's head, he wouldn't go get it, he'd let the hitter have a home run.

As a rookie in 1935, the 20-year-old Brown played three games against World Series veterans Dizzy Dean (28–12), Tommy Bridges (21–10), and Schoolboy Rowe (19–13). He drilled 4 hits in 12 at bats.

In the 1937 playoffs against Chicago's ace, Sug Cornelius, the two teams battled down to the ninth inning of the seventh game, tied 2–2. Brown's long fly scored the runner from third, and the Monarchs were champs.

In Puerto Rico in 1941 Willard hit .456, only to lose the batting crown to Gibson, with .480.

But in the '42 World Series against the Grays, Brown hit .412 to Gibson's .154. In the first game he blasted a triple to deep center in Washington, as the Monarchs won. In the third game, he lined a home run into right field in Yankee Stadium, as the Monarchs won again. In the fourth game, he cracked two long fouls out of Shibe Park, Philadelphia, then doubled to right to tie the score, as the Monarchs went on to win their fourth straight.

In the army in France, Brown slugged two home runs against Ewell Blackwell before 50,000 GIs in Marseilles to win for pitcher Leon Day. The Cardinals' Harry "The Hat" Walker recalled him as "a flim flam type—kind of flipped the ball underhand. I pitched against him on the Riviera. He like to killed me with a line shot, hit my glove, thank God, not my face."

In 1947 Brown was hitting .425, when he followed Larry Doby into the American League, signing with the St. Louis Browns along with his Monarch teammate, Hank Thompson. He hit the first black home run in league history, an inside-the-park blow against Hal Newhouser (17–17). Alas, it was his only one, and he was dropped after hitting only .179 in 21 games. His Kansas City teammates believe it was a mistake to bring him up in such a crucial, tension-filled role. It took a special man, a Jackie Robinson, to succeed, and Brown had neither Jackie's education nor his competitiveness.

Says O'Neil:

> Brown could have played major league ball. And it was proven that Hank Thompson could.
> The only reason he flunked in the American League, he was there for one reason: They thought that Willard and Hank Thompson would draw the people like Jackie did. They were looking for a franchise-saver, and when the people didn't flock to them, the Browns dropped them. The Browns were going to give Wilkinson [Monarch owner] so much money if they stayed, so when they didn't draw, the Browns would rather send them back than pay the money. Had they gone with any other franchise, they would have played.

Three of Brown's St Louis teammates—pitcher Les Moss, outfielder Al Zarilla, and third baseman Bob Dillinger—remembered him well. But a fourth Brownie, pitcher Bob Muncrief, curtly refused to talk about him at all, when I called him in his home in Texas.

"Brown was a great guy," said Moss from Florida. "We all had a heck of a time with him. I wish he'd come out and see me." The younger Thompson (22 years old) obviously had more potential than the 35-year-old Brown. "Neither one of them hit a heck of a lot"—Thompson hit .256—"but you could see Thompson had all the tools, which he proved when he went to the Giants for eight years." And, Moss continued, "you could see Brown had power. If he'd come to the big leagues when he was in his early 20s, he'd have been quite a ball player."

That winter Brown set the Puerto Rican record with 27 homers.

It was Brown's misfortune that he was brought to the white majors at the worst possible time. Two years later, when blacks were more widely accepted, he might have been a star. Indeed, Thompson was given a second chance with the New York Giants in 1949 and did become a star, topping 20 homers three times and hitting .302 in 1953 and .364 in the 1954 World Series.

In 1954 Willard Brown, nearing 40, was starring in the white Texas league, teaming with Bob Boyd, formerly of the Memphis Red Sox, to bring Houston a pennant for manager Harry Walker. Brown and Boyd were "Mr. Biff and Mr. Bang." In fact, Houston had the "Four Bs" that year:

	Age	BA	HR
Bob Boyd	27	.321	7
Ken Boyer	23	.319	21
Don Blasingame	22	.315	5
Willard Brown	39	.314	35

The next year Boyer and Blasingame went up to the parent Cardinals; Boyd and Brown stayed in Houston, each hitting .300. Boyd went up to the Orioles in '56 and gave them three .300 years. But there was no promotion for Brown. How he would have done if he had followed them is conjecture. Willard Brown never got a second chance.

Two decades later I found Brown in Houston in a small workshop, where he was sanding furniture to be refinished. His arms looked like Reggie Jackson's—two mahogany tree trunks. I saw Willard again at an old-timers' reunion in Ashland, Kentucky, where the other veterans nudged each other, smiled, and nodded toward him as he sauntered through the room. The same old nonchalant grace, they said.

In 1989 Brown was permanently hospitalized with incurable Alzheimer's disease.

The longest home run I've hit? Oh, I wish I knew; I hit so many of them. You ever been out to the old stadium here in Houston? There's a center-field fence there and a bakery behind that, and I hit one over the bakery. I hit it across the boulevard there. I don't know how far it was, I've hit some long shots, you know. I don't know how many I hit in all.

I used to watch the ball. I knew it was gone, I just wanted to see how far it would go. Those pitchers used to get kind of angry with me, say, "What you watching?"

I'd say, "I just want to see how far it's going, that's all."

Somebody wanted to know the most home runs Josh Gibson ever hit in a ball game. They say he hit four. I hit four two or three times. And they were all in major league parks. But I didn't pay them any attention. Our biggest series used to be playing against Josh and the Homestead Grays. Our shortstop Jesse Williams used to bet Josh a steak dinner that I'd hit more home runs than Josh. Josh never did win any steak dinners.

I hit two home runs off Bobby Feller in Yankee Stadium. I hit Feller pretty good. He could throw hard, but I could hit anybody could throw hard. Yeah. Another time I hit two off Feller in Wichita, one over center field, one over right field. They weren't looking for me to hit the ball to right field no way, but I could hit the ball pretty good there. I hit where they pitched. I'd reach out there. They said, "How come you hit that?"

I said, "Well, in our league you have to hit a whole lot like that." Some of the places you'd go, those umpires would call strikes up around your cap. I learned how to hit them to keep from being called out. I always used a 40-ounce bat, and anything I could get that big bat on, I could hit pretty good.

We'd barnstorm with Bob Feller's All Stars for two weeks in October, and they might win one game out of the two weeks. The fans, everybody, asked us to let them win one. They'd say, "Don't make them look too bad."

I'd say, "Well, they're major leaguers and they're supposed to run away from us, but it's the other way around."

I got started playing around our school league in Shreveport. I was born there in 1915.* My first contract was in 1934 with Monroe, Louisiana. I was shortstop and pitcher then. Hilton Smith was pitching there. The first baseman was Ted Mayweather, a good hitter. He hit like Buck Leonard; they both had that swing. He looked good striking out. He hit some balls, I don't know how far they went. I said he "hit 'em into the dark." But he broke his leg sliding into home, and he never was the same.

In 1935 the Monarchs got me. J. L. Wilkinson owned the Monarchs, and there was a great guy—a wonderful man, a wonderful man. He always got the best ball players. He got five of us from the Monroe Monarchs.

When I went to Kansas City, I couldn't go in the bar. All those old-timers would say, "If you want something, I'll bring you something out."

Kansas City wasn't an easy park to hit in. Center field, before they put a fence in, was around 440. It was 350 down the line. Then that hill in right field, I hit a couple out there. I hit a whole lot in left field over that parking lot, down where the trains go across the bridge there.

Bullet Joe Rogan was with them when I came up. Didn't have any wind-up, but he could throw hard, and he had a good curve ball. And he was a good hitter. He's the one started me hitting with a heavy bat.

---

*Brown told author Jack Etkin of *Innings Ago* that he was actually born in 1913 but changed it, because "it was the only way I could get to the major leagues. Four or five of us put our age down so we could make some more money. We were good enough, but age was against us." The *Macmillan Encyclopedia* gives his birth as 1921, obviously erroneously, since he began playing with the Monarchs in 1934.

I wasn't too much of a curve ball hitter, so he worked with me every day, every day. All the pitchers would get out there and pitch batting practice and throw me curve balls, nothing but curve balls. Because they knew I could hit the fast ball. Then I got so I could learn the rotation of the ball, and I got so I could hit curves just about as good as I could the fast balls.

I used to watch all the pitchers. If I was in the dugout, I'd just watch how he pitched the other guys, how he's got to pitch me. I'd take some pitches because I wanted to see the pitcher's delivery. A whole lot of times I used to take two strikes. But I didn't strike out too much; I could always get some of the ball anyway. I look at some of the hitters today, I say, "They don't follow the ball enough." A whole lot of balls they could hit they let go on by because they're not strikes. Most home runs you hit aren't strikes. You go and get the ball.

Willard Brown.

And I could hit to right field. They never could fool around with me like I see them now, all the infield on one side. Shoot, that would be a base hit for me every time I come up. They tried a shift a couple of times, but it didn't ever work. I'd laugh at them.

One pitcher in Birmingham threw the ball and it bounced, and I hit it over the left-field fence. He just took his glove and put it in his pocket and he quit pitching. He said, "It's time for me to quit."

I used to laugh at the infielders, because I hit some balls between their legs, right through 'em. I'd say, "Be careful, you'll get crippled."

I played against Dizzy Dean and Paul. They had Lon Warneke and Lou Fette pitching, Johnny Mize, Vernon Stephens, and Whitey Kurowski infield. Catching was Walker Cooper, and his brother Mort pitching. We didn't have nothing but our regular team—Satchel Paige, Hilton Smith, Connie Johnson, pitching; Frank Duncan and Joe Green, catching; Newt Allen, second. I was playing shortstop.

I started out at shortstop. I used to be pretty good at shortstop. They moved me to center field, and I was so good I played center field there for about 10 years. I had a pretty good arm until I got hit. Leroy Taylor came to bat and let the bat loose and hit me on my shoulder; it was sore for half a year. I never did get it right. I could throw but not as good as when I first came up. But I didn't let them take a whole lot of extra bases. I knew the fast guys running, I would come in and get the ball and get it back fast. If they started to go to third, I could throw them out. But it wasn't like when I first came up. I had a good arm when I first came up. Yeah.

We used to barnstorm a whole lot with the House of David. Used to go out to Canada about a month, come back to our league. A whole lot of times we used to win the league the first half, then we'd barnstorm. We didn't worry about the second half. We wanted somebody else to win the second half, we didn't care who, because we were going to beat 'em anyway in the playoff.

I went with the St. Louis Browns in 1947. The DeWitts had just gotten the team, but they didn't have much money no way. They took a look at me on a trial basis. They weren't drawing but 2–3–4,000 people. Then the Negroes were striking, because they didn't let the coloreds in the stands; they had to sit out there in the hot sun all the time. How you going to get people to come in the ball park out in the sun? We already got suntans. After Negroes got in the league, they changed that around.

You know, that's a team I never could understand. They didn't want to win. If I would get a hit, tie up the game, they didn't like it at all. I'd say, "Why?"

They said, "You didn't have to hit it. The other team has a chance to win the pennant, and we don't."

I said, "I ain't got nothing to lose out there. I'm trying to make the team."

There wasn't but one pitcher who would go out there to win— Ellis Kinder. He could have been on anybody's team and done way better than he did there. Every time he went out, he'd pitch a good game, I don't care against who. He'd tell 'em, "If you don't feel like playing, I don't want you to play, because I'm going to give it everything I've got, and I want you all to do the same thing."

I played in Puerto Rico about 14 winters. Won the batting championship about four or five times. They say I'm the Babe Ruth of Puerto Rico. I had quite a few records down there. Thirteen home runs was the league record with Josh, all those big guys. Satchel said, "You can hit more home runs than that."

When they told me the record, I said, "I could have hit that a long time ago." In 1947 I hit 28 home runs in 60 ball games. One of them

Willard Brown (left) with Jesse Williams.

was rained out, so that made 27. That hasn't been broken. And I don't think any of them are going to break it either. Three hundred fifty feet to left field, 420 to center, so you know it wasn't no small ball park.

They gave a Hudson car if you hit 25. I said, "You can give me the money," because they quit making the cars after that. I didn't want the car.

The next year Bob Thurman and I tied up at 18. I could have hit more than that, but we didn't need 'em.

I went to the Texas league in '53–'54–'55–56. I was the first black regular. Dave Hoskins, a pitcher, came in the year before I did. They said, "We don't have any Negroes in the league to play every day."

"Well, take me then. If I don't make it, you don't owe me anything." I did pretty good, hit over .300, 30-some home runs. And every year we won the championship, either Dallas or Houston.

We won the championship at Dallas, went to Nashville, won the Dixie Series. I guess I hit around five or six home runs in that series. You know, they've got the hill in Nashville in right field. You've got to know how to run up that hill. If you don't, you're going to slip down most of the time. The guy would hit the ball against the fence, should have had a double. I'd hold him to a single. They wanted to know how I did it: "How you playin' that wall so good?"

Houston got me the next year, and we played Atlanta in the series. Atlanta beat us; they shouldn't have though. After my first three games, they started walking me. They wouldn't throw strikes. The catcher would tell me, "You're not going to hit anything tonight."

I said, "Why?"

He said, "Watch and see. Just stay loose up there, because all the balls are going to be coming at you." I didn't get a chance to swing during the rest of the series.

Our manager, Dixie Walker,* was a pretty smooth guy. He was one of the Dodgers that didn't want Jackie Robinson, but he turned out to be all right. He treated me real fine, yes he did.

I hit about 35 home runs one year. Could have hit more than that, but I wasn't trying. I wanted to win instead of hitting home runs. When you need it, that's when I try, when you're behind.

I had some pretty good years, and I've seen the times when really I didn't know how good I could play, how good I could hit. Because I'd laugh at 'em if they get me out. It was all right with me, because a lot of times we'd be out in front anyway, and the quicker I could get the game over, the better. If I hit the ball, a whole lot of times it would be extra bases. I'd just stretch it anyway, go on and get throwed out, or I'd get in a chase, fool around there.

I would say that when we played in the Caribbean Series in 1950,

---

*Harry's brother.

that was my greatest thrill. We played in Havana, and all the teams would come in and play a round-robin elimination. If you lose two, you're out. We didn't lose a game.

I think I had 18 runs batted in, and that set a record. I hit about seven or eight home runs, and they haven't caught that record either. My last home run came off a boy who pitched for Washington, a knuckle baller, a Cuban, Conrado Marrero. I came in to pinch-hit with two men on base. He threw a couple of knuckle balls up there, and I said, "Shit, that's all he's throwing, I know I'm gonna get up there and hit another home run." There's a barn where they kept grain or seed, had a big old sign on top of it. The third pitch I hit right on top of that barn. Yeah, a knuckle ball, and he just looked at me all the way around the bases.

Willard Brown

b: 6/26/13, Shreveport, LA   BR TR   5'11", 200

Year	Team	PSN	G	AB	H	2B	3B	HR	BA	SB
1935	Kansas City	—	2	7	2	0	0	1	.286	1
1936	Kansas City	SS	7	30	11	0	0	1*	.367	2
1937	Kansas City	SS-OF	—	104	43	6	2	7*	.413	4
	Cuba	—	—	55	8	1	0	0	.145	0
1938	Kansas City	SS-CF	23	89	33	2	3	5*	.371	10
1939	Kansas City	LF	—	119	40	9	1	2*	.336*	4
1940	Mexico	OF	70	294	104	—	—	8	.351	13
1941	Kansas City	CF	—	90	30	6	4	2	.333	2
1942	Kansas City	CF	—	179	62	5	2	7*	.346	0
1943	Kansas City	CF	—	95	31	4	0	6*	.333	0
1944	U.S. Army									
1945	U.S. Army									
1946	Kansas City	CF	58	230	80	—	—	5	.348	13
	Puerto Rico	OF	—	254	99	—	—	—	.390*	—
1947	Kansas City	CF	50	211	71	—	—	—	.336	—
	St. Louis Browns	OF	21	67	12	3	0	1	.179	2
	Puerto Rico[b]	OF	—	115	52	—	—	27[a]	.452*	—
1948	Kansas City	OF	66	262	98	20	5	18*	.374	13
	Puerto Rico	—	—	—	—	—	—	18*	—	—
1949	Puerto Rico	OF	—	331	117	—	—	16*	.354*	—
1950	Ottawa	OF	30	128	45	7	1	1	.352	2
	Puerto Rico	No record								
1951	Dominican Republic	No record								
	Puerto Rico	No record								
1952	Dominican Republic	No record								
	Puerto Rico	No record								
1953	Dallas	OF	138	522	162	36	2	23	.310	3
1954	Dallas-Houston	OF	144	583	183	36	4	35	.314	2
1955	Houston	OF	149	544	164	34	4	19	.301	3
1956	Austin-San Antonio-Tulsa	OF	104	351	105	17	0	14	.299	2
	Topeka	OF	23	85	25	2	0	3	.294	—

Post-Season

Year	Team		G	AB	H	2B	3B	HR	BA	SB
1942	World Series		4	17	7	1	1	1	.412	1
1946	World Series		4	18	4	0	0	1	.222	0
1953	Caribbean Series		—	—	—	—	—	4	—	—

* Led league.
[a] Record.
[b] MVP.

Willard Brown vs. White Big Leaguers

Year	AB	H	2B	3B	HR	Pitcher
1935	5	2	1	0	0	D. Dean (28-12), P. Dean (19-12), Ryba (1-1)
	4	2	1	0	0	D. Dean, P. Dean, Ryba
	4	1	1	0	0	D. Dean, P. Dean, Ryba (M. Cooper)*
	4	3	0	0	0	Rowe (19-13), Bridges (21-10), Bowman (9-20), (Cooper)*
	4	0	0	0	0	Bowman, (Cooper)*
	4	2	0	0	0	Bridges, Rowe
1937	4	2	0	0	1	Warneke (18-11), Fette (20-10), Weaver (8-5), M. Brown (8-2)
	4	2	1	0	1	Fette, Weaver, Brown
	5	1	1	0	0	Brown, Feller, Fette, Weaver
1941	4	0	0	0	0	Feller (25-13), Heintzelman (11-11)
1942	3	2	0	0	0	Grodzicki, Piechota (Dean)
Totals	45	17	5	0	2	Average: .373

Recap

	PSN	G	AB	H	2B	3B	HR	BA	SB
Negro league	SS-CF	—	947	334	32	12	35	.342	36
Major league	OF	21	67	12	3	0	1	.179	2
vs. white big leaguers	OF	8	33	12	4	0	2	.364	0
Minor leagues	OF	—	2213	684	132	11	95	.309	12
Latin leagues	OF	—	763	276	0	0	61	.362	0
East-West games	OF	6	17	4	1	0	0	.235	1
Post-Season	OF	—	35	11	1	1	6	.335	1
Totals			4087	1338	175	24	200	.330	52

* Mort Cooper was not yet in the majors.

Black Eagle
MAX MANNING

Max Manning is one of those quiet men who doesn't talk about himself much. But "he was a terrific pitcher," says Gene Benson. "Half-sidearm, half-under-hand, he could throw hard."

"Manning was a control pitcher," Buck O'Neil says, "changed speeds well, wasn't over-powering, but he knew how to pitch."

Dodger pitcher Carl Erskine played with Manning in Cuba and recalls him as "a very studious kind of fellow."

I met Manning at a Negro league seminar conducted by Professor Larry Hogan at Union College, New Jersey and later got his story of pitching for the champion Newark Eagles of 1946.

I went to high school in Pleasantville, New Jersey outside of Atlantic City, and I had a wonderful coach named Emory Ty Helfrich, who had played third base in the old Federal league. As far as race was concerned, he wasn't a liberal. But his feelings about race were smothered by a lot of other things. He recognized talent when he saw it, and he took a special liking to me for some reason or other. I was the only black on the baseball team, and I had a third- or fourth-string suit, but he was going to have me on the team anyway.

The first time I went out on the field, the bases were loaded. In those days Pleasantville was kind of Ku Kluxie. My father was watching the ball game and told me he heard, "Why put him in? They can't think, they can't do anything. We're gonna lose this ball game." The first thing I did was pick the guy off third. That made two outs. I struck out the next guy, and we won it.

I pitched for the high school for four years, struck out 23 in one game, had some no-hit games, stuff like that.

In 1937 I got a letter from Max Bishop, who was a scout from the Detroit Tigers. I suppose in those days scouts didn't travel, they read accounts of games. He wrote me this letter, sent me a form to fill out: "Would you fill out this information, and looking forward to seeing you in the spring." I never answered it. I knew it was a mistake. I said, "Well, I'm not going to even bother with this." [Johnny Taylor of the New York Cubans had a similar experience.] Taylor was light. But there's no doubt about me! There's no way to mistake me for anything but black.

I used to go over to Atlantic City in the summer and play with the Johnson Stars. They were pretty much older guys: Pop Lloyd, Rats Henderson, Luther Farrell.

In my estimation, Pop Lloyd was one of the finest human beings I ever met. He was such a gracious kind of fellow, humble, kind, and gentle. It was always "young fellow this" and "young fellow that." He didn't drink, didn't smoke, didn't curse; he was really a role model. He was playing first base, and he could still hit the ball. He used to have a rag he'd oil the bat with. In a close game he'd say, "I guess I got to do something about this," and he'd get a hit and win the ball game.

The two people who meant the most for me in a baseball sense were Ty Helfrich and Pop Lloyd. They taught me how to pitch, how to stand on the rubber, all the little techniques.

Henderson was about done then. But you could see that the man had been a quality pitcher. He was very tricky. He could pick men off. I tend to watch people who knew how to do things, and one of the best things I saw him do was hold men on base, trap men off base—all those little trickly things.

Farrell* was one of the biggest, strongest pitchers I had ever seen. He was on the downside of his career, but you could see he had been a remarkable pitcher too. He wasn't very talkative, a quiet kind of guy, sort of like Pop Lloyd. Yes, he did drink. That's a sad story about a lot of good black ball players. I think there was a kind of despair. It was a hard life. Some ball players could overcome it, but it varied with the individual.

The Stars played at the New York Avenue Playground. New York Avenue and Adriatic. Had a tin fence around it. Short left-field fence. We used to have 400–500 people every Sunday. Big Boy Jones was the announcer. He was a very picturesque kind of guy, would bring a big megaphone and announce the batteries. A lot of people came out just to watch him.

Funny thing—from there I almost went to the Philadelphia Stars. In 1937 I pitched against the Camden Giants, a good semipro team, had a lot of old black players on it. Zeeny Nelson, the manager, said, "You know, I think you could make it in the Negro leagues. I'll see if I can get you a chance to play with the Philadelphia Stars. Would you like that? I'm going to talk to Ed Bolden [the owner], get you a tryout."

I went to their park. Here I was, a high school kid, a little country boy, had my shoes tied together so I wouldn't lose them. The Stars were playing the Baltimore Elite Giants, and I sat down at the end of the bench. The Stars were losing. Boojum Wilson was the roughest,

---

*He pitched a black World Series no-hitter in 1957.

meanest guy I ever saw, in appearance. Scared you to death. Boojum came off the field, cussing and carrying on. "Who is this young pitcher? That's why we're having so much bad luck!" I flew! I got on a bus and came home.

My father had gone to Lincoln University, and he said, "Why don't you go to college?" I said OK, and that fall I went to Lincoln.

It just so happened that Monte Irvin was there at the same time. He was a basketball player, and I played a little too. Monte was one of those fluid ball players who seem to do things effortlessly. Like Dick Lundy—that graceful style. Tremendous power, good speed, wonderful arm. He could play infield, and a good outfielder. He was on the heavy side, but all muscle. Weighed about 200 pounds. You don't look for a guy his size to have much speed, but he knew how to steal bases. Stealing home was no problem for him; he just seemed to have that knack.

Abe Manley, the owner of the Newark Eagles, came out to Lincoln University and talked to both Monte and me and arranged for us to come to the Eagles. That next spring I met the bus in Philadelphia—the "Blue Goose," they called it. We trained in Miami, and it was the longest ride I ever had in my life! Stopping and getting sandwiches and getting gas was all you could do: Cold cuts and sodas.

Dick Lundy was manager. He wasn't playing very much, but he was very graceful. The thing that impressed me about him was his fluid and smooth movements fielding ground balls.

My first game, I pitched against the Homestead Grays in Winston-Salem, North Carolina. I'll never forget it: I was scared to death! I had pitched a couple of exhibition games, but that game was really like a league game. By that time I had a certain confidence in myself as a pitcher. I felt I could do the job, and everyone said I could, which helped me out. They said, "You don't have anything to worry about, just throw hard." I struck out the first five men. That included Dave Whatley, Buck Leonard, Josh Gibson, Sam Bankhead, the whole bunch. And beat them that night.

Biz Mackey was one of the smartest catchers that I've ever pitched to. I remember one game against the New York Cubans. I think I shut them out 2–0. He came to me after the game, taking his shin guards off. "Heh, Millio, do you know how many curve balls you threw tonight?"

I said, "I don't remember."

He said, "One. I called for one curve ball. Your fast ball was so good tonight you didn't need a curve ball." The average catcher would change a lot, but he had the savvy to know that with location, the fast ball was all that was needed, really. To me the most important thing was where I was throwing it.

Ray Dandridge and I were pretty good friends. Dandridge had good hands. He'd smother the ball, say, "Come here!" grab it and throw you out. Very intelligent, knew how to play hitters. And always a good hitter. He'd adapt to the situation, whatever seemed necessary, pull it or hit to the right side to advance the runner.

Leon Day, that's my man! Good fast ball, good curve ball, good control. I felt about Leon the same way I felt about Dandridge—the same dedication, the same aggressive baseball. Leon was a complete athlete. He could bunt, he could run, he could play outfield, he could pitch. He was fast, he could field his position. I've seen him make plays—a bouncing ball hit to his right, go over and catch it. Do things the average pitcher wasn't about to do.

Very dry sense of humor. He's not a talker. But usually when he says something, it has a lot to it, it's pretty funny or right on the mark. It took a long time for me to understand Leon as a person. It's just like Mule Suttles and Boojum. Your first impression is that you'll never get

Max Manning.

to know the guy, because they seem stand-offish. But that's really not the case. Leon turned out to be one of my best friends.

The guy really deserves to be in Cooperstown. It bothers me, because these guys get older and die out. It just seems a shame that at least some of these ball players don't even get a chance to be voted on. If they don't elect them now, there will be so many of them elected posthumously.

When I first saw Mule Suttles, I was very young, and we played over in Bushwick. They used to say, "Kick, Mule, Kick, Mule!" Mule Suttles always had that little finger off the butt of the bat. He loved to hit the curve ball.

He hit a ball in Bushwich so far, I'd never seen anything like it! They had a flagpole in deep center field and a mound that went up to the pole. This Sunday they had just put in a brand new white ball, and Mule kicked! I just watched that thing go, I'd never seen anything like it in my life! Here I was, just out of the country. The sun was shining on it, and I can still see it right now in my mind's eye leaving that ball park in deepest center field.

I just stood in awe of that guy.

In the bus he'd have a seat all to himself. He was big, heavy. One seat was partly over the wheel, and that was his seat all the time. No one else could get near it.

Willie Wells was a remarkable shortstop—"Chico Chico." Weak arm, but he was very accurate and good at getting rid of the ball quick. Everyone thought they could beat it out: "He just got me by a step that time. If I run a little harder, I'll beat him." But they never did. It would be the same way the next time. It was always just by a step.

He was flamboyant in terms of dress. Suits and handkerchiefs and stuff. I never saw Willie Wells look tacky.

You talk about a dresser, Terris McDuffie was the same type of guy. And a good performer. McDuffie was a good pitcher, very egotistical. Terris McDuffie believed he could do anything in the world and would tell you that too. He was a loud sort of Satchel Paige—more talkative and louder and flamboyant. Satchel was confident, and he knew what he could do, and he would make statements once in a while. Terry would tell you *all* the time! A loudmouth, but I liked him.

Abe Manley was a real character. He loved to play cards, could spend a whole weekend without eating or sleeping, just playing cards.

He'd sit in the front seat of the bus. His feet would swell. It's funny how some things you remember a whole lot. I'd get on the bus and see how big his ankles were. I figured it was from riding and that it would happen to anyone. It was one thing that made me dislike the buses so much.

Guys would take pillows, put them behind their heads and go to sleep.

We started out getting 50 cents a day eating money, then it went to $1.00. Abe would sit up in the front with these dollar bills, and as you pass out, he'd give you a dollar, and you were on your way, do what you can with it. At that time you could get a real decent meal for 75 cents. We'd eat on the run. You get there and the stuff is a big knot in your stomach, but you had to get out there and play. We'd stop some place for a hot sandwich, but you couldn't go in and sit down, so someone would pass a bag out the back door.

Abe had his own way about some things, but he stayed mostly in the background.

As you know, Effa [his wife] would rule the roost. The whole women's approach to things is entirely different from a man. She was interested in appearances—uniform neat, shoes shined. She was particular about that. She had some people were her favorites, she'd mother them. Monte was one, Larry Dody was one, Lenny Pearson—people like that were her favorites. She never cared for me. I guess I used to look at her strange. She and I always seemed to be at it, particularly in terms of salary. I held out. If I had a good year, I felt I deserved an increase in salary, and she didn't want to give it to me.

The old Homestead Grays had such a reputation. But I don't remember having a whole lot of trouble with Josh or Buck Leonard. It was always the little guys that hurt me. Lick Carlisle playing second

Max Manning (rear, fourth from right) with the Newark Eagles.

base, and Whatley used to hurt me. I was a fast ball pitcher, and I threw Gibson mostly fast balls and kept them away from him.

Buck Leonard, I used to throw him curve balls. I liked to study hitters, how their stroke was. Instead of breaking curve balls down low, I'd just break it through his letters from his shoulder to his belt, and I could get him out that way.

Two people who reminded me of each other were Buck Leonard and Pop Lloyd; their characters were so similar—the quiet humbleness, the spartan-like kind of living. Buck never cursed, never drank. You'd always find him with a paper in his hand. In Mexico, if I wanted to find him, I'd go to the park, and he'd be sitting on a bench reading the paper, doing his crossword puzzle. He'd be in bed by nine o'clock.

Boojum Wilson? Strong! Boojum was strong! Boojum would stand up there and grab his bat and rub his hands around the butt of the bat. They used to say they could see sawdust coming out. Tough and rough. If you were an infielder and had the ball and Boojum was running, look out! He was going to try to make it.

He and Adolph Luque* were sort of the same way. Luque was probably one of the nastiest guys, other than Boojum, I ever met. In Cuba Mike Gonzalez was manager and Luque was coach. Gonzalez used to send Adolph Luque out to take the pitcher out. One thing Luque couldn't stand: pitchers walking batters. He would turn red and come out there, snatch the ball out of your hand and spit on your shoes, all around the mound, and cuss you out in Spanish. Boojum and Adolph Luque had gotten into some problems. Luque used to have a gun. They got into kind of an argument somewhere. Adolph Luque went over to his locker, took his gun and fired right in the ceiling. That was supposed to scare Boojum. Wilson just said, "Hmmm," reached up in his locker, got a gun, fired up in the ceiling, and said, "What about that?" That was the end of it.

I told Jud about that first time that I saw him. We used to kid each other and have a good time after that—as much as anyone could be a friend of Boojum. I was tall, so he used to call me "Look high and throw low."

When World War II came I went to England, France, Germany, the Philippines, Japan, the whole thing. Two and a half years. I was a truck driver on the fabulous Red Ball Express in France.

I came out in '46, had a good year that year, 15–1.‡ Only lost one game, the first game of the season. I said then, "This is going to be a

---

*Luque won 193 games for the Reds and Giants in the 1920s and '30s.
‡Manning's published record, probably incomplete, was 9–1. So far three victories are confirmed.

rough year." Then I won 15 straight. I've always been a hot weather pitcher; I could never pitch in cool weather. The more I sweat, the better.

Every time we went to Baltimore, me and Joe Black would always hook up in a duel. We had some pretty tough duels. One time we played in Omaha on a Friday night, and we left Omaha for a double header in Baltimore on Sunday. We rode and we rode, and we rode. We got to Baltimore just in time. We had to dress in the bus. We pulled into the park, Bugle Field. After all that riding, guess who had to pitch? Me. What amazes me is how present day ball players will squawk about a flight to Los Angeles and complain about jet lag. They really don't know what hardship is: No trainers, no hot water, and still get out and play.

Larry Doby was with us that year. Larry was quite an athlete—he was a super athlete. He was very adaptable, could play different positions. When I first saw him, I thought he was going to be one of the best second basemen I had ever seen. Very aggressive and intense, a lot of fire and spirit. But sensitive. I think the difference between Newark and the Cleveland Indians was the way we accepted him. First of all, the Eagles were looking for a good ball player, and everybody could see that he was one, and that readiness to accept him made him blossom. He got to be the big joker, the big laugh getter, he was a very outgoing guy. The first two or three days he came to the ball club, most of the guys he didn't know. But once he saw he was going to be accepted with open arms, he blossomed. I liked Larry a lot.

I think he lost some of that somewhere down the road. I think the experience with Cleveland bothered him a little bit. I think he's been hurt and doesn't know how to deal with it. He always was a somewhat sensitive guy.

Satchel Paige had a team played against Bob Feller that fall, and I played with him for two weeks. I had more money in my pocket than I ever saw in my life. I pitched in Dayton against the All Stars. They beat me 2–1. I struck out 14, struck out Charlie Keller three times. Spud Chandler [20–8] is the guy that beat me. We were leading 1–0. Chandler comes up in the ninth with a man on and hits the ball— Spud Chandler, the pitcher!—hits the ball over the short right-field fence.

Strangely enough, Phil Rizzuto [.257] was the only one I had any trouble with. He hit me like he owned me. He would be coming off the field, and I would be going out, and as we would pass each other, he'd say, "Big Max, Big Max." That's all he'd say.

That's when I knew I could have played in the majors. Even though I lost, it didn't seem like a loss to me, because of how effective I was.

I remember one trip we made from Philadelphia to Havana. We got on the train in Philadelphia, and we had to stay in a colored only compartment. We couldn't even leave to get some food. When we finally arrived in Cuba, we were treated as heroes. We could stay at any hotel, eat at any restaurant.

The winter of '46 I played in Cienfuego, Cuba. Carl Erskine and Max Surkont were on that team—Danny Gardella, Solly Hemus, Chuck Connors, "the Rifleman." Martin Dihigo was manager. In terms of personality, Dihigo reminded me a lot of Pop Lloyd. He was a marvelous physical specimen—height, weight, broad shoulders. You could see the power that this man had. One regret I have is that I never saw Martin Dihigo play in his prime.

Max Lanier [ex-Cardinal] pitched for Alamandares. I beat him 1–0. It was 0–0 going into the ninth, we were the home team.

Martin Dihigo hit for me, and Lanier walked him and forced in a run to win the ball game. I'm a gung-ho guy, and I happened to pass Max Lanier and said something to him: "Tough luck." I thought he'd bite my head off! He gave me a nasty look and muttered something. I said, "OK, if that's the way you feel about it. I still won the ball game."

Max Manning (right) with Johnny Davis (left).

That game gave me a big boost. I always had an inner confidence in myself in terms of major league competition. I never had any inner doubts in my mind about that.

If you could pitch and win down there, you could pitch and win anywhere. Carl went to Brooklyn and had a good year.

Gene Benson was a slap hitter, used to always hit me pretty good. Carl pitched against him and could always get him out. I said, "What do you throw Benson?"

He said, "I throw him a straight change." He showed me how to, and that became part of my repertoire.

We got to be good friends. When we had the Hall of Fame ceremony for me in Glassboro, he wrote a beautiful letter of commendation. Carl was a very decent guy.*

In 1948 a guy named Alex Pompez [owner of the New York Cubans and scout for the New York Giants] called me in Newark and left a message for me to call him in New York. He said, "How would you like to play with the Giants?" They'd already signed Monte. I said, "I'd like it, but I'm trying to figure out what you've got to do with me. I think it should come from Mrs. Manley, because she has my contract, and I'm playing for her, and she should tell me the Giants are interested in me." I'm being loyal to Effa, and she hates my guts.

He said, "OK, then." And that was the end of that. I never heard another word about it. At that time I had confidence in how good I was and felt, what the heck, it would soon happen again to me. But I never got another offer.

Unfortunately, I'd had a shoulder separation in the spring of '48. My arm used to swell. Very painful. I went to a doctor in Philadelphia. He had operated on Ewell Blackwell, but he said there wasn't much he could do about me.

After that I went to Venezuela, then to Canada. I struggled through a ball game, but it was really too painful for me to think about continuing. I knew I had to do something. I still had the rest of my life to get on with.

My wife said, "Why don't you go back to school and become a teacher? The GI Bill of Rights would pay your tuition."

It was the best decision of my life.

I graduated from Glassboro State College and taught for 28 years after that. In fact, I'd rather be known as a teacher than a ball player. I taught sixth grade for about 20 years. It's a difficult grade, but a very

---

*Erskine remembers Manning as "a very studious kind of a fellow." Carl joined the Dodgers in 1948, one year after Jackie Robinson. He feels the experience with Manning in Cuba was "a good training ground" for playing on an integrated team.

interesting grade. Having four kids of my own, I get attached to getting them started in the right direction, which is what teaching is all about.

The movie *Bingo Long,* in my estimation, was very inaccurate. I said, "I can't see anything about black ball that I know in that picture at all." One guy's wearing the shirt, and one guy's got the pants. The players I know didn't play like that.

"Never Look Back" [about Satchel Paige] on TV—I think they tried, but they still didn't come out right. They had Josh Gibson with a cigar in his mouth, they had Buck Leonard batting right-handed, and he was a left-hander. It would seem to me you ought to at least be accurate.

I don't think about myself very much. I have a whole lot of other things to take my mind off those things. I never look back, I always live for tomorrow. But I think about all the other people, like Willie Wells, who is blind. I worry about these guys who I know what they could do, the quality of ball they played. I think it's a damn shame. Some of these guys that I know, it was a real treat to see them perform. Seems like a shame that people have to get old. You think of all the beautiful things they've done. Like Oscar Charleston: He was finished when I saw him, but you could just see the tremendous talent the guy had. If I could just have seen this guy in his prime!

The sad commentary is that there are so many ball players who had the ability to match any major leaguer that never played. It's a shame that so many great black ball players, who are Americans and participated in the great American sport, will not gain the recognition they deserve.

I've always believed everything happens for a reason, and I've always been a here-and-now person. I can't worry about what might have been. The only one I have to prove anything to is myself, and I knew I was capable of pitching in the major leagues.

Some guys I played with are bitter about what they missed. But as far as I'm concerned, I have no reason to feel bitter, at least not about life. I'm very happy about my whole life. I've often been asked what I would do different with my life if I could do it all over, and I honestly think I would do it all the same.

Max Manning

	b: 11/18/18, Rome, GA	BR TR 6'4", 185	
Year	Team	W–L	Team Rank*
1939	Newark	2-6	2nd
1940	Newark	7-2	3rd
1941	Newark	2-4	1st
1942	Newark	6-6	3rd
1943	U.S. Army		
1944	U.S. Army		
1945	U.S. Army		
1946	Newark	9-1	1st
	Cuba	4-8	
1947	Newark	15-6	1st
	Cuba	10-8	
1948	Newark	10-4	unknown
	Cuba	5-12	
1949	Cuba	8-5	

Post-Season

1946	World Series	1-1

Recap

Negro league	54-29
Cuban league	27-33
Post-Season	1-1
East-West games	0–1
Totals	79-64

* Overall won-lost percentage in a six-team league.

The Millers' Giant Killer
DAVE BARNHILL

Dave Barnhill could have been a major league pitching star except for three things: He was too little, too black, and too old. He overcame the first, almost overcame the second, but couldn't lick the third. When the big league gates were finally opened in 1947, Dave was 33, just too old to go through them.

By his own estimate, Dave said, "I weighed 125–126 pounds—after it had snowed on me." But he could throw like a man twice his size.

"He had smoke!" Cool Papa Bell said.

"He had a live fast ball," says Buck O'Neil. "It was amazing. He'd throw it around your waist, it would come up to your armpits."

"For a little man," outfielder Jimmy Crutchfield agreed, "there were days when he could throw as hard as Satchel."

"He was right up there with Slim Jones and Satchel Page," Buck Leonard said. "He threw just as hard as anybody. He was one of the best we had in our leagues."

Three years younger than Leonard, Barnhill was born in 1914 in Greenville, North Carolina, near Leonard's hometown, Rocky Mount. "Barnhill was a number-one pitcher around there," Buck recalled. "We went to Greenville to play, and he blinded us! Man, we didn't do nothing with him. Oh, he was throwing that ball! We couldn't understand how such a little fella could throw the ball the way he could throw it.

"A fellow named Bill Bryan, a colored fellow used to run a white barber shop, got Barnhill to come to Wilson to pitch for his team. And he cut more heads! Boy, he beat everybody. He came out here to play us one Fourth of July morning, beat us about six or seven to nothing. He was top pitcher around here."

Leonard would return with the famous Homestead Grays, who tried to take Dave north with them. Dave turned them down. "Well, he had a girl over here, see," Leonard explained. "That had a whole lot to do with it. I think she told him not to leave."

Barnhill eventually did reach the black majors with the New York Cubans. In 1941 he pitched three innings in the East-West game, gave up two hits, and got two himself in two at bats.

The next year the white commissioner, Kenesaw Mountain Landis, "threw a bombshell" by saying there was no ban against blacks in the major leagues.

The black press jumped on it and quoted Leo Durocher, manager of the defending champion Dodgers, as saying he'd jump at the chance to have some black players. Paul Waner of the Pirates agreed. On July 24 a telegram arrived for Dave:

HAVE JUST ARRANGED WITH WILLIAM BENSWANGER, PRESIDENT OF THE PITTSBURGH PIRATES, A TRYOUT FOR YOU WITH THE TEAM IN PITTSBURGH SOON. CONGRATULATIONS. WON'T YOU PLEASE GET IN TOUCH WITH ME SO WE CAN MAKE FULL ARRANGEMENTS.

NAT LOWE
SPORTS EDITOR
DAILY WORKER

"I know there will be problems," Benswanger told the press, "but after all, somebdy has to make the first move." He worried that if he hired a black and then dropped him, he would be accused of discrimination.

His manager, Frank Frisch, was skeptical. "I don't believe there's anything to it," he scoffed. "But I'm only the manager. I do what I'm told." In the end, Frisch proved to be right. Dave got no tryout, and the Pirates finished with a 66–81 mark, 36½ games behind the Cards.

That summer Dave pitched three more innings in the East-West game, giving two hits and striking out four. Satchel Paige also pitched three innings, giving five hits, with one strikeout.

In 1943 Dave hooked up against Satch as starting pitchers in the East-West game before 52,000 fans. Both went three innings, with Satchel on top 1–0 when they left. In his nine total all-star innings, Dave gave just two runs.

After a sore arm, Barnhill teamed with Louis Tiant, Sr. to pitch the Cubans to the 1947 pennant. In the black World Series that fall, he beat Cleveland 6–0.

In Cuba that winter, Dave hooked up with Connie Marrero, later of the Washington Senators, in a 15-inning duel. Marrero was backed up by Monte Irvin, Sam Jethroe, Gene Benson, and Pee Wee Butts. Dave struck out 15 and walked only two before the game was called with the score 0–0.

The next winter, 1948, Barnhill returned to Cuba, experimenting with a new pitch. Although Dave hotly denied it, Buck Leonard insisted:

> I was on the same team with Barnhill down in Marianao, Cuba in 1948, and he was cutting the ball. He could sail that ball. The ball came up to the plate, would break just like a curve ball. You can look at the spin on a curve ball, but his ball didn't have any spin on it, because that little burr on the cover will cause it to curve. Just a little nick, cut the cover just a little bit. The wind would get in there and cause the ball to curve. If he held the burr up, the ball would go down. If he turned the cut side down, the ball would go up.
>
> Minnie Minoso was playing third base for us. He was cutting the ball for Barnhill.

> *One morning they had some kind of celebration down at the picture show. Barnhill was the leading pitcher, and they were going to give him a plaque. The commissioner of baseball in Cuba told Barnhill, "I'm going to ask you a question." Somebody had told him Barnhill was cutting the ball, and he asked him about it, and Barnhill said no—you knew he was going to say no—no, he wasn't cutting the ball. Never had cut the ball. But he was.*
>
> *Now when he first started out, he didn't do that.*

Says Gene Benson:

> *Dave Banhill was the hardest throwing little man. Almost as hard as Satchel. He had a lot of heart.*
>
> *But it was a strange thing. We were at a reunion, we were talking about Dave Barnhill, and they said, "and he cut the ball too."*
>
> *The next day I told him, "Barnhill, they're telling me you cut the ball."*
>
> *Barnhill started laughing, I thought he never would stop laughing. You know what he told me? "Benson, I was cutting it to pieces. You guys dragging those bats up there, you going to put me out of business if I didn't do something."*

At last in 1949, at the age of 35, Dave Barnhill got his big chance, an offer from the New York Giants to report to their Minneapolis farm, along with infielder Ray Dandridge. They were the first two blacks in the Association. The headlines in Dave's scrapbook tell the story:

MINNEAPOLIS WELCOMES BARNHILL AND DANDRIDGE
BARNHILL PITCHING PUZZLES AA BATTERS
BARNHILL TO BE HARD TO BEAT NOW
BARNHILL LOOMS AS STOPPER
BARNHILL YIELDS 2 RUNS IN 4 WINS WITH MINNEAPOLIS

Dave beat Kansas City 12–1 on a two-hitter. He shut out Columbus in "a brilliant piece of clutch-pitching," the Minneapolis Tribune wrote. He beat Milwaukee, giving one run in five innings of relief. He shut out Columbus again on four hits, making a total of only two runs in 32 innings. Dave had half the team's shutouts. Vern Kennedy, a veteran of the American League, had one.

Roy Hughes, veteran of the Indians and Cubs, played second base for the Millers. Barnhill "was sort of a spindly guy," he recalled, "a thin-framed guy with skin over his bones. But vivacious. He wanted to win. And to play. And he loved the game."

Jack Harshman, who would go on to pitch for the White Sox and Orioles, was Dave's teammate at Minneapolis. "Ray was very quiet, so was Dave," Harshman says. "That's why they were chosen to be the first. Dave had a quirkish way of taking his stretch, like he was wrapping yarn or pulling taffy. He'd run his hands a complete circle around each other, then come to a complete stop with his hands in the proper position. Not that it was illegal, it was just unique.

*"One time in St. Paul he pitched a shutout, and they got 11 hits off him.
He was in trouble constantly and wormed his way out every time."*

*The Millers were floundering in fifth place, 18½ games behind, needing
a win over Walter Alston's St. Paul club in order to get into the playoff. Dave
won the game in what Hughes called "a masterpiece," a gutsy example of
clutch-pitching.*

*That gave Dave a 7–10 record for the year and put fourth-place Minneapolis
in the playoff against Al Lopez' Indianapolis Indians. Lopez recalled the game well:*

*"All of a sudden I see where Barnhill struck out 14 in St. Paul, goes some
place else, strikes out about 15. Something wrong here some place. Now he's
going to pitch against us. Turns around to the outfield. I called for the ball.
Every time he turned around, I said, 'Heh, watch what he's doing to that ball
there!' I still don't know whether he was doing anything or not, but I think he
was."*

*"I never saw him cut the ball," says Harshman, who also played first base.
"If there was something happening out there, I'd be the first to find out. It was
certainly a secret to me."*

*"Any cut got on there, Barnhill didn't do it," Hughes grinned. "It would
be up to me or one of the other players."*

*Dave won his game 6–5 over Mel Queen, a 22-game winner, though
Indianapolis won the series four games to three.*

*Al and Dave met in Miami at an old-timers' game 32 years later.
According to Lopez, they had a good laugh together.*

*In 1950 Minneapolis won its first pennant in 15 years, as Barnhill
posted an 11–3 record (his .786 W–L percent was second best in the league),
and Dandridge won the MVP. They beat Lopez' Indians by four games. "The
biggest surprise on the staff was Dave Barnhill, Negro ace,"* The Sporting
News *reported.*

*(Some comparable won–lost marks in the league: Harvey Haddix 18–6
and Clem Labine 11–7; Dave's teammate, future Hall of Famer Hoyt
Wilhelm, was 15–11.)*

I was playing with the Ethiopian Clowns out of Miami about 1939,
and the Kansas City Monarchs wanted me to go pitch behind
Satchel against the Toledo Mudhens. They were white and they were a
farm club of a major league team.

I often wondered why the Monarchs wanted me.

Satchel would pitch three or four innings, a drawing card. Well,
he wasn't letting those boys do anything. He gave one hit, struck out
nine or 10.

The Toledo manager came to Frank Duncan [the Monarchs'
manager] said, "We're a major league farm club here. How about

taking Satchel out and putting somebody else in so we can have everything kind of even up?"

I was down in the bull pen, just slinging the ball. Duncan said, "What about that little guy down there in the bull pen?"

He said, "OK, put him in."

Duncan called me from the bull pen. "You warm?"

I said, "Yeah, I'm warm."

The first batter comes up. I wheeled around, turned my back on home plate—Luis Tiant must have got that move from me when I was in Cuba—and came back and turned loose a fast ball. The man ain't took his bat off his shoulder yet. That man didn't even *move!* Just looked like he was dumbfounded! Three straight. The man ain't swung at any of them.

OK, I got three like that in the inning. In five innings, I struck out 11, didn't give any hits.

After the game, taking our shower, here comes the Toledo manager, told Duncan: "You think you're smart, don't you?"

Duncan said, "What do you mean?"

He said, "You said you were going to take Satchel out."

"Well, I did."

He said, "No you didn't. You just took him out, carried him behind the dugout and cut his legs off and put him right back in there!"

Oh boy, we had a big laugh about that.*

When Satchel pitched against other teams, he would only pitch three innings. If he got one run ahead, he would come out. But anytime he came to play the Cubans, I had to pitch against him, so he had to pitch nine innings. He didn't let my team get nothing, and I didn't let his team get nothing. We didn't have any of that foolishness about pitching three innings and coming out. My arm started hurting trying to beat Satchel. But he didn't beat me any more than I beat him.

I saw him at the old-timers' reunion at Ashland, Kentucky. Three or four of us were talking, and the guys said, "Yeah, Barnhill could *sail* that ball. He was cuttin' that ball."

Satchel said, "Look, that little man there didn't have to cut no ball. He could throw as hard as he wanted to."

Jackie was signed in '45. But he wasn't the first one supposed to have a tryout. I was! I was supposed to have a tryout with the Pittsburgh Pirates in 1942 with Roy Campanella and Sammy T. Hughes, a second baseman. But the Pirates chickened out.

Every owner was waiting for the others to make the first move.

---

*Buck O'Neil and Willard Brown confirm the story almost word for word.

Three years later Branch Rickey took a chance on Jackie Robinson. But Benswanger said he wouldn't even take a chance at all. Branch Rickey had guts. He would either be a goat or a star. And he ended up starring. Jackie Robinson made him the star. He could have made him the goat if he hadn't come through.

I know we were ready in 1942. I played against quite a few big leaguers in Cuba. I pitched against Bob Lemon. I played against Johnny Mize.

I was born in Greenville, North Carolina, 1914—October 30. The Wilson Stars from Wilson, North Carolina came to Greenville. I beat them and they wanted me with them. I was out in the tobacco field, and the owner of the Stars, a black guy, sent this white guy to get

Dave Barnhill.

me. He was about this big around—four feet wide. The man came up and said, "Skinny"—everybody used to call me Skinny—"I talked to your mother, and she said you can go to Wilson and pitch for Wilson. I gave her a dollar for your day's wage."

I never rolled so fast in a car in all the days of my life! A Hudson. I don't know if you know about the Hudson. I mean, he *drove* that car! Oh my goodness! When we got to Wilson, I was so glad to get out of that car!

He took me right to the hotel. The black guy I was going to play for, his grandmother and grandfather owned the hotel.

Ray Dandridge came down from Virginia to play. Later on he and I went to Minneapolis in the American association together in 1949. The greatest ball player ever put on a uniform. *Think* so? I *know* so! There's nothing he couldn't do. He wore a red handkerchief like a train engineer around his neck. He was playing first, and oh my, I don't care how bad you throw it in the dirt, he'd get it. Oh, that was the most beautiful ball player I've ever seen! I'll say that the rest of my life. Ray Dandridge was a hell of a ball player—excuse the expression.

And I never saw ball players with bats as long as that. The bats were this long! That's the way it looked to me, because I was pitching against them. My God, you could throw the ball over their heads or under their legs, they still could hit it.

Buck Leonard, who's in the Hall of Fame now, is from Rocky Mount. That's only 38 miles from Greenville, and I used to pitch against him. You could put a fast ball in a 30–30 rifle and you couldn't shoot it across the plate by him. That's right. Later on Josh was the toughest hitter I faced. But you could strike Josh out; you might throw a fast ball by him. But not Buck.

I'm going to tell you an incident happened in Rocky Mount. I'm playing first base. On a skin-back diamond, no grass, nothing—hard. Buck hit one right across my toe! It was about three weeks before I could get a shoe on. Boy, that was a hard hit. Man!

The Ethiopian Clowns came through in 1936. Down through the years they named them the Indianapolis Clowns, but the Ethiopian Clowns started right here in Miami. I pitched against them in Tarboro, North Carolina and beat them 7–2.

They left and they were gone two hours when there came a telegram and $200 in money and two tickets for me and my catcher. They hadn't said anything to me about joining the ball club.

I said, "Well, Johnny, we're going home"—we were only 14 miles from home—"and see if our parents will let us go."

My mother said, "Well, if you want to go, I give you permission to go. Whatever money you make, put it aside, so if anything happens, you have some money to come back home with. And if you don't, if something happens, write me and let me know, I'll send you money to bring you back home."

Johnny's father didn't want him to go, so I left anyway to meet the team in Olean, New York.

I got there a day ahead of time. I'm standing in front of the train station, a country boy, you know, never been out of town. I had a few dollars, but I didn't know anything about hotels. And it started getting dark.

Right across the street, in front of the station, I saw a U.S. flag waving. The city jail. I said, "This is the best bet then." I walked across the street, walked in the office, and the desk sergeant looked at me, said, "Just what can I do for you?"

I said, "A lot you can do for me, I'm hoping. Because I'm supposed to meet the Ethiopian Clowns, the baseball team."

He said, "Oh yeah, they're supposed to play here tomorrow."

I said, "Can you put me up until tomorrow?"

He said, "I think I can help you." He called his jailer, told him, "See if you can fix him up. He's meeting the Clowns here."

The jailer took my suitcase, put it behind the sergeant's desk, took me upstairs. About two or three cell doors were open. He said, "You can sleep in this one." When he said that, I was so happy, 'cause I was tired with all that train riding. I wanted to go to sleep. So I walked in there, and when I walked in, oh my goodness, he slammed the door just like I was in Alcatraz. Well, I was too tired to worry.

I got up the next morning, earlier than when I was working on the farm. I got up *early*. I heard someone sweeping (sweep-sweep). I said, "Heh!" Nobody said anything. (Sweep-sweep.) "Heh!" Nobody ain't said nothing. (Sweep-sweep.)

"Yeah?"

"How about coming up here, opening this door?"

"Oh, I'll be there directly." You know, you kind of get uneasy about that kind of stuff. He come up in a few minutes, said, "You didn't think I was coming up, did you?"

I said, "I didn't know what was happening."

He opened the door. I walked out. He gave me my bag.

As soon as I walked out on the sidewalk, here come two Cadillacs. I don't know if you're old enough to remember running boards; that's what they had. That's the way the Clowns traveled. The two Cadillacs pulled right in front of me and stopped. They carried me to a rooming house.

"Do you want something to eat?"

I said, "Sure I want something to eat!"

That night we played Oleans, that was a St. Louis Browns farm club. They said, "Do you think you can pitch tonight?"

I said, "Yeah, I can pitch."

The ball park, everybody warming up. When the game started, I beat 'em 5–1.

The Clowns played on percentage. You go to a town, they give you 60–40. If you beat the team, you get 60. All that had to be divided among the ball players. That's the reason we didn't carry any more than 14 ball players, because the less ball players that you carry, the more money you'll get.

And every time you beat a major league farm club, you come back with a bigger percentage and a bigger guarantee of the gate. And you're not going to be gone from there over four or five days before they want you right back there. So they wanted me to pitch back in Olean. But first we had go to all the way up through New York state. They wouldn't let me pitch, they were saving me for Olean. And boy, that was the worst thing that ever happened to me. When we got back to Olean, I haven't got those ball players out *yet!* They hit everything I threw their way! [Laughs.] You talk about it was rough! They almost killed me.

I told them, "Look, don't you *ever* save me to pitch against anybody. When it's my turn to pitch, let me pitch." So I pitched every fourth day and played first base the other three.

We'd come to the park with paint on our faces like a clown. Even the batboy had his face painted too. We wore clowning wigs and the

Dave Barnhill (left) with Buck Leonard.

big old clown uniforms with ruffled collars. My clowning name was Impo. We'd play "shadow ball," pretend to hit and throw without any ball at all. They'd "hit" the ball to me, I'd run to field it, I'd jump, turn a flip, grab and throw it like I'm throwing the ball to first base. They'd pay us extra money to do it over again, that's how good it was.

Then when we were supposed to get down to business, we pulled the clown suits off, and we had on regular baseball uniforms underneath. But we didn't change our faces. We played with the clown paint still on our faces.

Morris Palmore was also the manager, and Syd Pollack was the booking agent. The owner was my wife's daddy, Johnny Pierce. That's how I met her. After we got married, she didn't go around with the team. I wouldn't let her. There were too many guys on the ball club who wanted her, and I was the one that got her, and I didn't want to take a chance!

It was a beautiful life. I enjoyed it! We weren't making all that kind of money, but I enjoyed it, because I had just come out of North Carolina, hadn't been any place. I stayed with the Clowns three years.

I would have stayed longer, but Pollock was trying to get the team out from under my dad-in-law. I told him, "Look these people are trying to get this team away from you. Go have this team copyrighted." Then if anything happened to him, the team would belong to my wife.*

Buck Leonard was with the Homestead Grays then. He tried his best to get the Grays to get me. But they said I was too small.

In 1939 the New York Cubans wanted me. There were so many ball clubs that used to beat the Cubans, and we were beating some of them, so they wanted me, and I left with them.

We played the Homestead Grays, and I just washed them away. I beat a big old guy named Roy Partlow, about six foot. Buck Leonard went and told the Grays' owner, "That's the same little guy you said was too small."

We were drawing good, because the Polo Grounds [the New York Giants' stadium] was the New York Cubans' home grounds. The Black Yankees were playing in Yankee Stadium.

Look at the crowds we had! Our East-West game was drawing more than the major league All-Star game. When I walked out of the clubhouse and saw all those people, then I wanted to put on my best show. That ain't no time for being nervous.

Later Silvio Garcia played short. One of the greatest ball players ever left Cuba. Used to be a pitcher. One day he was sitting in the

---

*The plan was never carried into effect.

dugout, a ball came off the bat, broke his pitching arm, so he started playing short. And he was a great shortstop. Oh my God, he could hit.

Showboat Thomas was first base. How did he play first? As good as he wanted to. As good as he wanted to.

Later Minnie Minoso played third base. Oh my God, he was a great ball player. We loved him. When the ball was hit to him, the pitcher had to lay down on the ground, because Minoso threw the ball all the way to first base about four feet off the ground.

Tetelo Vargas was center field. Oh man, he'd run like he stole something, and I don't mean bases.

But he wasn't as fast as Cool Papa Bell. *Lightning* wasn't as fast as Bell.

Cool Papa Bell sitting in front of his locker. Take off one piece of clothing, sit there awhile. Take off another, sit there awhile. Pull his pants off. Put his leg up on a stool, start wrapping it with gauze. When he got through, he looked like a mummy.

He'd pat you on the back: "Young man, you'll be all right. Don't worry." When he gets through patting you, talking to you, he's put on all his adhesive tape—and he's trying to console *you*.

"The old man don't feel too good tonight." Get out on the ball field, hit one of those high hoppers. He's gone! When you hear him saying that in the clubhouse, don't believe it, because he's going to run all over you.

He was a beautiful person. Yes he was. Cool Papa Bell. He was a lovable person. And still is. And always has been. I love him. My goodness, that's one beautiful man.

Mule Suttles of the Newark Eagles hit the highest home runs I ever saw in my life. We went to "school" in the clubhouse before the game. They said, "Don't throw nothing down here at the knees to Mule." In the first game our pitcher, Bill Anderson, threw the first ball right down there. Mule swung. The bat flew all apart. The ball went 400 feet, behind the fence.

Second game, I'm pitching. Jose Fernandez, our manager, says, "Don't throw nothing down there. You see what happened to Anderson." But I was stubborn. I was going to challenge him. I had to satisfy myself. I threw three balls there. Mule dragged his bat back to the clubhouse. I didn't believe any man in the world could hit my fast ball down there.

Josh Gibson was with the Grays. Ain't no man in the world hit a ball farther or harder than Josh Gibson. He was the greatest. As far as I'm concerned, he was the greatest. Every time we hit a town, some young kid would say, "Heh, see over there? Josh done hit one right there." And that was about four blocks from the ball park where he was pointing.

One Sunday we were playing the Homestead Grays. There was a cemetery beyond the fence. I threw Josh a curve ball. When the ball broke, his hand slipped off the bat and he just followed through with one hand and hit the ball in the cemetery. I've never seen a ball hit that hard before in my life. If Josh hadn't died early, when Jackie Robinson went up, the New York Yankees never would have let Josh out of New York. They would have taken him. You know so!

Jesse Williams was the greatest shortstop I ever saw. When I pitched that game against Toledo, the only reason they didn't get a hit was Jesse Williams, the Monarchs' shortstop. One guy hit the ball right behind the box. I just knew it was a base hit. When I looked around, here was Jesse Williams coming across second base, picked it up, ball, dirt and everything, fired to first base, and Buck O'Neil there was stretching for the out.

When Jackie Robinson came to the Monarchs as a shortstop in 1945, he was sitting on the bench—Jesse Williams was playing short-stop. Jackie couldn't carry Jesse Williams' glove.

But the big leagues got the right man in Jackie. Because the stuff that Jackie took, Jesse wouldn't have taken. They threw black cats in Jackie's face and everything. Jesse would still be in the penitentiary right now if they had done that to him. He'd be pulling time right now.

When Jackie Robinson went to the Dodgers, that's what broke up the Negro league. They fought so long, so hard to get blacks in the majors. That was a big mistake. The fans followed that one man instead of following the rest of the teams, so the league folded. We pushed to get one up there, should have pushed to get more up there. But we didn't. Just pulled the league down completely. The fans stopped going to the ball games. We had nothing going for us then. Not one thing. We had to give it up.

Carl Hubbell [former great New York Giant pitcher and then a scout] talked to Alexander Pompez, the guy that owned the Cubans, said, "We need a third baseman and a pitcher."

Pompez said, "I don't have anybody I figure you could use but Barnhill and Dandridge." I'll say, whether you like it or not, I was a pretty good pitcher. And Dandridge was a darn *great* third baseman.

So Hubbell said, "Well, I want Barnhill and Dandridge."

Pompez called me down to the office, said, "You and Dandridge are going to Minneapolis [the Giants' farm club]. "I just sold you to the Giants." He never did tell me how much. I wish he had, so I could get a little of that too.

Dandridge and I flew to Minneapolis. I don't think I flew no more either! I didn't like flying. They picked us up from the airport. Wouldn't take us to the hotel, carried us straight to the ball park, where they were playing a double header. Dandridge and I sat at the end of the bench. When the Minneapolis team came off the field, they were all sitting way down on the other end of the bench.

Tommy Heath, the manager, asked us, "Do you think you all can play in the second game?"

I told him, "Yeah, I can play. The only thing, I'm a little shook up from the airplane ride from New York." I went out there, and Dandridge was at second base. We did good. We did beautiful. I won, and Dandridge got a few base hits. After that, when we came off the field, instead of me and Dandridge sitting here by ourselves, the ball team just spread out all over the dugout. The whole dugout was mixed.

Oh man, I had some experiences with that ball club. Yes sir, *good* experiences. They treated me and Ray like we were on the ball club. Well, we *were* on the ball club. It wasn't who was black, who was white.

We didn't have any trouble in the hotels. The only hotels we couldn't stay with the ball club were Kansas City and Louisville. All the other towns, we stayed with the ball club. In Louisville we stayed in a black hotel. In Kansas City we stayed with Willard Brown's wife, because he was in Mexico. There was no problem; there was no problem at all. Everything was cool when I was there. Everything by then was kind of smoothed out. It was lovely. Yes it was. Lovely.

In the playoff we had to play Indianapolis with Al Lopez managing. He made a whole lot of stink about me. Yeah. Every time I took

Dave Barnhill (center) with Ray Dandridge (left) and Willie Mays.

the ball and rubbed it up, Al Lopez would run out and hold up the game. They thought I was cutting it on my belt.

But there's the umpire right there looking at me. Heath told me, "Dave, it looks like that's *worrying* 'em when you turn your back and rub up the ball. Continue on doing it."

Al Lopez: "Hold it! Hold it! He scratched the ball!"

Umpire said, "Now look here. If you walk out here one more time, hold up the game, I'm going to forfeit the game to Minneapolis." That's the only thing stopped him from going out there.

But every time I'd cross the foul line after the inning was over, when I'd go by him, he'd just call me all kinds of names. But that didn't bother me. They were calling me that out there in the Negro leagues.

We beat them three straight in Indianapolis. Came back to Minneapolis, we only had to win one more game. For the fourth game I was pitching. Jack Harshman [later of the White Sox] was on first base. I hit a triple down the left-field line, and when he made his turn at third base, he missed third base. People in the stands were hollering to go back and touch third. But he was in the dugout, and they put him out. And they beat us four straight.

In 1950 I played against Mickey Mantle and Whitey Ford. I popped Mantle up.

Leo Durocher was going to call me and Ray Dandridge up to finish the season. My manager told me, "You and Dandridge will go up at the later part of the season." But we got in the playoffs, and they wouldn't call us. I've never been so mad in all the days of my life! I could have had a cup of coffee and a cookie in the big leagues. We won the championship. They gave each of us a ring, but I was so mad, because I didn't get to play with the Giants.

Willie Mays joined Minneapolis in 1951. Tommy Heath came to me, said, "Dave, you're going to have to take the car, pick up Willie Mays at the station, because nobody on the team knows him but you."

I said, "OK." I brought him to the ball park, bags and all, and introduced him to Tommy Heath.

When Willie came to bat in batting practice, if the pitcher threw it inside, he'd hit it over the left-field fence; if he threw it down the middle, he'd hit it straight away over the center-field fence; if he threw it on the outside, Mays would hit it over the right-field fence. We had a clubhouse beyond the center-field fence, and he was hitting it over the clubhouse. But to tell you the truth, Mays wasn't the type of hitter in the Negro leagues that he was when he went to the majors. In the Negro leagues, the pitchers didn't like you to come in there and take advantage of them at bat. They'd throw at your head, at your legs.

When he got to Minneapolis, the pitchers would be pitching to spots. The ball would come up around home plate. He'd just stand there and bang on it. He was hitting .470-something when he was with us. The infielders were all glad when Durocher called him up to the Giants, because he was knocking their gloves off.

He was a center-fielder. The left-fielder and right-fielder didn't have much to do. He was catching everything.

What I liked about Mays, he didn't smoke or drink. Dandridge, Mays, and I would go to the Elks, sit down, have a couple of beers. Willie would get him a Coke, sit there and have just as much enjoyment as Dandridge and I drinking our beer.

I stayed with Minneapolis four years, 1949–52. Jack Harshman played first base for us. I could hit pretty good. I could hit from both sides. One day Tommy Heath called me, said, "Dave, get some bats and swing them." I was going to hit for Harshman, the regular first baseman—and I'm a pitcher.

Harshman: "They're scraping the bottom of the barrel now"—talking about me. Well, I could see his point. He'd been playing first base all season. So I went up to hit. Guess you know, I won the ball game. Hit me a triple, won the game. Who was the first one came out and shook my hand? Jack! He called me everything but the Child of God!

Oh my goodness, there were some beautiful days back then. I can say that I'm a very, very lucky guy.

Dave Barnhill.

Dave "Impo" Barnhill

b: 1/30/14, Greenville, NC   d: 1/8/83, Miami, FL   BL   TR   5'7"   155

Year	Team	W–L	Team Rank[a]
1941	NY Cubans	5–8	4th
1942	NY Cubans	5–5	4th
1943	NY Cubans	15*–3	5th
1944	NY Cubans	2–1	2nd
1945	NY Cubans	1–3	3rd
1946	NY Cubans	6–0	6th
1947	NY Cubans	4–0	2nd
	Cuba	10–8	
1948	Cuba	13*–8	
1949	Minneapolis	7–10	
	Cuba	0–3	
1950	Minneapolis	11–3	
1951	Minneapolis	6–5	
1952	Miami Beach	13–8	
1953	Ft. Lauderdale	1–1	

Recap

Negro league	38–20
Cuban league	23–19
Minor leagues	38–27
East-West game	0–1
Totals	99–67

* Led league.
[a] Overall won-lost percentage in a six-team league.

When Red Sox Were Black
VERDELL MATHIS

"You talk about Lefty Grove and Whitey Ford and Rube Waddell and those guys," catcher Larry Brown once told me. "We had a left-hander here in Memphis as good as those guys. His name was Verdell Mathis."

Slight and spindly, Verdell Mathis hardly looked the part of one of the best left-handers in America in the 1940s. But there are many who say he was.

He may also have been the greatest pitcher ever to come out of Tennessee.

"Verdell Mathis had so much heart," Gene Benson said. "He wasn't a big guy, but he had a lot of heart."

Wrote the 1945 Negro Baseball Pictorial Yearbook: *"The most over-powering pitcher now active is Verdell Mathis, the Memphis left-hander who mystified the East's touted sluggers at Chicago" in the East-West game of 1944.*

Mathis had tamed the East stars Josh Gibson, Buck Leonard, Cool Papa Bell, Roy Campanella, and Ray Dandridge, all of whom are now in the Hall of Fame. As Campanella's manager, George Scales, moaned, "It don't look like a team like that should beat our club."

Although a lefty, Mathis had little trouble with right-handers like Gibson, Campanella, Bell, and Dandridge. Larry Brown recalled:

> *Josh Gibson—now, you had to try to trick him. One day in Zanesville, Ohio I told Mathis, "Heh, Lefty, be careful with this guy. He's been hitting that ball out of all those ball parks." So Verdell got in the box and just lobbed the ball up and Josh took his cut. Next pitch he lobbed it in, Josh fouled it off. I said, "Don't try to trick him, just throw the ball through the middle of the plate." Josh thought I was kidding him. And he swung, taking his natural cut. Struck him out.*
>
> *Same thing we did to Campanella in Baltimore. He was in the clubhouse changing, so I said, "Heh, Campy, they tell me you been hittin' the ball over the fence." I said, "What kind of pitchers have you been hittin? We got some pitchers out West you never looked at before in your life."*
>
> *Well, Campanella came up to bat and I told Verdell, "Say, Lefty, don't try to trick him, just throw your curve ball, let him see what he can do with it." Campanella thought I was trickin' him. I wasn't trickin' him! The first pitch was right in there, strike one. Next pitch I said, "Don't try to trick him, throw him the same thing." Fast ball this time, right in there. He leaned forward as if to bite on it. Strike two. The next pitch Lefty threw the ball and it bounced on the ground. Campanella swung at it. I trapped the ball and threw to first base. I said, "Shoot, you all been tellin' me about how good these eastern ball clubs are."*

When I met Verdell Mathis some 30 years later, on a warm summer evening in Memphis, he was coaching a city recreation team before an enthusi-

astic crowd of blacks and whites. Later, at his home, he spoke in a velvety voice, his face creased with a perpetual gentle smile. He was still trim and lithe, apparently ready to go out and pitch a few innings any time.

I remember when I was a kid, even in grade school, I used to buy the old Pittsburgh *Courier,* and I always would admire Satchel Paige, and I used to say to myself, "You know, I'd like to be like this guy."

Every year while I was in grade school, when the visiting team would come to Memphis, I would make it down to the hotels where they were stopping, and I'd be batboy for the visiting teams, because I always did love basball. In fact, it must have been a gift, because I don't ever remember learning how to play baseball; it looked like I knew from the beginning how to catch and throw a ball. Anyway, I would always be the batboy for those teams, and I just stayed around them all the time. And I would always manage to hustle up enough money to get that Pittsburgh *Courier,* because I knew something was going to be in there about Satchel. I would just look at his picture all the time and read about this guy, and I always wanted to be like him.

I never dreamed I'd ever get to pitch against him.

I joined the Memphis Red Sox in 1940, and every time we'd play the Kansas City Monarchs, I'd go find Satchel. We'd sit down and discuss baseball: How to pitch. And he would always tell me: "Control." That guy was pretty tough. You know, I used to stand up there at the plate and let one or two pitches pass me, and actually the ball had a little buzz, a hum. He could throw that hard!

Satchel and I hooked up many a day. One time in New Orleans I beat him 1–0 in 11 innings.

In Chicago it was Satchel Paige Day at Wrigley Field. The crowd was about 30-some thousand people. They had a big van to take away the stuff they had given him. I got a traveling bag—a little traveling bag. I beat him that day 2–1. I drove in the winning run. Oh, I could hit too. I could play first base, I could play outfield, and I played all those positions very well.

And we had a hook-up in Kansas City. Oh, we had about 25–30,000 people. The town went wild that night. I told Larry Brown, "Larry, I feel good. I'm gonna get him tonight." I went over in Satchel's clubhouse, and his trainer was working on him.

Satchel said, "Lefty, what you doin' over here?" He said, "I know: You gonna pitch tonight. I know Larry Brown: he's gonna pitch you. He's gonna try and beat me tonight." And I beat him that night 2–1, and the whole city went wild—just that quick—when they heard it was over, everybody knew about that game, and the whole town celebrated.

I remember in Dallas one Sunday it was awful hot. Satchel beat me down there.

The toughest pitcher I faced, black or white, was Satchel Paige.

But we had a lot of tough pitchers. We had this other boy in Kansas City, Hilton Smith. He was so tough, it wasn't even funny.

But major games, I didn't lose 'em against any pitcher on any team. I didn't want anybody to beat me. I had determination.

I played with Memphis my entire career, 20 years, and Larry Brown was my teammate from the beginning of my career until the end. For 12 straight years we were roommates. Larry always told me, "Look, you can become a star, but you've gotta do what I tell you to." So every night or every morning when we knew we were going to play that night, we'd get up early and we'd sit on the side of the bed and Larry would say, "We're playing so-and-so team today." Larry knew every hitter in the league, always did. "We're going to pitch so-and-so this way, and so-and-so like this." And that's what we did for years.

I remember one time in Allentown, Pennsylvania we were playing the Washington Homestead Grays—Josh Gibson, Buck Leonard, and those guys. They had a shortstop—a good one—named Chester Williams. He said, "Come on in here, we're gonna run you to death." I

Verdell Mathis.

wasn't supposed to pitch that day, but Chester Williams kept "woofin'," you know, kidding you, trying to get a rise out of you. I didn't like that. I didn't like no team to start woofin' about they were gonna do this or that. So our pitcher was warming up, and Chester Williams kept beefing and going on, so I got up off the bench, said, "Give me that ball." I went and took the ball away from Evans and warmed up four or five pitches. They got one run off me, and that was a home run Buck Leonard hit in the first inning. I wasn't quite warm. But by the bottom of the ninth, when the game was over, we beat 'em 7–1. Chester Williams *cried* all the way to the dressing room. He said, "This just ain't fair. How *can* you do this?" I stopped him from woofin' though.

I started three East-West games in Comiskey Park. They would put Josh Gibson and Roy Campanella in the lineup together, they wanted all the right-handed power they could get. They would put Campanella on third and let Gibson catch. But that didn't make no difference to me. I was happy. And in these three All-Star games, ain't nobody made a score on me yet.*

Right-handers couldn't hit me, because of my screw ball. I was happy when they put eight right-handers in the lineup. I knew I had a good chance of winning that game.

Gibson and Willard Brown, they were two tough ones. Willard Brown could hit any pitch, just like Gibson. You couldn't fool them— don't think you're gonna fool them. Josh will hit you with one hand as quick as he will with two.

I'm gonna tell you how I pitched to Josh Gibson. Now, the only thing you have to do with a man like Gibson, you have to be careful *and don't make no mistakes!* You try to throw the ball where you want to. I always used the screw ball on Gibson, low and away. He never hit a home run off me.

One year the Baltimore Elite Giants were beating everything out East. Campanella played for them, and he and I were good friends. They were laying for us that Sunday, and Campanella brought three bats, three brand new 36-inch bats, and started woofin' at Larry. He said, "You know who these are for—these are for Lefty." And he shook them at Larry.

So the game got under way, and Larry told me, "Now, Lefty, I tell you how I want you to pitch him: Don't throw him nothing but change-up curve balls. When you put in your fast ball, you tighten him up, you get him back from the plate." I struck Campanella out three times. The last time, the ball made a bounce in front of the plate, and he struck at that. I beat them 5–0.

---

*One run, unearned, scored off him.

Larry used to carry me down to Mexico. All the top players were on Mexico City, they were the champions for three or four straight years. Larry and I were on Tampico. We went to play Mexico City, and they had Josh Gibson, Willie Wells, Ray Dandridge, Ray Brown, Barney Brown, Lazaro Salazar.

Willie Wells said, "You all brought that left-hander down; I heard about him. But I don't see how you all gonna beat us tomorrow."

We had a double header, one at 10:00 in the morning, one at 3:00 in the afternoon. That's the way they play down there. So the next day the game got under way. I beat Ray Brown the first game, and when 3:00 came that afternoon, I told Larry, "You know, I feel pretty good. Give me the ball." I beat 'em the second game. And the Pasquel brothers [owners of the league] turned the city over to us.

I developed my pick-off move from Lefty Tiant [father of the Red Sox pitcher] with the New York Cubans. I used to watch him close, very close. He was so good, he could throw to first and the batter would swing. Even at home or in the hotel room, I used to go through that motion. That's the way I learned it very well. Every chance that I got I would practice that move to first base.

I caught Jackie Robinson off base several times. He could bunt the ball excellent well. You gotta know how to be in position against that guy.

I could pick so many men off base, Larry used to say, "Let *me* throw some of these men out." In that case, I don't worry about throwing to first base, because I'm going to throw three off pitches

Verdell Mathis (bottom, fourth from left), with Jackie Robinson and others in Venezuela, 1945. Robinson kneels on left, next to Gene Benson. In the back row are Roy Campanella (second from left) and Buck Leonard (far right).

[pitch outs]. If he doesn't go the first time, if he doesn't go the second time, he's gonna go the third time. Three pitch outs in a row. If I throw one off pitch, they're not going to think you're going to throw another. And if you throw two off pitches, they know darn well you're not going to throw the third off pitch, so they're gone. Larry's got 'em. And then I'd throw three straight strikes—and could throw the curve on any pitch I want, on the 3–2 pitch, and get it over.

I tell you, a fellow like Cool Papa, he was smart. If he knew you could really hold men on base, he couldn't take the chance that he took on the other pitchers. When a man like Cool Papa got on, I really had to have my best move. Men like Cool Papa, Sam Jethroe, I'd never lob a ball to first base. I would actually throw there at him, to let him

Verdell Mathis.

know I'm trying to get him now, right away. I might throw over there two or three times, but my throws were *active*. Then when I make throws to the plate, he ain't going.

Bushwick—you've heard of the Brooklyn Bushwicks? In those days they were great. I went over there and I'll tell you what happened: They had a hell-fire team over there, and I pitched against this boy Marius Russo, who went to the Yankees. I beat him. I hit a home run. They had a sign said "God Bless America" in the outfield about 420 feet from home. I hit the ball on that sign. I beat 'em that first game. The second game I played left field seven innings, then I had to relieve the next two innings. In the double header I got seven-for-nine.

In 1946 I barnstormed with Satchel against Bob Feller's All Stars. Stan Musial couldn't get out there, he was playing in the World Series. The day after the World Series he flew out there for the night game. We had to turn people away. He made more money in the first night in Wrigley Field, Los Angeles, than he made in the World Series. Stan Musial came to me that night and said, "You know what? I should have been out here all the time."

Dayton, Ohio—you know that was a good baseball town. And the Homestead Grays were a big favorite there. But no matter who we played there, the only way they would book our team a game, I had to pitch. Now, I didn't know anything about that. But every team that we carried to Dayton, I beat 'em. So we decided to put our team against the Homestead Grays. They had been beating us, and Larry told me, "You know, you're gonna have to pitch." So we had a turn-away crowd there that particular night. They had a pitcher, Frank "Groundhog" Thompson. I beat him.

It was a funny thing, last summer this fellow who sponsored the games, he and his wife were on a vacation, and they stopped at our hotel in Memphis. One of the other bellmen roomed him, so he asked the bellman did he know me?

The bellman said, "Yes, he's downstairs—you must be kidding."

He said, "Well, send him up here."

So I went on up, I said, "Well, I'll be doggone," I said, "Gee whiz." And we had a long conversation.

He said, "Where is Larry?" I said Larry was down at another hotel. So after all this long talk, he told me what happened. Now, this is what was happening:

This man was giving Larry $20 every time our team come there. "This is for you," he said, "you have to save Mathis to pitch here because the people don't want to see nobody but him." Now Larry was getting $20.

I said, "You must be kidding."

He said, "Yeah, that's true, that's true." So Larry and I and him got together before he left and we talked the situation over. I told Larry he owed me half of those $20.

Verdell "Lefty" Mathis

b: 11/18/21, Crawfordville, AR		TL	5'11", 150
Year	Team	W–L	Team Rank*
1940	Memphis	2-2	3rd
1941	Memphis	2-4	unknown
1942	Memphis	5-5	unknown
1943	Memphis	5-3	6th
1944	Memphis	9-9	4th
1945	Memphis	8-10	6th
1946	Memphis	1-5	5th
1947	No record		
1948	Memphis	7-11	3rd

Recap

Negro league	39-49
East-West games	2-0
Totals	41-49

*Overall won-lost percentage in a six-team league.

Cherokee
JOHNNY DAVIS

*Johnny Davis looked and sounded exactly like a tanned Walter Matthau when
I interviewed him in his home in Fort Lauderdale in the 1970s.*

*As an outfielder-pitcher on the Newark Eagles in the 1940s, he joined
Monte Irvin and Larry Doby to make a potent 1–2–3 punch. In 1946 they
ended the record string of nine straight pennants by Josh Gibson, Buck
Leonard, and the Homestead Grays, then upset Satchel Paige and Hank
Thompson's Kansas City Monarchs in the black World Series in seven games.
Johnny drilled two doubles in game seven, one of them driving in Irvin and
Doby to beat the Monarchs 3–2.*

*Newark's Ray Dandridge calls him "a double duty" man, meaning he both
hit and pitched. Ray says Johnny started pitching when "I carried him back to
Mexico one time. On account of that he was a double duty man."*

*In the pitcher's box, Davis hurled a no-hitter in Puerto Rico in 1944, and
was strikeout king and MVP in '47–'48.*

*In the batter's box, Davis hit .345 for the Eagles in 1944, was second to
Josh Gibson in homers in '45, and second to Irvin in '47. He drilled two hits in
one game against Bob Feller in 1946, slugged .381 in Venezuela in 1950–
51, topped the Puerto Rico winter league in homers the next winter, and broke
the home run record in the Florida International league in '52.*

*And, says Irvin, if Davis had concentrated on either hitting or pitching,
he could have been even better.*

*Wilmer "Red" Fields of the Grays, another "double duty" man, insists that
Davis was a better pitcher than hitter.*

*As for his hitting, "He couldn't hit that curve ball, but he could kill that
fast ball," Fields continues. "He could hit that fast ball as good as anybody and
as far as anybody too." Fields, a fast ball pitcher, winces at the memory. "When
you make a mistake against him, he could hurt you. When I say hurt, I mean
hurt."*

*Eagles pitcher Leon Day agrees that Davis was a good fast ball hitter—
"don't try to throw that fast ball by him. He hit the ball a long way."*

*"He was a strong guy," says Monarch first baseman Buck O"Neil. "Kind
of weak on the breaking pitch, but you couldn't hang the curve ball. If you get it
in the wrong place, he'd hit it a long ways."*

Newark pitcher Rufus Lewis says he saw Johnny lean away from one of Satchel Paige's fast balls and still line it over first base for a triple. "Anyone else would have scored," Lewis says. "He was slow."

"I remember him as being very, very strong," says another Newark pitcher, Max Manning. "I remember one ball he hit. The shortstop jumped to try to catch it. It knocked his glove into left field. I've seen balls hit a lot deeper, but this was hit like a bullet."

Davis went on the famous Satchel Paige-Bob Feller tour of 1946, when Feller's all-star pitching staff held him to a sub-.200 average. However, when the clubs reached Kansas City, the Yankees' Spud Chandler had a 2–0 lead in the ninth, when he put two men on, and Johnny drove one over the left-field wall to win it 3–2.

"He used to act kind of wildish," Manning said. "he was really a big kid more than anything else. He'd do a lot of kiddish things. He loved to drive the bus. He liked to be alone, but he was a good mixer too."

Davis had a variety of nicknames, all related to Indians. Some called him Cherokee. Manning called him "Indian." Josh Gibson watched him slug a home run into Washington's distant bleachers, and when Johnny circled the bases and jumped on home plate with both feet, Josh called out the paratroopers' cry of "Geronimo!" and the name stuck.

The first time I faced Satchel Paige, I hit a drive to center field. The center-fielder had to go back about 40 feet to catch it. When I got back to the bench, I asked our manager, Biz Mackey, "Who's that guy pitching?"

He said, "Satchel Paige."

I said, "Big deal"—but I got impressed later.

'Forty-five they voted me to go out there to Chicago to the East-West game. I was nervous. You know, you get out there with all them ball players been playing for 20 years, 15 years. Here I am, just started in '42 or '43, going to the East-West game in two years. There's guys been in the league 10 years never got out there. But I got two hits.

We got $200 a man for that day. They used to give you a watch and $50. They had 55,000 people out there. Josh Gibson told Tom Wilson [league president] that we weren't getting enough money for playing that ball game. Tom said, "What do you want?"

We said, "We want $200 a man." Three ball players from each team. What's that, 18 men? What's 200 bucks?

Tom Wilson said, "I can't give you that, I gotta talk to the owners."

"Well, if you don't give us $200 a man, you're not gonna have no ball game." Sure enough, they agreed on it. That's $600 to me,

Dandridge, and Terris McDuffie. You know how much the Eagles got left? Five grand. Just for sending three ball players there. Shoot, he's got $5,000, he gives us $600—and he didn't want to pay us that!

Naw, I didn't grow up in reform school. Orphan homes, not reform school. I didn't quite make it that high.

Just about like Babe Ruth. He come from St. Mary's, and I come from the Catholic Protectory. Look at the money he made!

I'd run away from the homes. I probably was looking for something, but who in the heck knows what I was looking for? Maybe I was trying to find my mother. I was seven or eight. Just take off and run. Cops'd find me. "Where ya live?"

"I don't know." OK, back in another home.

I was in the Catholic Protectory in the Bronx, I was in an orphan house out on Staten Island, and in between times I'm placed with this family and that family and this family and that family. One would tell

Johnny Davis.

me that this was wrong, and this one over here would say, "That's all right, go ahead." You get sort of mixed up, you know. And I would take off.

One man I lived with out in Long Island, every Friday I had to go with him. He had a little pickup truck, and he cut the back of it off and put ice and fish in it and sold butterfish and porgies and stuff. He would clean the fish and scale 'em, and I'd deliver them to the people and get the money. I don't know if you're old enough to remember: Butter used to come in a big tub about three feet high; you want butter, the grocer would cut you off a chunk, put it in a little container and weigh it. One pound was 10–12 cents, something like that. One day he brought home one of them butter tubs filled with chitlins. Chitlins are hog innards, the guts. What they do, they make crackling out of them. He said, "I want you to clean these." You take the chitlin and you squeeze all the crap out of it, then you cut it and turn it inside out and you wash it. Then you fry it, and it makes like potato chips. I picked up one of them and squeezed. And that's where I left it. He hasn't seen me from that day to this one.

The cops caught me on Coney Island, said, "Where you live?"

I said, "I don't have a home." So back to the Catholic Protectory I went. I was about 12 or 13, I guess.

A lot of kids up there were run-aways and guys who stole maybe an apple or something, and they put them in there for six months. I was there for six *years*. I had no place to go. Who's gonna take me? Anybody want to take you, you got to be a little cute one; they want one that's not too old, or one that's not too fat. I just stayed there. I didn't mind.

Shoot, I used to ring the Angelus at 12:00. Get the string and pull the bell down. Everybody stops what they're doin', then you go for lunch.

I never had any visitors, but when other kids would get visitors, I'd go in there and visit with their mothers too.

I got a good education. In the Catholic Protectory you go to school regular hours. It didn't go any higher than the ninth grade. After you learned all you could in ninth grade, you couldn't go out in the street, you didn't have no place to go. So we were learning algebra, trigonometry, geometry, and I got a pretty good education up there.

I was an altar boy up there too, so I had to learn Latin. Picture me being an altar boy?

If you didn't make it out of there, you went to Elmira, a reform school. They had Jeep Lanza, Two Gun Crowley, Johnny Rizzo, Machine Gun Kelly—before they became Machine Gun Kelly and all that. They all went up to Elmira, because they were tough guys. They were all mixed up with Dutch Schultz and Murder Incorporated. The brothers at the Protectory wouldn't stand for too much. You got too much for them, shoosh, up you go.

I was the biggest kid in my division. When I got to the highest division, that's when I started to play baseball. We used to play not baseball, but stickball. You can't play baseball on concrete, because you slide, you tear your butt up. Or sometimes we'd throw the ball up, hit it with your hand.

The Lincoln Giants played at the Catholic Protectory in the afternoons, but we were in school. They wouldn't let us go to see them play. But we went out there one Sunday, and we saw one game, and after that we didn't see them any more. But I heard about them. I heard about [Frank] Wickware—the Red Ant, could throw that ball through a brick wall—and Smokey Joe [Williams], Pop Lloyd, George Scales. There were some great ball players back in those days.

When I was 17 they sent me "outside the walls"—really, it was no walls—and I was working with a cement mason. He sent me over to get two bags of portland cement that weighed 94 pounds, and I'm pushing the wheel barrow and said, "What the heck am I doing this for?" So I left the wheel barrow right there. I found a dime, went up and put it in the subway and went to Coney Island. They caught me, brought me back. The next day they place me out with some lady in Long Island.

That's when I got in the merchant marine. A fellow and I—Roland—we were both six foot, and we went down to become longshoremen. We went on the docks, and the bos'n gave us little chipping hammers to chip the paint. Friday comes, they're short one man. They asked Roland, "You want to go?"

Roland looks at me, says, "You go on this trip, and I'll try to get on the Pennsylvania Railroad." I think he's still there.

The man said, "How old are ya?"

I said, "I'm 17."

He says, "You want to go on this trip?"

"Yeah."

He says, "OK, you're 18."

I always wanted to see what's on the other side of the street—different people, different places, different foods. I got seasick before I left New York. Only a 4,000-ton ship. A 21-day trip. What do you pay for a 21-day trip now? $6,000–$7,000.

I was an ordinary seaman. I've still got my license in the back room. I'm qualified to serve on vessels from 500 gross and up.

We only had two Americans. The rest of them were from Venezuela, Guayana, couldn't none of them speak English. That's where I learned how to speak Spanish. Pretty soon I was speaking Spanish like a native. Didn't take me long, because I had French and Latin when I was in the Protectory.

We ate good on the way down, but on the way back we didn't eat too good, because the passengers got all the good food. The most we'd eat was a lot of sandwiches. So I got me a fishing pole and caught me some fish. Dunk your garbage over and drop your line in. A lot of fun.

Eighteen years old, and I'd seen half the world already.

I stayed in the merchant marine from '36 to '39, till [union boss] Buzz Curran called a strike. We couldn't get off the ship, so we had to take a tugboat across the East River. I said, "That's enough for me."

That's when I ran into Al Campanis up there in Central Park. He saw me playing, asked me if I wanted to go up to Schenectady and play for the Mohawk Giants. I told him, "Man, I can't just play baseball, they don't pay nothing up there."

"Get a job too." He called up this guy, Hank Bozzi, up in Schenectady. So I got out of the merchant marine and went up there and worked for American Locomotive and started playing baseball.

Johnny Davis (#16) being greeted by teammates.

It's cold up there. Ah God, is it cold! Got to work one morning 24 below zero. My ears fell down like that. Everybody laughing at me. And this finger here curled up, and I couldn't straighten that son of a gun out for anything.

[Davis eventually was signed by Newark Eagles owner Effa Manley.]

It was just a continuous scuffle. Play here this afternoon, another game tonight, ride 600 miles, play somewhere else. Sometimes you put on the uniform, it was still wet. You'd pick up a sweatshirt sometimes, and phew! You couldn't hang your socks up, you had to put them in your suit roll. You'd take them socks out and see green mold—ha! Until we got the new bus. Then we could hang the uniform up in the back of the bus, because the engine was in back. The heat would sometimes dry it out. But we played. Doggone, we played.

When I first started playing baseball, you *needed* drugs to stay awake! But we never thought about drugs or anything. We were Mrs. Manley's boys. The worst thing we did was take a Coca Cola bottle, drink half of it, and fill it up with whiskey. Lenny Pearson, by the time he got off the bus, he didn't know where he was. But he played. He played.

Abe Manley was kind of easy-going. Mrs. Manley was the toughie, 'cause she handed out the money on pay day. We were her boys. She always wanted you to look like a ball player. She didn't want you walking down the street in a pair of jeans or an old shirt. "You are my ball players, and you're going to look like my ball players"—clean shirt, shined shoes. Had to comb your hair and brush your teeth— ugh. Matter of fact, we loved it better when we were on the road. Then we could wear anything.

She had a lot of faith in that ball club. But you couldn't say nothing to her. She had an apartment house in Crawford Street, and she'd get you down there and, boy, she'd blast you. Maybe you didn't have clean white socks on your uniform, or you looked sloppy on the field, or your shirt was torn, "and I didn't like the way you did this." What could you say? You'd sit there, and after she was all through, say, "Aaaah." Well, you were representing something in Newark. You walk down the street, you had to look, not like a bum, you had to look halfway decent. You can't blame her for that.

But she knew about baseball like I knew about shooting a rocket up in the air. And Abe didn't either. Neither one of them did. Abe had his favorites, she had hers. She was chummy with Jimmy Hill and Larry Doby. Me? No way. I stayed as far away from that woman as I could. When she had a meeting, I stayed in the back of the room.

They called me Cherokee. Ray Dandridge was Squatty, 'cause he was so short. Monte Irvin was Muggsy; Doby, LD; Jimmy Wilkes,

Seabiscuit [a race horse]; Max Manning, Doctor Cyclops. Biz Mackey was the Silver Eagle. Pearson, we used to call him Gold Tooth. We'd say, "Go ahead and smile, Horse, show us that golden tooth again."

Nineteen-forty-six I was supposed to go to the All-Star game again. We were out in Oklahoma. Our next stop was South Bend, Indiana. You know how far South Bend is from Oklahoma? It's a long ride! Guess who wound up driving the bus from Oklahoma to South Bend? Me. Stayed in the hotel, and I caught the train from South Bend to Chicago.

In 1946 the Eagles would have beat anybody. We wanted to play the Brooklyn Dodgers [National League runners-up]. Wouldn't play us—would not play us. Matter of fact, we went over there to play a pick-up team, first time I'd been to Ebbetts Field. Rex Barney was pitching. First pitch he threw, he threw it up on the stands. I guess you know that got everybody loose. You don't know where he's going to throw the next one.

[Johnny signed with the San Diego Padres in the Pacific Coast league in 1952.]

When I went out there, I drove my car, a '48 Buick. It cost me $77 from Newark. The next day I went out to the ball park and Cookie— he was the trainer—said, "OK, Davis, come here. What'd it cost you to come out here?" I had written down everything: Two stops, one in Indianapolis, one in Dallas. With gas, it run to $77. He took the thing and tore it up.

I said, "Whatta ya doin'?"

He says, "You come out here first class on a train. In a compartment at $385. Now, three days at seven and a half dollars a day, that's $22.50 You're gonna be in spring training for two weeks at seven and a half bucks a day." He gave me close to $600.

I looked at my little $77, said, "Shucks, this is the place for me!" *Ha*-ha! This is the place! I'm lookin' at him countin' that money. Every time he put another $10, my eyes got as big as this.

You know, I'll tell you something funny. Back on the Eagles we got a buck and a half a day for expense money. I was still eatin' for a buck and a half! Couldn't get outta the habit! I'd get up in the morning, go downstairs, have corn flakes or sausage and eggs for 85 cents or 90 cents, something like that. The rest I put in my pocket. I might have supper for a dollar. At the end of the week I had saved myself 30 or 40 dollars.

Lefty O'Doul managed the Padres. Once a week he'd come in and have a fishin' pole, a camera, a flashlight, something interesting, and he'd put your name in a hat. He'd pull out: "Aha! So-and-so, you won a fishin' pole!" Everybody was together on the team. We were leading the league there for about three weeks.

I was only one home run behind Max West [formerly of the Braves] for the league lead. They wanted me to go to the Chicago White Sox and hit behind Eddie Robinson.

But I broke my leg.

There wasn't any more chance for me after that. Who's gonna pick you up when you're about 35 years old? Nobody wants you then, you're too old.

A guy came over there from Santo Domingo, wanted me to play for the last month. I told him, "I can't even run."

He said, "I don't care if you run or not. Come on." He handed me 1200 bucks, so I went.

I got married in '52 in Puerto Rico. Back in those days when you took a girl out, you took her brother or her sister, make sure there wasn't any fooling around. Called chaperones. I came down to Florida, went up to Montgomery, back to the Dominican Republic.

I haven't hurt anybody, they haven't hurt me. Only got hurt once in my life, that's when I broke my ankle. No, twice—Dan Bankhead hit me in the head with a curve ball.

I'd love to have gone up to the majors just to see what it was like. But I look at it this way: When I was with the Eagles, we went all over the country. We stayed in hotels, if we could find one. The major

Johnny Davis sliding into home plate defended by Quincy Trouppe.

leaguers couldn't go to Puerto Rico, couldn't go to Mexico, Canada. I went to all them places. All expenses paid. I got some pictures here of Mount Hood, Mount Whitney. We're up 18,000 feet, I'm shooting things out of the window.

I regret not going to the majors. Just a little. At the rate I was going, I believe I could have gone up there and kept on doing what I was doing.

In Kansas City in '46 Bob Feller's team was leading us in the ninth inning with two outs and a man on, and I hit Spud Chandler's fast ball over the left-field fence. I picked Phil Rizzuto up at shortstop and carried him piggy-back from shortstop to third base, and we both slid in at home plate together.

Johnny "Cherokee" Davis

b: 2/6/18, Newark, NJ* d: 11/17/82, Ft. Lauderdale, FL BR TR 6'3", 215

Year	Team	PSN	G	AB	H	2B	3B	HR	BA	SB
1941	Newark	—	—	40	10	0	0	1	.250	1
1942	Newark	OF	—	33	10	0	0	0	.303	0
1943	Newark	OF	—	77	20	4	1	3	.260	0
1944	Newark	OF	47	142	49	8	1	4	.345	1
1945	Newark	OF	38	138	44	14	3	6	.319	1
1946	Newark	OF	59	216	73	—	—	9	.338	3
	Cuba	OF	—	109	26	—	—	—	.238	—
1947	Newark	OF-P	—	262	69	13	—	13	.263	3
	Cuba	—	—	188	57	5	4	0	.303	—
1948	No record									
1949	No record									
1950	No record									
1951	Drummondville	—	120	421	146	28	1	31	.347	—
1952	San Diego	—	61	167	44	9	1	6	.263	—
1953	Ft. Lauderdale	—	140	514	165	18	2	35	.321	—
1954	Montgomery	—	40	133	35	4	0	8	.263	—

Post-Season

1946	World Series		7	24	7	3	0	0	.292	1

* Date and place not certain; may have been born in Ashland, VA.

Johnny Davis vs. White Big Leaguers

Year	AB	H	2B	3B	HR	Pitcher
1945	2	2	0	0	0	Hal Gregg (18-13)
	2	1	0	0	0	Ralph Branca (5-6)
1946	4	0	0	0	0	Bob Feller (26-15)
	4	0	0	0	0	Spud Chandler (20-8), Feller
	3	1	0	0	0	Bob Feller
	5	0	0	0	0	Feller, Dutch Leonard (10-10)
	3	0	0	0	0	Feller, Chandler, Lemon (4-5)
	5	0	0	0	0	Feller, John Sain (20-14), Lemon
	4	2	1	0	0	Feller, Sain
	4	1	0	0	0	Feller, Chandler
	4	1	0	0	1	Feller, Chandler
Totals	40	7	1	0	0	Average: .175

Recap

	G	AB	H	2B	3B	HR	BA	SB
Negro league	—	912	275	39	5	36	.302	9
Minor leagues	361	1235	390	59	4	80	.316	—
Winter leagues	—	297	83	5	4	0	.279	—
vs. white big leaguers	10	40	8	1	0	1	.200	0
East-West games	3	7	2	0	0	0	.286	0
Post-Season	7	24	7	3	0	0	.292	1
Totals		2515	784	107	13	117	.304	10

Pitching

		W-L
1946	Newark	1-1
1947	Newark	0-1

The Big Red Gray
WILMER FIELDS

Wilmer "Red" Fields is a big, cheerful man, bubbling with good humor. Four decades ago he was a double-threat man for the Homestead Grays, starring both in the pitcher's box and at the plate.

A light-skinned man (hence the nicknames "Red" and "Chinky"), Fields was "the man who integrated the Homestead Grays," Ted "Double Duty" Radcliffe likes to chuckle.

When I first began researching the Negro leagues, I wrote an article on Josh Gibson for the Washington Post Magazine. *The morning the story came out, I got a call from Wilmer, who introduced himself as Josh's teammate—and said he lived right in Manassas, the same town I lived in! I hadn't even known about him!*

In the years since then, we have appeared together on radio and before SABR and other groups. Every time I think I have mined him for every story in his bag, he pulls a new one out that I haven't heard yet.

"Red Fields, he had a lot of nerve," said Tom "Pee Wee" Butts of the Elite Giants. "He could stand a beating. Most pitchers can't come back when you get three or four hits off them, but he could. That's what I call hanging in there. Most fellows get shaky and blow up, but it looked like he could come back with more. Had a chance to win his own game at bat too."

"Most of those old pitchers were good hitters," Grays manager Vic Harris said. "When we put Fields on third, he was as good as any third baseman fielding that we had. And a good hitter."

Wilmer's main rival on the Grays was 6'7" pitcher Garnet Blair. They had been rivals in college in Virginia in both basketball and baseball before joining the Grays. Their rivalry continued on the Grays: "I beat you pitching yesterday," or, "I beat you hitting."

Chuckled Harris: "If Fields won his game, Blair was going to try to win his, going to out-pitch Fields, and vice-versa." While Harris gleefully watched the competition, the Grays' poor foes squirmed.

I came up to the Grays in 1940, and it was like going into battle when we went into Griffith Stadium or one of the other major league parks. The people saw real baseball. In a double header you saw two pitchers who could pitch and hit that ball too. I remember sitting in the dugout of Griffith Stadium. The other team had to come through the home dugout and walk across the field to the other dugout, and I'd watch them walk by and look at each one and think, "What's he going to throw me today?"

It was interesting when Satchel used to pitch against the Grays, just to see him and Josh Gibson battle each other—you know, see which way Satchel would pitch him. Josh was strong—strong and gifted. He had arms like this.

I can remember every game Satchel ever pitched against us. He beat me one time real bad 9–4. He used to pitch five innings, then this boy Hilton Smith would come in. But if Satchel had us 1–0, he'd want to stay in and go nine, and that's when we'd get him. One time he had us 4–0 in Forbes Field, Pittsburgh, but when the ninth inning came, we had him 9–4.

Oh, Satchel Paige was something, he was something! He used to come up to my room in Puerto Rico when we played down there. He pitched for Santurce, and I was playing for San Juan. I was playing the outfield one night, a Puerto Rican boy was pitching, and I hit him out for a home run. So in the sixth inning, they brought Satchel in to protect a two-run lead. And he threw Les Layton, who used to play for the Giants—he threw Les three straight fast balls knee high, I mean with something on them—phew! phew! phew!

I was next up, and we knew each other, see. I had to get the lightest bat I could find. He threw me a fast one, and I missed it, and he hollered to me, "Aw, you can't hit." I knew he was going to throw the same pitch, and I hit it out of there, and I went around the bases and said, "Old man, go back home." In Latin American countries when you do something like that, they give you money—you know, through the chicken wire fence in front of the stands. A guy gave me $100 through the fence. I never will forget it.

I was born in Manassas in 1922. See this big field out here in front of the house? There was nothing out there then. We'd go out there every afternoon and play. Make a rag ball, tennis ball, anything. There was always a good crowd to watch us. I didn't see how a person could play ball and get paid. I prayed to the Lord for a chance to play professional ball.

I was playing with a team down in Fairfax, and a fellow with the team knew a guy who was connected with the Grays, and they gave me an opportunity. Oh lord, I showed up with these "peg" pants. If you didn't have uniform pants from the factory, you rolled up a regular pair real tight. They must have seen me coming and thought, "What is this coming?" Here I am 17, and the closest one in age to me out there is 25. It was almost like foreign soil to me. I pitched against a semipro team in Boston, Virginia. I made a million mistakes, but they kept me.

I could throw pretty good. I was strictly a fast ball pitcher. I'd throw a curve ball every now and then, and I got two or three hits.

I wasn't a starter. I was just *there*, pitching exhibition games. The Grays didn't care about a country boy like I was: You didn't know anything. This is the way you were treated. Rookies had to sit in the back of the bus. There was no riding up front. And when we young guys made a mistake, the others would get all over us. They'd get in that bus after a game, going from Washington to Pittsburgh, and they'd start talking about the game, especially if it was a crucial game—not crucial, but an interesting game, say 1–0, 2–1. They wouldn't be afraid to tell each other: "You should have done this, you

Wilmer Fields with the Toronto Maple Leafs.

should have done that. . . . Why did you throw him a curve ball? You should have thrown a fast ball."

But those bus trips used to go fast. We used to talk all night: "This guy throws this and that and that, but he never throws me that pitch." We'd talk about everything in the league. Or there'd be singing, or you could watch the scenery. It went fast.

You had to be in good shape to play then. Do all that traveling, get out and play a double header. When we'd get to a big town we'd get a good meal. But sometimes we'd get two hot dogs. You couldn't hardly play a double header on two hot dogs. And one time in Newark we got ahold of some bad hot dogs.

Did any of the guys tell you about how we used to eat on the bus? That was one of the biggest parts of our life to me. We called it a "Dutch lunch." Everyone had his box under his seat: bread, baloney, ham, tomatoes, sandwich spread, and a knife. We called it our "frigidaire."

I remember one night we stopped at a filling station in Mississippi to get gas. I was sitting up front with Josh. They used to call me "Chinky," and Josh said, "Here, Chinky, get us some sandwiches, wear my hat." A few minutes later, R.T. Walker jumps up and runs in there to tell me to get him a sandwich too. The proprietor looked at him and said, "Get out of here." Then he took another look at me and said, "You too, get out of here, both of you get out of here!" I thought it was funny at the time. I still think it's funny.

We had a pretty good quartet on the team. I remember one time the Mills Brothers were up there in New York in the hotel where the team was staying. They'd sing a number, and the Homestead Grays would sing the same thing. Our best voices were Jerry Benjamin, Buck Leonard, Lick Carlisle, Jelly Jackson, Eudie Napier, and Vic Harris. They'd sing spirituals, barber shop numbers. You had to do something, those trips were so long. From Pittsburgh to New York is about 400 miles. We'd play cards, casino, whist, pinochle. Sometimes they'd play a whole trip. It was very seldom a whole lot of money. Back in those days there wasn't a whole lot of money.

A couple of players would take turns helping the driver on long trips. When one guy got sleepy, another would take over and drive for him. During the game the driver would take a nap and be ready to go again when the game was over. We're just lucky we never had any bad accidents, I guess.

The most respected man I met in baseball was Sam Bankhead.*

---

*Bankhead, the oldest brother of Dodger pitcher Dan Bankhead, was considered the best of five baseball-playing brothers. Sam never saw Dan pitch in the

He was a wonderful person. He'd help anybody. When you did wrong, he'd tell you, but he'd tell you in such a way, it took effect. He never hollered or whooped. On the bus he never was the type of person to raise his voice or start a disturbance. He had so much confidence in himself. He had confidence in me. I know he drank some, but he was a wonderful man. I'm sorry you met him when you did. I think about him all the time now.

Bankhead in the movies? They ought to get in touch with me to talk about it. I could help his cause. He should get all the respect he

Wilmer Fields (left) with Thurman Tucker (center) and Garnet Blair.

---

majors, perhaps out of bitterness at being passed over, and ended his days as a garbage man in Pittsburgh. When I interviewed Bankhead, he was living in one of the worst parts of the Pittsburgh ghetto. Soon after that, he was shot to death in a barroom fight. He is the model for Troy Maxson of the Broadway show, "Fences," by August Wilson, soon to be made into a motion picture with Eddie Murphy.

deserves. He was a wonderful person, not only to me but to every person.

I went in the army in 1943, and when I came out in '46, I wanted to prove myself. Double Duty Radcliffe was talking about he was going to win more games than anybody. I didn't know, maybe he could. Shoot, he won less!

I tried harder to prove myself. That was my best year. Any time we played in a major league ball park, they gave me the ball, even if I had only one-two days rest. The only game I lost was in Dayton; Johnny Vander Meer [the Cincinnati Reds] beat me 1–0. Dayton was a good baseball town. We'd usually get pretty good crowds there, so we'd usually pitch a good pitcher there. Vander Meer had just pitched against Pittsburgh and won 1–0. I guess they gave him $700 to pitch against us. He brought Ray Meuller from the Reds to catch him. I knew Meuller wouldn't guess on a curve and take a chance of getting hit if it was a fast ball, so I just threw him curves all day long. Vander Meer, I think he struck out 12, and I struck out 11. He allowed three hits, I allowed four. He beat me with control, good control. Like throwing darts. Didn't look like his curve ball was that big, but he threw it where he wanted it. That was the last game of the year for me.

Josh and I were real close. I didn't know anything about him smoking dope. I knew about drinking. I could have sat right beside somebody and couldn't smell dope. But how could he be doing something wrong and hit the ball that hard? He hit it so hard it would *bend*.

Luke Easter was supposed to be our power hitter to replace Gibson. But you know, the first year he came with the Grays in '46, he couldn't hit the side of the wall? Then in Venezuela he hit .302. When he came back to the Grays he hit .378. Have you ever been to the Polo Grounds? Do you remember Jose Santiago, a little Puerto Rican who used to pitch for Cleveland? He got behind Luke, 3–0, and Luke hit it into the center-field stands, and that's 487 feet away. He hit it like a shot. And it went up in there, it didn't stop at the fence. That's the hardest hit ball I've seen.* I saw him in Cuba hit the 3–0 pitch to right field. The right-fielder got his glove on it and it took him right on back. Oh, he was strong. That winter he went with us to Puerto Rico and hit .402.

I hit the ball pretty good too. Very few pitchers in the Negro leagues that couldn't hit—very, very few. Sometimes we would move them around; they'd play the outfield two or three innings, get to swing the bat. Sometimes they would bet a beer or something that they

---

*Only three other men ever reached the same spot—Hank Aaron, Joe Adcock, and Lou Brock.

would get more hits than somebody else. You know, it makes a big difference when you look down that lineup and you've got nine good bats in it. I don't know why pitchers don't practice hitting more. If you're a pitcher, and you've got two balls against you, you know you're going to get your pitch, with a .290 hitter coming up after you. I used to take advantage of guys in that situation.

Sam Bankhead was managing, so I said, "Look, Bank, let me play third base sometimes so when I go to Puerto Rico I can play third base and pitch and get more money." He said OK.

I hit .400 in 1948, the year Luke Easter hit .403. Bob Thurman, who went to Cincinnati, hit .314.*

The black World Series we played the Birmingham Black Barons in different places in the South. I pitched in New Orleans, Pelicans Park. They were in New Orleans, waiting for me. A sports writer said, "What do you think your chances of winning are?"

Bankhead said, "Chinky's coming down, we'll win."

I drove down to New Orleans in a 1947 Chevrolet, took me 25 hours. When I got there, I was confused, disoriented. I was shaking. I was in such bad shape out there pitching, the fast ball wouldn't go straight, it would run the other way. I never threw a running fast ball before in my life.

On Piper Davis, I was keeping it up on him. He couldn't hit the high pitch, he was waiting for the curve.

I struck out Artie Wilson‡ three times. And he hit from the left side too. But because my fast fall ran, that's how I got him out. He couldn't hit the inside pitch low.

There wasn't nothing to it. The final score was 14–1, if I'm not mistaken. Luke hit a homer or a triple. That's when Cleveland grabbed him. [The Grays won the series in five games.]

Willie Mays got one base hit the whole Series, a curve ball that hung up in his eyes that R.T. Walker threw him. In fact, he didn't play that much. They wouldn't even send him out there against me.

I don't like to name any names, but some guys went up to the major leagues who couldn't hit that ball in the Negro National league. There's a lot I could name who hit a lot better in the American League than they did in the Negro leagues. We'd be playing a game and somebody would say, "So-and-so went to Cleveland today." We'd say, "What! *Him?*" Al Smith went to Cleveland, hit .300 a couple years. Used to play for the Cleveland Buckeyes in the Negro league. It was a big surprise that he did so well.

---

*Published, unconfirmed.
‡Wilson preceded Mays to the New York Giants. He was released in 1954 in order to make room for Willie.

Minnie Minoso was a real hustler, but he couldn't hit the curve ball away from him or the fast ball on his handle high. That's the way I worked him all the time. He never hit me till the last year.

Sam Jethroe, I didn't have any trouble with him; he couldn't hit the low fast ball. I didn't have any trouble with Hank Thompson. I didn't have any trouble with Junior Gilliam. He could field—you know he could field! But he always said, "If I could hit, I'd be in the majors." He hit .265 in the majors.

Or take a guy like Campanella. He became an entirely different player in the major leagues. The first time I saw him, he didn't get any hits, but he was a good defensive player.

I don't think the Newark Eagles ever beat me a ball game. Monte Irvin, Johnny Davis, Lenny Pearson, they didn't bother me. But the man who hit me was Larry Doby, because he was a good fast ball hitter. Doby hit me hard a couple of times, but straight to someone. He didn't pull it now, but there was something on it. He hit me in Trenton right before he went to Cleveland. I was trying to get that fast ball by him. If only I had the knowledge then that I have now.

Willard Brown was rough on me! I'd have to come in on his handle as much as I could. But down in Puerto Rico I didn't get it in far enough. And he didn't leave it in the ball park! One time in Caracas I came from the side. He hit it, buddy—he hit the curve ball like he owned it. Willard Brown didn't just hit me, he hit everybody, I have to give him credit. I sure would like to have seen him when he first came up.

Wilmer Fields being congratulated in Caguas, Puerto Rico.

In the winter of 1948–49 I went back to Puerto Rico. Fellows like Lew Burdette, Joe Black, Doby, Brown, Irvin, Gilliam. You always saw good pitching. I pitched and played third base or outfield and hit fourth, fifth, or sixth in the lineup. The three years I was there I hit .327, .329, and .332. It made me Player of the Week several times. We'd go to a movie theater, they'd introduce us, my wife and I.

Mayaguez was a contender. I beat them 4–0 in 11 innings. I hit a triple with the bases loaded. Artie Wilson was the only one got a hit. He got three hits off me; they were all to shortstop. He could not pull the ball.

At that time I was throwing hard, 90 miles an hour or better. Dan Bankhead [of the Dodgers] was on the same pitching staff. He said, "Heh, Chinky, don't work so fast."

I said, "I want to get it over with." I was just blowing it past them.

We won the Puerto Rican Series and played in the Caribbean playoff against Cuba, all those Cuban major leaguers—Al Gionfrido [of Brooklyn] and old Roberto Torres, used to play for Washington. I gave them three hits that night. Minoso got two of them. The score was 6–0 at that time. I threw him a fast ball, he hit it.

In Mayaguez, Puerto Rico I pitched two ball games within 24 hours. In fact, one ball game I went 11 innings. The first one was a 2–2 tie. The next one Johnny Davis beat me 2–1 with a base hit in the 11th. Man, it was hot that day! That team I was with, it was rough: You get two runs, you better be satisfied.

Once, with the Grays, I pitched three games within 24 hours—Saturday night, Sunday afternoon, Sunday night. That must have been like 1949. We were barnstorming against the New York Black Yankees. The first one was in Dayton, Ohio. Any place you could draw a crowd, they wanted to win. About the fourth or fifth inning Bankhead asked me would I go in and pitch and hold them. The next one was against a local team, went about seven-eight innings; they called that one because we were beating them so badly. The third ball game R.T. Walker was supposed to pitch, but he was late. Bankhead said, "Chinky, would you start it?" I said yeah. I went about six innings. Well, you had to make a living. They wanted me to come back Tuesday. I told them, "No, you want me to do all this, you have to up my salary."

I wasn't denied a chance in the majors. I had five offers, even from the Yankees. I sent the money back.

Artie Wilson talked to Charlie Dressen of the Yankees to get me out to Oakland. Cookie Lavagetto was playing third then, and I'd just got done playing third in Puerto Rico and had the best fielding average in the league. So Charlie Dressen called me every night for a week, wanting me to go out there. He told me, "I'll give you $2,000 bonus if you stay a month." So I finally said OK. Dressen sent me $500 to catch the plane and go out. Well, my sister drove me to Washington, and halfway there I told her to turn the car around, I'm going home. I sent the money back.

I pitched for the Grays that weekend in the Polo Grounds. I knew I could have made it in the majors. There's no doubt in my mind. But I preferred black baseball, I was more comfortable doing it. I know we traveled a lot, but the money situation wasn't that great in the majors or Triple-A. The starting salary in the majors was $4,500. I could pick up $4,500-plus in four months with the Grays.

In Santurce they had that revolution, must have been 1950–51. I told my wife, "Let's get out of this place!" We came home for two weeks. They wanted me in Venezuela, I hit about .390 for two months.

Terris McDuffie of Newark: He used to say he was the second-best dresser in New York—him and Sugar Ray Robinson. He was always sharp as a tack. But he'd go around with a jacket with THE GREAT TERRIS MCDUFFIE written on the back. Now you know, you just don't do that. I used to put out a little extra effort to beat guys like that. One time down in Maracaibo, Venezuela, he threw me two balls outside and I hit them for a homer and a triple. Then he threw one inside and I doubled. The next Sunday he pitched us all inside. We didn't get but four hits off him, and I got three of them. I got me a 34½-inch bat and just waited for those inside pitches. You know, baseball is a lot of guessing. So he woke me up at 6:00 in the morning before he got his plane—he was going back to the States—woke me up, said, "You really can hit."

Somebody saw his passport down there. That was in 1950, and he was 49 years old. He had an 11–1 record. McDuffie would let us have one run, two runs, no runs, something like that. One day we decided to bunt on him, move him around, make him work. We could see him out there panting on the mound. We scored five or six runs off him, but he beat us anyway.

I came up with Toronto in 1952. Jack Kent Cooke [later the owner of the Redskins] called me every three or four days while I was playing in Venezuela. He ended up offering me $14,000 to come to Toronto. Cooke was a great man. He treated my wife and I so good; he was one of the greatest guys.

Went to spring training in Jacksonville. My wife and I stayed in a black hotel.

When I walked in the clubhouse, I asked the clubhouse man to get me a chair. In black baseball we used to call each other Hoss, so I said, "Heh, Hoss, get me a chair."

He looked at me, said, "Who you calling Horse?"

Our trainer said, "Oh, go on, get him a chair." Instead of getting a chair, he went out and got a shotgun.

I was the last one to come out of the clubhouse. He was sitting on the hood of his car with a gun. I just kept on walking. I saw some crows, some blackbirds, up on some telegraph wires. After my back was to him, the shot went off. He knocked off a blackbird. That bird fell down at my feet. I didn't even look back. I just kept on walking. That was enough for me!

In Puerto Rico I had been playing the outfield and pitching and I was having a pretty good year so they called me "The Great One." When I came to Toronto, the papers picked it up. So I went to the sports writers and told them, "We'll do away with that now." Yeah, they don't care about how great you are when you go up there. There's always somebody better than you are. I hit .300 until that last day. They pitched a guy against me who was throwing that sinker ball and I didn't catch a whiff of it. I ended up about .291.

In 1952–53 I had a real good year in Venezuela. I was playing third base. Here's who I was playing beside—Chico Carresquel. You talk about making it rough on a person, he made it rough—playing beside the best fielder in the American League? I had to come up with my *hitting*. I hit .350 and led the league in home runs and runs batted in. We won 17 straight.

I was in spring training 1953, and an owner in the Dominican Republic kept calling me and saying, "Give me your price." We went back and forth until it was up to $2,200 a month. That was a lot of money in the '50s, so I left Toronto in spring training. In Latin America you played three or four games a week, you lived in a hotel and were about five minutes from the ball park. But if you didn't produce down there, you were sent home in a hurry.

If you're talking about playing against major league ball players, one year in Colombia, South America they had the whole Baltimore roster down there—Jim Gentile, Brooks Robinson. When I tell you this, you won't believe it, but the whole winter he played ball down there, Robinson did not pull the ball once to the left side of the field. He didn't hit a ball over 300 feet the whole winter. But look—he could pick up *dust!* His arm wasn't that great, and he looked like a snail running. But he could pick up dust. He hit .319 down there; I hit .320.

In 1957 I was voted most valuable player in the national semipro tournament in Wichita. I was playing for Fort Wayne. I hit five homers out in that short series; I think I tied the record for the amount of games played. The year before that, we lost to a team from Texas. Clint Hartung—remember him, used to play for the Giants?—played for them. We used to go around together, eat together, go to the movies together. You can tell when a guy's a regular guy.

I played in Canada in the Intercounty league and hit over .400 twice.

In all I put in 25 playing seasons, summer and winter. That's a whole lot of rolling. I think I made just as much money as quite a few of those guys in the majors, so I'm satisfied. I look back, and I see I came through that kind of baseball without too much effort. If I didn't do it pitching, I did it hitting.

My greatest thrill? I hit one in Mexico City in 1958, the last year I played. Have you ever been to that park? If you ever get a chance, look at dead center field, where they have a scoreboard. I hit one past that scoreboard, must have gone 525 feet. Bases loaded. The only one had ever been hit out there, and Mays and all of them had been there. The night before, this boy came in to relieve; he threw me a curve ball, and I hit it on the handle. And I'm a pretty good curve ball hitter. Next day I had a 37-ounce bat—I use a heavier bat against curve ball pitchers. He threw the same pitch, and I swung. Ask Alonzo Perry the longest ball he ever saw hit; he was there.

I wish you'd seen that one.

Wilmer "Red" Fields
Pitching

---

b: 8/2/22, Manassas, VA   BR TR   6'3", 215

Year	Team	PSN	W–L	Team Rank*
1940	Grays	No record		
1941	Grays	No record		
1942	Grays	No record		
1943	U.S. Army			
1944	U.S. Army			
1945	U.S. Army			
1946	Grays		10-2[a]	3rd
1947	Grays		4–4	4th
	Puerto Rico		5–5	
1948	Grays		7–1	unknown
	Puerto Rico		10–4	
1949	Grays			
	Puerto Rico		13–6	
1953	Dominican Republic		5–2	
1955	Canada semi-pro		4–0	

Post-Season

1948	World Series		1–0	

Recap

Negro league	21–7	
Latin America	33–17	
Semi-pro	4–0	
Post-Season	1–0	
vs. white major leaguers	0–1	
Totals	59–25	

---

* Overall won-lost percentage in a six-team league.
[a] Confirmed to date. Unofficially 16 victories.

Wilmer "Red" Fields
Batting

Year ·	Team	G	AB	H	2B	3B	HR	BA	SB
1942	Grays	1	4	1	0	0	0	.250	—
1946	Grays	12	30	7	1	2	0	.233	0
1947	Grays	—	49	14	2	—	0	.286	0
	Puerto Rico	—	—	—	—	—	—	.330	—
1948	Grays	47	148	46	—	—	—	.311	—
	Puerto Rico	—	—	—	—	—	—	.328	—
1949	Puerto Rico	—	—	—	—	—	—	.330*	—
1950	Puerto Rico	—	—	—	—	—	—	.340	—
1951	Venezuela	—	—	—	—	—	—	.398	—
1952	Venezuela	51	207	72	2	8	2	.336ᵃ	2
1953	Toronto	51	165	48	10	1	2	.291	2
	Dominican Republic	—	—	—	—	—	—	.395	—
1954	Canada semi-pro	—	—	—	—	—	—	.379*	—
	Colombia	—	209	69	—	—	—	.330	—
1955	Canada semi-pro	—	—	—	—	—	—	.425*	—
	Colombia	—	216	69	—	—	—	.319	—
1956	Semi-pro	—	—	—	—	—	—	—	—
	Colombia	—	—	—	—	—	—	—	—
1957	Semi-pro	—	—	—	—	—	—	—	—
1958	Mexico	25	88	33	2	0	7	.375	0

Recap

	G	AB		2B	3B	HR	BA	
Negro league	231	68		3	2	0	.295	
Minor leagues	165	48		10	1	2	.291	
Latin America	632	210		2	8	2	.331	
East-West game	1	0		0	0	0	000	
Totals	1029	326		15	11	4	.317	

* Led in RBI; MVP.
ᵃ MVP.

League Leaders

League Leaders, East

Year	Player	BA	Player	HR	Pitcher	(W–L)
1923	Jud Wilson	.464	Charlie Mason	5	Rats Henderson	(13–12)
1924	George Scales	.422	Dick Lundy	13	Nip Winters	(16–3)
1925	John Beckwith	.404	Oscar Charleston	19	Nip Winters	(21–10)*
1926	Luther Farrell	.359	Martin Dihigo	11	Nip Winters	(18–6)
1927	Jud Wilson	.412	Oscar Charleston	12	Rats Henderson	(19–7)
1928	Pop Lloyd	.564	Pop Lloyd	11	Luther Farrell	(15–11)
1929	Chino Smith	.461	Chino Smith	23	Connie Rector	(18–1)
1930	Chino Smith	.429	John Beckwith	9	Pud Flournoy	(11–1)
1931	Jud Wilson	.358	John Beckwith	6	Porter Charleston	(14–3)
1932	Bill Perkins	.352	Gibson-Charleston	4	Bertram Hunter	(16–6)
1933	Leroy Morney	.419	Oscar Charleston	9	Bertram Hunter	(7–1)
1934	Jud Wilson	.361	Josh Gibson	12	Slim Jones	(18–3)*
1935	Turkey Stearnes	.430	Mule Suttles	10	Leroy Matlock	(17–0)
1936	Lazaro Salazar	.375	Josh Gibson	12	Webster McDonald	(10–1)
1937	Jim West	.421	Mule Suttles	8	Leon Day	(6–0)[a]
1938	Ray Dandridge	.417	Mule Suttles	8	Ray Brown	(11–0)
1939	Bill Wright	.402	Josh Gibson	16	Henry McHenry	(7–3)
1940	Pee Wee Butts	.390	Mule Suttles	8	Ray Brown	(15–0)
1941	Monte Irvin	.463	Monte Irvin	5	Ray Brown	(8–2)
1942	Willie Wells	.351	Josh Gibson	11	Bill Byrd	(10–1)
1943	Josh Gibson	.547	Josh Gibson	13	Dave Barnhill	(15–3)*
1944	Frank Austin	.390[b]	Gibson-Leonard	6[b]	Bill Ricks	(10–4)[b]
1945	Josh Gibson	.393[b]	Josh Gibson	8[b]	Roy Welmaker	(12–4)[b]
1946	Monte Irvin	.389[b]	Josh Gibson	11[b]	Wilmer Fields	(10–2)
1947	Luis Marquez	.417[b]	Monte Irvin	14[b]	Max Manning	(15–6)[b]
1948	Buck Leonard	.395[b]	Leonard-Easter	13[b]	Bill Byrd	(11–6)[b]

* Rats Henderson was 21–17 in 1925, Satchel Paige, 17–2 in 1934.

[a] SABR's Jim Riley has found typewritten stats for the Newark Eagles in the files of the Hall of Fame. No source or identification is given. They show Wells batting .386, Suttles 17 home runs, and Day 13–0.

[b] As published, not verified.

League Leaders, West

Year	Player	BA	Player	HR	Pitcher	(W–L)
1920	Cristobal Torriente	.450	Edgar Wesley	11	Bill Gatewood	(11–5)
1921	Charles Blackwell	.448	Oscar Charleston	15	Bill Drake	(20–10)
1922	Charles Blackwell	.387	Oscar Charleston	15	Bill Holland	(16–13)*
1923	Cristobal Torriente	.389	Wesley-Stearnes	17	Andy Cooper	(15–8)
1924	Dobie Moore	.470	Turkey Stearnes	10	Joe Rogan	(15–5)
1925	Edgar Wesley	.440	Wesley-Stearnes	18	Joe Rogan	(12–2)
1926	Mule Suttles	.418	Mule Suttles	26	Slap Hensley	(17–7)
1927	Red Parnell	.438	Turkey Stearnes	21	Bill Foster	(18–3)
1928	Pythian Russ	.406	Turkey Stearnes	24	Ted Trent	(17–4)
1929	Clarence Smith	.390	Willie Wells	27	John Williams	(19–7)
1930	Willie Wells	.404	Mule Suttles	20	Slap Hensley	(17–6)
1931	Nat Rogers	.424	Turkey Stearnes	8	Nelson Dean	(8–3)
1932[a]	Willie Scott	.385	Turkey Stearnes	5	Bill Foster	(14–6)
1933	One league only					
1934	One league only					
1935	One league only					
1936	Pat Patterson	.484	Brown-Strong	1	Ted Trent	(3–0)
1937	Neil Robinson	.533	Willard Brown	7	Hilton Smith	(5–5)
1938	Nat Rogers	.461	Willard Brown	5	Satchel Paige	(9–1)
1939	Willard Brown	.336	Stearnes-Strong-O'Neil	2	Hilton Smith	(9–3)
1940	Chester Williams	.473	Turkey Stearnes	5	Jack Matchett	(6–0)
1941	Lyman Bostock	.488	Ted Strong	4	Smith-Paige	(6–0)
1942	Ducky Davenport	.381	Willard Brown	7	Booker McDaniel	(9–1)
1943	Lester Lockett	.392	Willard Brown	6	Booker McDaniel	(9–1)

(Following compiled by Elias Baseball Bureau)

Year	Player	BA	Player	HR	Pitcher	(W–L)
1944	Sam Jethroe	.353[b]	Alec Radcliff	5[b]	Alfred Saylor	(14–5)[b]
1945	Sam Jethroe	.393[b]	Alec Radcliff	7[b]	Gentry Jessup	(15–10)[b]
1946	Buck O'Neil	.350[b]	Not yet compiled		Connie Johnson	(9–3)
1947	John Ritchie	.381[b]	Not yet compiled		Jim LaMarque	(12–2)[b]
1948	Art Wilson	.402[b]	Willard Brown	18[b]	LaMarque-Newberry	(14–5)[b]

* Johnny Meyers was 15–1.
[a] Southern league.
[b] As published, not verified.

Index